J. H. (John Henry) Middleton

Illuminated manuscripts in classical and mediaeval times

Their art and their technique

J. H. (John Henry) Middleton

Illuminated manuscripts in classical and mediaeval times
Their art and their technique

ISBN/EAN: 9783744640220

Printed in Europe, USA, Canada, Australia, Japan

Cover: Foto ©ninafisch / pixelio.de

More available books at **www.hansebooks.com**

ILLUMINATED MANUSCRIPTS IN CLASSICAL AND MEDIAEVAL TIMES,

THEIR ART AND THEIR TECHNIQUE

BY

J. HENRY MIDDLETON,

SLADE PROFESSOR OF FINE ART, DIRECTOR OF THE FITZWILLIAM MUSEUM,
AND FELLOW OF KING'S COLLEGE, CAMBRIDGE;
AUTHOR OF "ANCIENT ROME IN 1888",
"THE ENGRAVED GEMS OF CLASSICAL TIMES" &C.

CAMBRIDGE:
AT THE UNIVERSITY PRESS:
1892
C
[*All Rights reserved.*]

Cambridge:
PRINTED BY C. J. CLAY, M.A. AND SONS,
AT THE UNIVERSITY PRESS.

TABLE OF CONTENTS.

PREFACE AND LIST OF AUTHORITIES. Page xiii to xix.

LIST OF ILLUSTRATIONS. Page xxi to xxiv.

CHAPTER I. Page 1 to 10.
CLASSICAL MANUSCRIPTS WRITTEN WITH A STILUS.

Survival of classical methods in mediaeval times; epigraphy and palaeography; manuscripts on metal plates; lead rolls; tin rolls; gold amulets; Petelia tablet; waxed tablets and diptychs; tablets shown on gems and coins; tablets found in tombs; tablets from Pompeii; Consular diptychs; many-leaved tablets; the form of the waxed tablets; whitened boards used by the Greeks; late survival of tablets; "bidding the beads;" lists of members of guilds; wooden book in Norway; ivory tablets and diptychs; inscribed Anglo-Saxon lead tablet; "horn-books."

CHAPTER II. Page 11 to 30.
CLASSICAL MANUSCRIPTS WRITTEN WITH PEN AND INK.

Two forms of manuscripts, the roll and the codex; Egyptian Books of the Dead; Book of Ani; existing manuscripts on papyrus; the library of papyrus rolls found at Herculaneum; Herodotus on manuscripts; use of parchment; manuscripts on linen; inscribed potsherds or *ostraka;* manuscripts on leaves of trees; Greek libraries; Roman libraries; a list of the public libraries in Rome; Roman library fittings and decorations; recently discovered library in Rome; authors' portraits; closed bookcases; booksellers' quarter; cost of Roman books; slave scribes; librarii of Rome. The technique of ancient manuscripts; parchment and vellum; palimpsests; papyrus manuscripts; process of making papyrus paper; use of papyrus in Greece and Rome; ancient papyrus manuscripts; the qualities of papyrus paper; the form of papyrus rolls; the wooden roller; inscribed titles; coloured inks; use of cedar oil; black carbon ink, its manufacture and price; red inks and rubrics; purple ink; double inkstands; pens of reeds and of metal; Egyptian scribes' palettes, pen-cases, and pens.

CHAPTER III. Page 31 to 44.

CLASSICAL ILLUMINATED MANUSCRIPTS.

Use of minium; Egyptian miniatures; illuminations in Roman manuscripts; Greek illuminations; two sources of knowledge about classical illuminations; the Ambrosian *Iliad;* the Vatican Virgil; the style of its miniatures; later copies of lost originals; picture of Orpheus in a twelfth century *Psalter;* another *Psalter* with copies of classical paintings; the value of these copied miniatures.

CHAPTER IV. Page 45 to 61.

BYZANTINE MANUSCRIPTS.

The very compound character of Byzantine art; love of splendour; *Gospels* in purple and gold; monotony of the Byzantine style; hieratic rules; fifth century manuscript of *Genesis;* the Dioscorides of the Princess Juliana; the style of its miniatures; imitations of enamel designs; early picture of the Crucifixion in the *Gospels* of Rabula; the splendour of Byzantine manuscripts of the *Gospels;* five chief pictures; illuminated "Canons"; Persian influence; the Altar-Textus used as a Pax; its magnificent gold covers; the Durham Textus; Byzantine figure drawing, unreal but decorative; Byzantine mosaics; the iconoclast schism, and the consequent decadence of Byzantine art.

CHAPTER V. Page 62 to 79.

MANUSCRIPTS OF THE CAROLINGIAN PERIOD.

The age of Charles the Great; the school of Alcuin of York; the *Gospels* of Alcuin; the *golden Gospels* of Henry VIII.; the *Gospels* of the scribe Godesscalc; Persian influence; technical methods; the later Carolingian manuscripts; continuance of the Northumbrian influence; beginning of life-study; the *Gospels* of Otho II.; period of decadence in the eleventh century.

CHAPTER VI. Page 80 to 97.

THE CELTIC SCHOOL OF MANUSCRIPTS.

The Irish Church; Celtic goldsmiths; technical processes of the metal-workers copied by illuminators of manuscripts; the *Book of Kells*, its perfect workmanship and microscopic illuminations; copies of metal spiral patterns; the "trumpet pattern;" Moslem influence; absence of gold in the Irish manuscripts; the *Book of Durrow;* the monks of Iona; the Celtic missionaries to Northumbria; the *Gospels* of St Cuthbert; the Viking pirates; the adventures of St Cuthbert's *Gospels;* the Anglo-Celtic school; improved drawing and use of gold; Italian influence; the early *Gospels* in the Corpus library; the *Gospels* of MacDurnan; the *Book of Deer;* the *Gospels* of St Chad; the Celtic school on the Continent; the *Psalter* of St Augustine; Scandinavian art; the *golden Gospels* of Stockholm and its adventures; the struggle between the Celtic and the Roman Church; the Synod of Whitby; the Roman victory, and the growth of Italian influence; the school of Baeda at Durham.

CHAPTER VII. Page 98 to 105.

THE ANGLO-SAXON SCHOOL OF MANUSCRIPTS.

The Danish invasions; revival of art under king Alfred; the *Benedictional* of Aethelwold; signs of Carolingian influence; the Winchester school; St Dunstan as an illuminator; Anglo-Saxon drawings in coloured ink; Roll of St Guthlac; the great beauty of its drawings; Canute as a patron of art; the Norman Conquest.

CHAPTER VIII. Page 106 to 125.

THE ANGLO-NORMAN SCHOOL.

The Norman invasion; development of architecture and other arts; creation of the Anglo-Norman school; magnificent *Psalters;* the Angevin kingdom; the highest development of English art in the thirteenth century; Henry III. as an art patron; the rebuilding and decorating of the Church and Palace of Westminster; paintings copied from manuscripts; the Painted Chamber; English sculpture; the Fitz-Othos and William Torell; English needlework (*opus Anglicanum*); the Lateran and Pienza copes; Anglo-Norman manuscripts of the *Vulgate;* the style of their illuminations; manuscripts produced in Benedictine monasteries; unity of style; various kinds of background in miniatures; magnificent manuscripts of the *Psalter;* the Tenison *Psalter;* manuscripts of the *Apocalypse;* their extraordinary beauty; their contrast to machine-made art; English manuscripts of the fourteenth and fifteenth centuries; the results of the Black Death; the Poyntz *Horae;* the *Lectionary* of Lord Lovel; the characteristics of English ornament; the introduction of portrait figures; the Shrewsbury manuscript; "Queen Mary's Prayerbook;" the works of Dan Lydgate; specially English subjects; manuscripts of *Chronicles* and *Histories.*

CHAPTER IX. Page 126 to 146.

French Manuscripts.

The age of Saint Louis; archaism of costume in miniatures; French manuscripts of the fourteenth and fifteenth centuries; historiated Bibles; the ivy-pattern; the *Horae* of the Duc de Berri; the *treasure-book* of Origny Abbey; the Anjou *Horae;* costly and magnificent French *Horae;* their beautiful decorations; their numerous miniatures; the Bedford *Breviary;* the Bedford *Missal;* various styles in the same manuscript; manuscripts in *Grisaille;* manuscripts of secular works; Cristina of Pisa; *Chronicles* and *Travels; Romances* and *Poems;* Italian influence in the south of France; the growth of secular illuminators; the inferiority of their work; cheap and coarsely illuminated *Horae;* manuscripts of the finest style; use of flowers and fruit in borders and initials; influence of the Italian Renaissance; the *Horae* of Jehan Foucquet of Tours.

CHAPTER X. Page 147 to 153.

Printed Books with painted Illuminations.

Horae printed on vellum in Paris; their woodcut decorations; the productions of the earliest printers; the Mazarine Bible; the Mentz *Psalter;* illuminators becoming printers; Italian printed books with rich illuminations; the colophons of the early printers; the books of Aldus Manutius; invention of Italic type; manuscripts illustrated with woodcuts; blockbooks; the long union of the illuminators' and the printers' art.

CHAPTER XI. Page 154 to 182.

ILLUMINATED MANUSCRIPTS OF THE TEUTONIC SCHOOL AFTER THE TENTH CENTURY.

Revival of art in Germany in the eleventh century; the *Missal* of the Emperor Henry II.; the designs used for stained glass; the advance of manuscript art under Frederic Barbarossa; grotesque monsters; examples of fine German illuminations of the twelfth century; their resemblance to mural paintings; the school of the Van Eycks; the Grimani *Breviary;* Gérard David of Bruges; examples of Flemish miniatures; the use of gold; grotesque figures; the influence of manuscript art on the painters of altar-pieces; the school of Cologne; triptych by the elder Holbein; book illuminated by Albert Dürer; Dutch fifteenth century manuscripts; their decorative beauty; their realistic details; illumination in pen outlines in blue and red.

CHAPTER XII. Page 183 to 205.

THE ILLUMINATED MANUSCRIPTS OF ITALY AND SPAIN.

Italian art slow to advance; its degraded state in the twelfth century; illuminators mentioned by Dante; *Missal* in the Chapter library of Saint Peter's; the monk Don Silvestro in the middle of the fourteenth century; his style of illumination; the monk Don Lorenzo; Fra Angelico as an illuminator; Italian *Pontifical* in the Fitzwilliam library; manuscripts of the works of Dante and Petrarch; motives of decoration; Italian manuscripts after 1453; introduction of the "Roman" hand; great perfection of writing, and finest quality of vellum; the illuminators Attavante, Girolamo dai Libri, and Liberale of Verona; manuscripts of northern Italy; their influence on painting generally; Italian manuscripts of the sixteenth century, a period of rapid decadence; Giulio Clovio a typical miniaturist of his time; the library of the Vatican; its records of the cost of illuminating manuscripts. The manuscripts of Spain and Portugal; the manuscripts of Moslem countries, especially Persia.

✓CHAPTER XIII. Page 206 to 223.

THE WRITERS OF ILLUMINATED MANUSCRIPTS.

Monastic scribes; the great beauty of their work, and the reasons for it; their quiet, monotonous life; examples of monastic humour; no long spells of work in a monastery; care in the preparation of pigments; variety of the schemes of decoration; the *scriptoria* of Benedictine monasteries; their arrangement in one alley of the cloister; the row of *armaria;* the row of *carrels;* the *carrels* in the Durham cloister described in *the Rites of Durham;* the scribes of other regular Orders. Secular scribes; the growth of the craft-guilds; the guilds of Bruges; their rules, and advantages to both buyer and seller; the production of cheap *Horae;* wealthy patrons who paid for costly manuscripts; women illuminators, such as the wife of Gérard David; the high estimation of fine manuscripts. Extract from the fourteenth century accounts of St George's at Windsor showing the cost of six manuscripts. Similar extract from the Parish books of St Ewen's at Bristol in the fifteenth century, giving the cost of a *Lectionary*.

CHAPTER XIV. Page 224 to 238.

THE MATERIALS AND TECHNICAL PROCESSES OF THE ILLUMINATOR.

The vellum used by scribes, its cost and various qualities; paper made of cotton, of wool and of linen; the dates and places of its manufacture; its fine quality. The metals and pigments used in illuminated manuscripts; fluid gold and silver; leaf gold, silver and tin; the highly burnished gold; leaf beaten out of gold coins; the goldsmith's art practised by many great artists; the *mordant* on which the gold leaf was laid; how it was applied; a slow, difficult process; laborious use of the burnisher; old receipts for the mordant: the *media* or vehicles used with it; tooled and stamped patterns on the gold leaf; the use of tin instead of silver; a cheap method of applying gold described by Cennino Cennini.

CHAPTER XV. Page 239 to 256.

THE MATERIALS AND TECHNICAL PROCESSES OF THE ILLUMINATOR (*continued*).

The coloured pigments. The vehicles used; blue pigments, ultramarine; its great value; story told by Pliny and Vasari; *smalto* blues; "German blue;" Indigo and other dye-colours; how they were made into pigments; green pigments; terra verde, verdigris, smalt, leek-green; red pigments, *minium* red lead, vermilion, red ochre (*rubrica*); *murex* and *kermes* crimson; kermes extracted from scraps of red cloth by illuminators; madder-red; lake-red; purples; yellow pigments, ochre, arsenic and litharge; white pigments, pure lime (*Bianco di San Giovanni*), white lead, *biacca* or *cerusa*. Black inks, carbon ink and iron ink (*incaustum* or *encaustum* and *atramentum*); red and purple inks; writing in gold; the illuminator's pens and pencils; the lead-point and silver-point; red chalk and *amatista*. Pens made of reeds, and, in later times, of quills; brushes of ermine, minever and other hair, mostly made by each illuminator for himself; list of scribes' implements and tools. Miniatures representing scribes; the various stages in the execution of an illuminated manuscript; ruled lines; writing of the plain text; outline of ornament sketched in; application of the gold leaf; the painting of the ornaments and miniatures; preparation for the binder.

CHAPTER XVI. Page 257 to 264.

THE BINDINGS OF MANUSCRIPTS.

Costly covers of gold, enamel and ivory; the more usual forms of binding; oak boards covered with parchment and strengthened by metal bosses and corners; methods of placing the title on the cover; pictures on wood covers; stamped patterns on leather; English stamped bindings; bag-like bindings for portable manuscripts; bindings of velvet with metal mounts; the costly covers of the Grimani *Breviary* and other late manuscripts. The present prices of mediaeval manuscripts; often sold for barely the value of their vellum; modern want of appreciation of the finest manuscripts.

APPENDIX. Page 265 to 270.

Directions to scribes, from a thirteenth century manuscript at Bury St Edmund's.

Note on Service-books by the late Henry Bradshaw. Extract from the Cistercian *Consuetudines*.

Painting on panel by a fifteenth century artist of the Prague school; it represents St Augustine as an Episcopal scribe. The background and the ornaments of the dress are stamped in delicate relief on the *gesso* ground and then gilt. This picture, which is now in the Vienna Gallery, was originally part of the painted wall-panelling in the Chapel of the Castle of Karlstein.

PREFACE.

THE object of this book is to give a general account of the various methods of writing, the different forms of manuscripts and the styles and systems of decoration that were used from the earliest times down to the sixteenth century A.D., when the invention of printing gradually put an end to the ancient and beautiful art of manuscript illumination.

I have attempted to give a historical sketch of the growth and development of the various styles of manuscript illumination, and also of the chief technical processes which were employed in the preparation of pigments, the application of gold leaf, and other details, to which the most unsparing amount of time and labour was devoted by the scribes and illuminators of many different countries and periods.

An important point with regard to this subject is the remarkable way in which technical processes lasted, in many cases, almost without alteration from classical times down to the latest mediaeval period, partly owing to the existence of an unbroken chain of traditional practice, and partly on account of the mediaeval custom of studying and obeying the precepts of such classical writers as Vitruvius and Pliny the Elder.

To an English student the art-history of illuminated manuscripts should be especially interesting, as there were two distinct periods when the productions of English illuminators were of unrivalled beauty and importance throughout the world[1].

In the latter part of this volume I have tried to describe the conditions under which the illuminators of manuscripts did their work, whether they were monks who laboured in the *scriptorium* of a monastery, or members of some secular guild, such as the great painters' guilds of Bruges or Paris.

The extraordinary beauty and marvellous technical perfection of certain classes of manuscripts make it a matter of interest to learn who the illuminators were, and under what daily conditions and for what reward they laboured with such astonishing patience and skill.

The intense pleasure and refreshment that can be gained by the study of a fine mediaeval illuminated manuscript depend largely on the fact that the exquisite miniatures, borders and initial letters were the product of an age which in almost every respect differed widely from the unhappy, machine-driven nineteenth century in which we now live.

With regard to the illustrations, I have to thank

[1] See pages 97 and 113.

Mr John Murray for his kindness in lending me a *cliché* of the excellent woodcut of the *scriptorium* walk in the cloisters of the Benedictine Abbey of Gloucester, which was originally prepared to illustrate one of Mr Murray's valuable *Guides to the English Cathedrals*.

The rest of the illustrations I owe to the kindness of Mr Kegan Paul. They have previously appeared in the English edition of Woltmann and Woermann's valuable *History of Painting*, 1880–7.

I have to thank my friend and colleague Mr M. R. James for his kindness in looking through the proofs of this book. He is not responsible for the opinions expressed or for the errors that remain, but he has corrected some of the grosser blunders.

J. HENRY MIDDLETON.

KING'S COLLEGE, CAMBRIDGE.

BOOKS ON ILLUMINATED MSS.

THE following are some of the most important works on this subject, and the most useful for the purposes of a student. Many others, which deal with smaller branches of the subject, are referred to in the following text.

Bastard, *Peintures et Ornemens des Manuscrits, classés dans un ordre Chronologique*, Imper. folio, Paris, 1835, &c.; a very magnificent book, with 163 plates, mostly coloured.

Birch and Jenner, *Early drawings and illuminations*, London, 1879; this is a useful index of subjects which occur in manuscript miniatures.

Bradley, J. W., *Dictionary of Miniaturists and Illuminators*, 3 vols. 8vo. London, 1887-1890.

Chassant, *Paléographie des Chartes et des Manuscrits du XIme au XVIIIme Siècle*, 12mo.; a useful little handbook, together with the companion volume, *Dictionnaire des Abbréviations Latines et Françaises*, Paris, 1876.

Denis, F., *Histoire de l'Ornementation des manuscrits;* 8vo. Paris, 1879.

Fleury, E., *Les Manuscrits de la Bibliothèque de Laon étudiés au point de vue de leur illustration*, 2 vols., Laon, 1863. With 50 plates.

Humphreys, Noel, *Illuminated Books of the Middle Ages*, folio, London, 1849; a handsome, well-illustrated book.

Humphreys, Noel, *The Origin and Progress of the Art of Writing;* sm. 4to., with 28 plates; London, 1853.

Kopp, *Palaeographia Critica,* 4 vols. 4to., Manheim, 1817–1819; a book of much historical value for the student of Palaeography.

Lamprecht, K., *Initial-Ornamentik des VIII.-XIII. Jahrh.,* Leipzig, 1882.

Langlois, *Essai sur la Calligraphie des Manuscrits du Moyen Age et sur les Ornements des premiers livres imprimés,* 8vo. Rouen, 1841.

Monte Cassino, *Paleografia artistica di Monte Cassino,* published by the Benedictine Monks of Mte. Cassino, 1870, and still in progress. This work contains a very valuable series of facsimiles and coloured reproductions of selected pages from many of the most important manuscripts in this ancient and famous library, that of the Mother-house of the whole Benedictine Order.

Reiss, H., *Sammlung der schönsten Miniaturen des Mittelalters,* Vienna, 1863–5.

Riegl, A., *Die mittelalterl. Kalenderillustration,* Innsbruck, 1889.

Seghers, L., *Trésor calligraphique du Moyen Age,* Paris, 1884; with 46 coloured plates of illuminated initials.

Shaw, Henry, *Illuminated Ornaments of the Middle Ages from the sixth to the seventeenth century;* with descriptions by Sir Fred. Madden; 4to. with 60 coloured plates, London, 1833. A very fine and handsome work.

„ „ *The Art of Illumination,* 4to. London, 1870; with well-executed coloured plates.

„ „ *Hand-book of Mediaeval Alphabets and Devices,* Imp. 8vo. London, 1877; with 37 coloured plates.

Silvestre, *Paléographie Universelle,* 4 vols., Atlas folio, Paris, 1839–1841. This is the most magnificent and costly work on the subject that has ever been produced.

The English Edition in 2 vols., Atlas folio, translated and edited by Sir Fred. Madden, London, 1850, is very superior in point of accuracy and judgment to the original French work. A smaller edition with 72 selected plates has also been published, in 2 vols. 8vo. and one fol., London, 1850.

Waagen, G. F., *On the Importance of Manuscripts with Miniatures in the history of Art*, 8vo. London (1850).

Westwood, J. O., *Palaeographia Sacra Pictoria*, royal 4to. London, 1843-5. This is a very fine work, with 50 coloured plates of manuscript illuminations selected from manuscripts of the Bible of various dates from the fourth to the sixteenth century.

" " *Illuminated Illustrations of the Bible*, royal 4to. London, 1846. This is a companion work to the last-mentioned book.

" " *Miniatures and Ornaments of Anglo-Saxon and Irish Manuscripts*, fol., London, 1868; with 54 very finely executed coloured plates of remarkable fidelity in drawing. The reproductions of pages from the *Book of Kells* and similar Celtic manuscripts are specially remarkable.

Wyatt, M. Digby, *The Art of Illuminating as practised in Europe from the earliest times*; 4to. London, 1860; with 100 plates in gold and colours.

The best work on the form of books in ancient times is Th. Birt, *Das antike Buchwesen in seinem Verhältniss zur Literatur*, 8vo., 1882.

The publications of the Palaeographical Society, from the year 1873, and still in progress, are of great value for their well-selected and well-executed photographic reproductions of pages from the most important manuscripts of all countries and periods.

xxi

LIST OF ILLUSTRATIONS.

Fig. 1, page 33. Part of the drawing engraved on the bronze *cista* of Ficoroni, dating from the early part of the fourth century B.C. A beautiful example of Greek drawing.
„ 2 „ 37. Miniature of classical design from a twelfth century *Psalter* in the Vatican library.
„ 3 „ 39. Painting in the "House of Livia" on the Palatine Hill in Rome.
„ 4 „ 41. A Pompeian painting of Hellenic style, as an example of Greek drawing and composition.
„ 5 „ 43. The Prophet Ezechiel from a Byzantine manuscript of the ninth century A.D.
„ 6 „ 49. Miniature from the Vienna manuscript of *Genesis*.
„ 7 „ 51. Miniature from the manuscript of the work on *Botany* by Dioscorides, executed at Constantinople about 500 A.D. for the Princess Juliana.
„ 8 „ 58. Mosaic of the sixth century in the apse of the church of SS. Cosmas and Damian in Rome.
„ 9 „ 60. Miniature from a Byzantine manuscript of the eleventh century; a remarkable example of artistic decadence.
„ 10 „ 63. An initial P of the Celtic-Carolingian type, of the school of Alcuin of York.
„ 11 „ 64. An initial B of the Celtic-Carolingian type.
„ 12 „ 66. Miniature of Christ in Majesty from a manuscript of the school of Alcuin, written for Charles the Great.
„ 13 „ 68. A cope made of silk from the loom of an Oriental weaver.
„ 14 „ 71. King Lothair enthroned; a miniature from a manuscript about the year 845 A.D.

xxii LIST OF ILLUSTRATIONS.

Fig. 15 page 73. Illumination in pen outline, from a manuscript written in the ninth century at St Gallen. It represents David riding out against his enemies.

Figs. 16 and 17, pages 74 and 75. Subject countries doing homage to the Emperor Otho II.; from a manuscript of the *Gospels*.

Fig. 18, page 77. Miniature of the Evangelist Saint Mark; from a manuscript of the *Gospels*.

„ 19 „ 78. Miniature of the Crucifixion from a German manuscript of the eleventh century; showing extreme artistic decadence.

„ 20 „ 91. Miniature from the *Gospels* of MacDurnan of the ninth century.

„ 21 „ 100. Miniature from the *Benedictional* of Aethelwold; written and illuminated by a monastic scribe at Winchester.

„ 22 „ 127. A page from the *Psalter* of Saint Louis, written about the year 1260, by a French scribe.

„ 23 „ 130. Miniature representing King Conrad of Bohemia, with an attendant, hawking.

„ 24 „ 132. Scene of the martyrdom of Saint Benedicta from a *Martyrology* of about 1312.

„ 25 „ 134. Miniature of the Birth of the Virgin painted by the illuminator Jacquemart de Odin for the Duc de Berri. The border is of the characteristic French or Franco-Flemish style.

„ 26 „ 142. Miniature executed for King René of Anjou about 1475.

„ 27 „ 145. Miniature of the Marriage of the B. V. Mary from a French manuscript of about 1480, with details in the style of the Italian Renaissance.

„ 28 „ 146. Border illumination from a *Book of Hours* by Jacquemart de Odin which belonged to the Duc de Berri; see fig. 25.

„ 29 „ 155. A page from the *Missal* of the Emperor Henry II.

„ 30 „ 156. Figure of King David from a stained glass window in the Cathedral of Augsburg, dating from 1065.

„ 31 „ 157. Miniature from an eleventh century manuscript of the *Gospels*, by a German illuminator.

„ 32 „ 159. An initial S, illuminated with foliage of the Northumbrian type, from a German manuscript of the twelfth century.

„ 33 „ 160. Miniature of the Annunciation from a German manuscript of the beginning of the thirteenth century.

LIST OF ILLUSTRATIONS. xxiii

Fig. 34 page 161. Page of a Kalendar from a German *Psalter* of about 1200 A.D.

" 35 " 163. Initial Y from a German manuscript of the beginning of the thirteenth century, with a most graceful and fanciful combination of figures and foliage.

" 36 " 164. Paintings on the vault of the church of St Michael at Hildesheim, closely resembling in style an illuminated page in a manuscript.

" 37 " 166. Miniatures of Italian style from a German manuscript of 1312, showing the influence of Florentine art on the illuminators of southern France.

" 38 " 168. Miniature symbolizing the month of April from the Kalendar of the Grimani *Breviary*, executed about 1496.

" 39 " 170. A page from the *Book of Hours* of King René, painted about 1480.

" 40 " 171. A page from a *Book of Hours* at Vienna, of the finest Flemish style.

" 41 " 173. Marginal illumination of very beautiful and refined style from a manuscript executed for King Wenzel of Bohemia about the year 1390.

" 42 " 174. Miniature of Duke Baldwin, painted about the year 1450 by an illuminator of the school of the Van Eycks of Bruges.

" 43 " 176. Retable painted by Martin Schöngauer, in the style of a manuscript illumination.

" 44 " 177. An altar-piece of the Cologne school, showing the influence of manuscript illumination on the painters of panel-pictures, especially retables.

" 45 " 179. Wing of a triptych, with a figure of St Elizabeth of Hungary, painted by the elder Hans Holbein; this illustrates the influence on painting of the styles of manuscript illumination at the beginning of the sixteenth century.

" 46 " 180. Illuminated border drawn by Albert Dürer in 1515.

" 47 " 185. Illumination from an Italian manuscript executed for the Countess Matilda in the twelfth century; this illustrates the extreme decadence of art in Italy before the thirteenth century.

" 48 " 187. Miniature of Saint George and the Dragon from a *Missal*, illuminated about 1330 to 1340 by a painter of the school of Giotto.

" 49 " 196. An illuminated border from a manuscript by Attavante, of characteristic north-Italian style.

LIST OF ILLUSTRATIONS.

Fig. 50 page 198. A miniature from the Bible of Duke Borso d'Este, painted between 1455 and 1461 by illuminators of the school of Ferrara.

„ 51 „ 201. A Venetian retable by Giovanni and Antonio di Murano, in the style of an illuminated manuscript.

„ 52 „ 208. Grotesque figure from a French manuscript of the fourteenth century.

„ 53 „ 209. Miniature of a comic subject from a German manuscript of the twelfth century, representing a monastic scribe worried by a mouse.

„ 54 „ 213. View of the scriptorium alley of the cloisters at Gloucester, showing the recesses to hold the wooden *carrels* for the scribes or readers of manuscripts.

„ 55 „ 219. Picture by Quentin Matsys of Antwerp, showing a lady selling or pawning an illuminated manuscript.

Frontispiece. Painting on panel by a fifteenth century artist of the Prague school; it represents Saint Augustine as an Episcopal scribe. The background and the ornaments of the dress are stamped in delicate relief on the *gesso* ground and then gilt. This picture, which is now in the Vienna Gallery, was originally part of the painted wall-panelling in the Chapel of the Castle of Karlstein.

CHAPTER I.

CLASSICAL MANUSCRIPTS WRITTEN WITH A STILUS.

BEFORE entering upon any discussion of the styles and methods of decoration which are to be found in mediaeval manuscripts and of the various processes, pigments and other materials which were employed by the mediaeval illuminators it will be necessary to give some account of the shapes and kinds of books which were produced among various races during the classical period.

The reason of this is that classical styles of decoration and technical methods, in the preparation of paper, parchment, pigments and the like, both survived to greater extent and to a very much later period than is usually supposed to have been the case, and, indeed, continued to influence both the artistic qualities and the mechanical processes of the mediaeval illuminator almost down to the time when the production of illuminated manuscripts was gradually put an end to by the invention of printing.

Survival of methods.

The word *manuscript* is usually taken to imply writing with a pen, brush or *stilus* to the exclusion of inscriptions cut with the chisel or the graver in stone, marble, bronze or other hard substance. The science of *palaeography* deals with the former, while *epigraphy* is concerned with the latter. The inscribed clay tablets of Assyria and Babylon might be considered a sort of link between the two, on account of the cuneiform writing on them having been executed with a stilus in soft, plastic clay, which subsequently was hardened by

The pen and the stilus.

baking in the potter's kiln, but it will be needless to describe them here.

Writing on metal. **Manuscripts on metal plates.** Another form of writing especially used by the ancient Greeks, which falls more definitely under the head of manuscripts, consists of characters scratched with a sharp iron or bronze *stilus* on plates of soft tin, lead or pewter, which, when not in use, could be rolled up into a compact and conveniently portable cylinder.

A considerable number of these inscribed lead rolls have been found in the tombs of Cyprus; but none of them unfortunately have as yet been found to contain matter of any great interest.

Lead rolls. For the most part they consist either of monetary accounts, or else of formulae of imprecations, curses devoting some enemy to punishment at the hands of the gods. We know however from the evidence of classical writers that famous poems and other important literary works were occasionally preserved in the form of these inscribed tin or lead rolls. Pausanias, for example, tells us that during his visit to Helicon in Boeotia he was shown the original manuscript of Hesiod's *Works and Days* written on plates of lead; see Paus. IX. 31. Again at IV. 26, Pausanias records the discovery at Ithome in Messenia of a bronze urn (*hydria*) which contained a manuscript of the "Mysteries of the Great *Tin rolls.* Deities" written on "a thinly beaten plate of tin, which was rolled up like a book," κασσίτερον ἐληλασμένον ἐς τὸ λεπτότατον, ἐπείλικτο δὲ ὥσπερ τὰ βιβλία. This method of writing would be quite different from the laborious method of cutting inscriptions on bronze plates with a chisel and hammer, or with a graver.

A scribe could write on the soft white metal with a sharp stilus almost as easily and rapidly as if he were using pen and ink on paper, and the manuscript thus produced would have the advantage of extreme durability.

We may indeed hope that even now some priceless lost work of early Greece may be recovered by the discovery of similar lead rolls to those which Cesnola found in Cyprus.

Some very beautiful little Greek manuscripts, written on *Gold* thin plates of gold, have also been discovered at various *amulets.* places. The most remarkable of these were intended for amulets, and were rolled up in little gold or silver cylinders and worn round the neck during life. After death they were placed with the body in the tomb. Several of these, discovered in tombs in the district of Sybaris in Magna Graecia, are inscribed with fragments from the mystic Orphic hymns, and give directions to the soul as to what he will find and what he must do in the spirit-world.

The most complete of these little gold manuscripts, *Petelia* usually known as the Petelia tablet, is preserved in the *tablet.* gem-room in the British Museum. The manuscript consists of thirteen hexameter lines written on a thin plate of pure gold measuring 1½ inches by 2⅜ inches in width; it dates from the third century B.C.[1]

In classical times, manuscripts were of two different forms; first, the *book* form, πίναξ, πινάκιον or δελτίον, in Latin *codex* (older spelling *caudex*); and secondly the roll, κύλινδρος, βίβλος or βιβλίον, Latin *volumen*[2].

Manuscripts on tablets. Both the Greeks and the Romans *Waxed* used very largely tablets (πίνακες, Lat. *tabulae* or *cerae*) of *tablets.* wood covered with a thin coating of coloured wax, on which the writing was formed with a sharp-pointed *stilus* (γραφίς) of wood, ivory or bronze. The wax was coloured either black or red in order that the writing scratched upon it might be clearly visible. The reverse end of the stilus was made flat or in the shape of a small ball so that it could be used to make corrections by smoothing out words or letters which had been erroneously scratched in the soft wax.

These tablets were commonly about ten to fourteen inches in length by about half that in width. The main surface of each tablet was sunk from $\frac{1}{8}$ to $\frac{1}{16}$ of an inch

---

[1] See *Jour. Hell. Stud.* Vol. III. p. 112.
[2] It was not till quite a late period that the word βίβλοι was used to mean another form of book than the roll. The word σανίς is also used for a tablet; see p. 30.

in depth to receive the wax layer, leaving a rim all round about the size of that round a modern school-boy's slate. *Waxed diptychs.* The object of this was that two of these tablets might be placed together face to face without danger of rubbing and obliterating the writing on the wax, which was applied in a very thin coat, not more than $\frac{1}{16}$ of an inch in thickness. As a rule these tablets were fastened together in pairs by stout loops of leather or cord. These double tablets were called by the Greeks πίνακες πτυκτοί or δίπτυχα (from δίς and πτύσσω) and by the Romans *pugillares* or *codicilli*. Homer (*Il*. VI. 168) mentions a letter written on folding tablets—

πόρεν δ' ὅ γε σήματα λυγρά
Γράψας ἐν πίνακι πτυκτῷ.

Tablets on coins and gems. Representations of these folding tablets occur frequently both in Greek and in Roman art, as, for example on various Sicilian coins, where the artist's name is placed in minute letters on a double tablet, which in some cases, as on a *tetradrachm* of Himera, is held open by a flying figure of Victory.

A gem of about 400 B.C., a large scarabaeoid in chalcedony, recently acquired by the British Museum, is engraved with a seated figure of a lady holding a book consisting of four leaves; she is writing lengthwise on one leaf, while the other three hang down from their hinge.

Some of the beautiful terra-cotta statuettes from the tombs of the Boeotian Tanagra represent a girl reading from a somewhat similar double folding tablet.

On Greek vases and in Roman mural paintings the *pugillares* are frequently shown, though the roll form of manuscript is on the whole more usual.

Tablets from tombs. Some examples of these tablets have been found in a good state of preservation in Graeco-Egyptian tombs and during recent excavations in Pompeii.

Part of a poem in Greek written in large uncial characters is still legible on the single leaf of a pair of tablets from Memphis in Egypt, which is now in the British Museum. Though the coating of wax has nearly all perished, the sharp stilus has marked through on to the wood behind the wax, so that the writing is still legible. Its date appears to be shortly before the Christian era[1].

Some well preserved *pugillares* found in Pompeii are now in the Museum in Naples; the writing on them is of less interest, consisting merely of accounts of expenditure. Though the wood is blackened and the wax destroyed, the writing is still perfectly visible on the charred surface.

Pompeian tablets.

A more costly form of *pugillares* was made of bone or ivory[2]; in some cases the back of each ivory leaf was decorated with carving in low relief.

A good many examples of these tablets, dating from the third to the sixth century A.D., still exist. These late highly decorated *pugillares* are usually known as *Consular diptychs*, because, as a rule, they have on the carved back the name of a Consul, and very frequently a representation of the Consul in his *pulvinar* or state box presiding over the Games in the Circus. It is supposed that these ivory diptychs were inscribed with complimentary addresses and were sent as presents to newly appointed officials in the time of the later Empire.

Consular diptychs.

In some cases the ancient writing-tablets consisted of three or more leaves hinged together (τρίπτυχα, πεντάπτυχα &c.); this was the earliest form of the *codex* or *book* in the modern sense of the word. The inner leaves of these *codices* had sinkings to receive the wax on both sides; only the backs of the two outer leaves being left plain or carved in relief to form the covers.

Many-leaved tablets.

When the written matter on these tablets was no longer wanted, a fresh surface for writing was prepared either by smoothing down the wax with the handle of the stilus, or else by scraping it off and pouring in a fresh supply. This is mentioned by Ovid (*Ar. Am.* I. 437); "cera......rasis infusa

---

[1] A fine set of five tablets is preserved in the coin room in the Paris Bibliothèque Nationale; see *Revue Archéol.* VIII. p. 461.

[2] A well-preserved example of Roman *pugillares* formed of two leaves of ivory, now in the Capitoline museum in Rome, is illustrated by Baumeister, *Denkmäler*, I. p. 355.

Waxed tablets.

tabellis¹." These tablets were sometimes called briefly *cerae;* the phrases *prima cera, altera cera,* meaning the first page, the second page. The best sorts of wooden writing-tablets were made of box-wood, and hence they are sometimes called πυξίον. In addition to the holes along one edge of each tablet through which the cord or wire was passed to hold the leaves together and to form the hinge, additional holes were often made along the opposite edge in order that the letter or other writing on the *tabulae* might be kept private by tying a thread through these holes and then impressing a seal on the knot. Plautus (*Bacch.* IV. iv. 64) alludes to this in mentioning the various things required to write a letter,

Effer cito stilum, ceram, et tabellas et linum.

In some cases wooden tablets of this kind were used without a coating of wax, but had simply a smooth surface to receive writing with ink and a reed pen. Many examples of these have been found in Egypt. The writing could be obliterated and a new surface prepared by sponging and rubbing with pumice-stone.

Whitened boards.

Among the Greeks wooden boards, whitened with chalk or gypsum, were often used for writing that was intended to be of temporary use only. Charcoal was used to write on these boards, which were called λευκώματα or γραμματεῖα λελευκωμένα². Public advertisements and official announcements were frequently written in this way and then hung up in a conspicuous place in the *agora* or market-place of the city.

Thus some of the inscriptions of the fourth century B.C., found at Delos mention that every month a λεύκωμα was suspended in the *agora*, on which was written a statement of the financial management and all the expenses of the Temple

---

[1] Lucian, who lived in the second century A.D., mentions (*Vita Luc.* II.) that when he was a boy he was in the habit of scraping the wax off his writing-tablets and using it to model little figures of men and animals. Probably he was not the only Roman school-boy who amused himself in this way.

[2] Charcoal or crayon-holders of bronze with a spring clip and sliding ring, exactly like those now used, have been found in Pompeii. These and other writing materials are illustrated by Baumeister, *Denkmäler*, Vol. III. p. 1585.

of the Delian Apollo during the past month. Finally, at the *Sacred accounts.* end of the year, an abstract of the accounts of the Temple was engraved as a permanent record on a marble *stele*. This was also the custom with regard to the financial records of the Athenian Parthenon, and probably most of the important Greek temples. In connection with the sacred records, the Delian inscriptions mention, in addition to the λευκώματα, other forms of tablets, the δέλτος and the πίναξ, and also χάρται or writings on *papyrus;* manuscripts of this last kind will be discussed in a subsequent section[1].

Late survivals of writing on tablets. Before passing on to *Late survivals.* describe other forms of classical manuscripts, it may be interesting to note that the ancient waxed tablets or *pugillares* continued to be used for certain purposes throughout the whole mediaeval period, down to the sixteenth century or even later. Many of the principal churches, especially in Italy, but also in other countries, possessed one or more diptychs on which were inscribed the names of all those who had in any way been benefactors either to the ecclesiastical foundation or to the building. In early times, during the daily celebration of Mass, the list of names was read out from the *diptych* by the Deacon standing in the gospel ambon; and the congregation was requested or "bid" to pray for the souls of those whose names they had just heard.

The "bidding prayer" before University sermon at Oxford *"Bidding the beads."* and Cambridge is a survival of this custom, which in the fifteenth century was termed "bidding the beads," that is "praying for the prayers" of the congregation. In some cases fine specimens of the old ivory *Consular diptychs* were used for this purpose in Italian churches till comparatively late times, but as a rule they fell into disuse before the eleventh or twelfth century, as the list of names became too long for the waxed leaves of a diptych, and so by degrees vellum rolls or else *codices,* often beautifully written in gold and silver letters, were substituted. One of the most splendid of these lists, the

---

[1] An Athenian inscription (*C. I. A.* i. 32) mentions accounts and other documents written on πινάκια καὶ γραμματεία.

Liber vitae of Durham, is now preserved in the British Museum; *Cotton manuscripts*, Domit. 7. 2.

For many other purposes, both ecclesiastical and secular, the classical waxed tablets were used in England and on the Continent, especially for lists of names, as for example in great Cathedral or Abbey churches the list for the week of the various priests who were appointed to celebrate each mass at each of the numerous altars.

List of guild-members. The British Museum possesses a very interesting late example of a waxed tablet which in shape, size and general appearance is exactly like the Roman *pugillares*. This is an oak tablet, about 20 inches long by 10 inches wide, covered with a thin layer of wax protected by the usual slightly raised margin about half an inch wide. Along one edge are three holes with leather loops to form the hinges; the other leaf is lost. On the wax is inscribed a list of the names of the members of a Flemish guild; each name is still as sharp and legible as the day it was written. The form of the writing shows that it belongs to the end of the fifteenth century. Such tablets were used both by the trade guilds of the middle ages and by the religious guilds formed for the cult of some special Saint.

Wooden Book. The most interesting mediaeval example of the classical form of manuscript made up of several leaves of waxed tablets was found a few years ago in a blocked-up recess in the old wooden church at Hopperstad in Norway. It was enclosed in a casket of wood covered with leather, and thus it still remains in a very perfect state of preservation; it is now in the University Museum at Christiania. The book consists of six tablets of box-wood, coated with wax within the usual raised margin, and hinged with leather thongs. The outer leaves are decorated on the back with carving mixed with inlay of different coloured woods.

Bestiary. The manuscript itself which is written on the wax is a *Bestiary*, dating, as its style shows, from the latter part of the thirteenth century, though the book itself is probably older. It contains lists of animals in Latin with a Norwegian translation, and it is copiously illustrated with drawings of scenes from agricultural and domestic life, executed in fine outline on the wax with a sharply pointed stilus. In every detail, except of course in the character of the writing and drawings, this book exactly resembles an ancient Greek or Roman many-leaved wooden book, πολύπτυχον, a very striking example of the unaltered survival of ancient methods for an extraordinarily long period.

During the mediaeval period, sets of ivory tablets hinged together were frequently made for devotional purposes. This form of manuscript has no layer of wax, but the writing is executed with a pen on the thin smooth leaf of ivory. Each leaf has its margin raised, like the ancient *pugillares*, to prevent the two adjacent surfaces from rubbing together.

Ivory tablets.

These ivory tablets usually contain a set of short prayers, and they are frequently illustrated with painted miniatures of sacred subjects exactly like those in the vellum manuscripts of the same date.

The South Kensington Museum possesses a very beautiful example of these ivory books; it is of Northern French workmanship dating from about the middle of the fourteenth century. It consists of eight leaves of ivory, measuring 4⅛ inches by 2⅜ inches in width. The six inner pages are extremely thin, no thicker than stout paper, and have paintings on both sides, the two covers are of thicker substance, about a quarter of an inch, and are decorated on the outside with beautiful carved reliefs.

Tablet with eight leaves.

This remarkable work of art has on the inner leaves fourteen very delicately executed miniatures of sacred subjects, single figures of Saints and scenes from Christ's Passion, painted in gold and colours in the finest style of French fourteenth century art, evidently executed by some very skilful illuminator.

Tablets like this with as many as eight ivory leaves are rare, but a very large number of beautiful ivory diptychs still exist, with carved reliefs on the outside of very graceful style and delicate execution. Most of these diptychs date from the fourteenth century, and are of French workmanship, but

Ivory diptychs.

they were also produced in England at the same time and of quite equal merit in design and execution.

Inscribed lead tablet.   *Manuscripts on lead plates,* like those of the ancient Greeks, were occasionally used in mediaeval times.

A single lead leaf of an Anglo-Saxon manuscript from Lord Londesborough's collection is illustrated in *Archaeologia,* Vol. XXXIV, Plate 36, page 438. This leaf measures 6½ inches by 5 inches in width. On it is incised with a stilus in fine bold semi-uncial writing the beginning of Aelfric's preface to his first collection of *Homilies,* which in modern English runs thus :—" I, Aelfric, monk and mass-priest, was sent in King Aethelred's time from Aelfeage the Bishop, the successor of Aethelwold, to a certain minster which is called Cernel, &c." At the top of the page there is a heading in large Runic characters. Aelfric was sent by Aelfeage Bishop of Winchester to be Abbot of Cerne in 988 or 989, and this interesting page appears to be of contemporary date. It was found by a labourer while digging in the precincts of the Abbey of Bury St Edmunds. Along one edge of the leaden page there are three holes to receive the loops which hinged the plates together, but the other leaves were not found.

Horn-books. *Horn-books.* One form of wooden tablet continued in use, especially in boys' schools, till the sixteenth century. This was a wooden board, rather smaller than an ordinary school-boy's slate, with a long handle at the bottom ; on it was fixed a sheet of vellum or paper on which was written or (in the latest examples) printed *the Alphabet, the Creed, the Lord's Prayer* or such like. Over this a thin sheet of transparent horn was nailed, whence these tablets were often called " horn-books." A good example dating from the sixteenth century is now preserved in the Bodleian library at Oxford.

CHAPTER II.

CLASSICAL MANUSCRIPTS WRITTEN WITH PEN AND INK.

To return now to classical forms of manuscripts, it appears to have been a long time before the *book* or *codex* form of manuscript was extended from the wood and ivory tablets to writings on parchment or paper.

It seems probable that throughout the Greek period manuscripts on paper or vellum were usually, if not always, in the shape of a long roll; and that it was not till about the beginning of the Roman Empire that leaves of parchment or paper were sometimes cut up into pages and bound together in the form of the older tablets. During the first two or three centuries of the Empire, manuscripts were produced in both of these forms—the *codex* and the *volumen;* but the *roll* form was by far the commoner, almost till the transference of the seat of government to Byzantium.

The roll form of MS.

The codex form.

The roll form of book is the one shown in many of the wall paintings of Pompeii; but on some sarcophagi reliefs of the second century A.D. books both of the *roll* and the *codex* shape are represented[1].

Having given some account of the various classical forms of manuscript in which the writing is incised with a sharp *stilus*, we will now pass on to the other chief forms of manuscript which were written with a pen and with ink or other pigment.

Writing with a pen.

[1] See, for example, a relief on the sarcophagus of a *scriba librarius* or library curator which is illustrated by Daremberg and Saglio, *Dict. Ant.* I. p. 708. The scribe is represented seated by his book-case *armarium*, on the shelves of which both *volumina* and *codices* are shown.

Books of the dead.

Manuscripts on papyrus; the oldest existing examples of this class are the so-called *Rituals of the Dead* found in the tombs of Egypt, especially in those of the Theban dynasties; the oldest of these date as far back as the sixteenth or fifteenth century B.C.[1]

They are executed with a reed pen in hieroglyphic writing on long rolls of papyrus, and are copiously illuminated with painted miniatures illustrating the subject of the text, drawn with much spirit and coloured in a very finely decorative way. Immense numbers of these Egyptian illuminated manuscripts still exist in a more or less fragmentary condition. One of the most perfect of these is the *Book of the Dead of Ani,* a royal scribe, dating from the fourteenth century B.C., now in the British Museum. An excellent facsimile of the whole of this fine illuminated manuscript has been edited by Dr Budge and published by the Trustees of the British Museum in 1890.

Egyptian psalter.

Manuscripts of this important class are not very accurately described as *Rituals of the Dead;* as Dr Budge points out they really consist of collections of *psalms* or *sacred hymns* which vary considerably in different manuscripts.

They appear to have been written in large numbers and kept in stock by the Egyptian undertakers ready for purchasers. Blank spaces were left for the name and titles of the dead person for whom they were bought.

Thus we find that the names are often filled in carelessly by another hand than that of the writer of the manuscript, and some examples exist in which the spaces for the name are still left blank.

Another of the finest and most complete of the funereal *papyri* is preserved in the Museum in Turin; see Pierret, *Le livre des Morts des anciens Egyptiens,* Paris, 1882.

Use of papyrus.

Papyrus seems to have been used for manuscripts more than any other substance both by the Greeks from the sixth century B.C. and by the Romans down to the time of the later Empire. Some very valuable Greek manuscripts on papyrus are preserved in the British Museum; among them the most

[1] The ancient method of manufacturing papyrus paper is described below, see page 22.

important for their early date are some fragments of Homer's *Iliad* of the third or second century B.C. Another papyrus manuscript in the same collection dating from the first century B.C. contains four *Orations* of the Athenian Orator Hyperides, a contemporary and rival of Demosthenes. In the last few years the important discovery has been made that in certain late tombs in Egypt, dating from the Roman period, the mummied bodies are packed in their coffins with large quantities of what was considered waste paper. This packing in some cases has been found to consist of papyrus manuscripts, some of which are of great importance. In this way the newly discovered treatise by Aristotle on the *Political Constitution of Athens*, and the *Mimes* of Herondas were saved from destruction by being used as inner wrappings for a coffin of about the year 100 A.D.[1]

Existing Greek MSS.

Other important manuscripts may yet be found, now that careful search is being made in this direction.

Unfortunately the large library of manuscripts, consisting of nearly 1800 papyrus rolls, which was discovered about the middle of the last century in the lava-buried town of Herculaneum, has not as yet been found to contain any works of much value or interest. These rolls are all charred by the heat of the lava, which overwhelmed the town, and the work of unrolling and deciphering the brittle carbonized paper necessarily goes on very slowly. The owner of this library appears to have been an enthusiastic student of the Epicurean philosophy in its later development, and his books are mainly dull, pedantic treatises on the various sciences such as mathematics, music and the like, treated from the Epicurean point of view, or rather from that of the Graeco-Roman followers of Epicurus.

Herculaneum library.

All these manuscripts appear to be of about the same date, not many years older, that is, than the year 79 A.D., when the eruption of Vesuvius overwhelmed Herculaneum and Pompeii in the same catastrophe. They are written in fine bold uncial

[1] Some very interesting fragments of the *Antiope* of Euripides have been brought to England by Mr Flinders Petrie, and have been edited by Dr Mahaffy in a collection entitled *The Flinders Petrie Papyri*, Dublin, 1891.

14 MANUSCRIPTS ON PAPYRUS AND PARCHMENT. [CHAP. II.

Papyrus rolls.

characters without illumination or ornament of any kind on rolls of papyrus nine or ten inches in breadth. In their present burnt and shrunken condition the rolls average about two inches in diameter, but they were probably larger than that in their original state; see *Palaeo. Soc.* Pl. 151, 152; the other published 'facsimiles' of the Herculaneum manuscripts are not perfectly trustworthy.

Herodotus on MSS.

In the time of Herodotus (c. 460 B.C.) *papyrus paper* (βιβλία or χάρται)[1] appears to have been used by the Greeks almost to the exclusion of parchment or other kinds of skin. In his interesting section on the introduction of the art of writing into Greece by the Phoenicians, Herodotus (V. 58) remarks that the Ionians in old times used to call *papyrus rolls* διφθέραι or "*parchment*," because they had once been in the habit of using skins of sheep or goats for manuscripts, at a time when *papyrus* paper was not to be had; and, Herodotus goes on to say, "Barbarians even now are accustomed to write their manuscripts on parchment."

Use of parchment.

Manuscripts on parchment; this old use of parchment for manuscripts was again introduced among the Greeks by Eumenes II., king of Pergamus from 197 to 159 B.C. At this time men had forgotten that parchment had ever been used for books, and so Varro, quoted by Pliny (*Hist. Nat.* XIII. 70), tells us that Eumenes *invented* this use of parchment; the real fact being that he re-introduced an old custom, and stimulated the careful preparation of parchment for the sake of the great library which he was anxious to make the most important collection of manuscripts in the world.

Varro tells us that he was driven to this use of parchment by the jealousy of the Egyptian King Ptolemy Epiphanes, whose enormous library at Alexandria was the only existing rival to the Pergamene collection. One of the Greek names

Pergamena.

for parchment, *Pergamena*, was derived from the fact of its being so largely made for the Pergamene Kings Eumenes and Attalus, both of whom were not only great patrons of

---

[1] The book-market in Athens was called τὰ βιβλία, i.e. οὗ τὰ βιβλία ὤνια; see Pollux IX. 47. Lucian, in his treatise *Adversus Indoctum*, gives an interesting account of the Greek book-buyers and book-sellers in his time; see § 1 and § 4.

CHAP. II.] MANUSCRIPTS ON LINEN AND POTSHERDS. 15

literature and collectors of ancient manuscripts, but were also enthusiastic buyers of pictures, statues, rich textiles and works of art of every class. The other word for parchment used for manuscripts is *membrana*.

Manuscripts on linen; in ancient Egypt hieroglyphic manuscripts with sacred hymns and portions of the so-called *Ritual of the Dead* were frequently written with a reed pen on fine linen. These manuscripts, which are often found among the mummy wrappings of burials under the Theban Dynasties, are usually illustrated with pen drawings in outline, not painted miniatures like those on the papyrus rolls. These drawings are executed with much spirit and with a beautiful, clean, certain touch.

Linen MSS.

The early Italian races, Latins, Samnites and others, appear to have used linen very frequently for their manuscript records and sacred books. Among the public records mentioned by Livy as having once been preserved with the Archives in the Capitoline Temple of Juno Moneta were some of these early linen manuscripts (*libri lintei*); see Liv. IV. 7, 13, 20. Livy also (X. 38) describes an ancient manuscript, containing an account of the ritual customs of the Samnites, as a *liber vetus linteus*. In historic times, however, *papyrus* and *parchment* appear to have superseded *linen* in ancient Rome.

Early MSS. in Italy.

Ostraka Manuscripts. For ephemeral purposes, such as tradesmen's accounts and other business matters, writing was often done with a pen and ink on broken fragments of pottery (ὄστρακα). An enormous number of these inscribed potsherds, mostly dating from the Ptolemaic period, have been found in Egypt, and especially on the little island of Elephantine in the Nile a short distance below the first cataract.

Inscribed potsherds.

Among the Greeks too, writing on potsherds was very common; especially when the Athenian tribes met in the Agora to record their votes for the exile of some unpopular citizen, whence is derived the term *ostracism* (ὀστρακισμός).

The word *liber* as meaning a *book* is supposed to be derived from a primitive custom of writing on the smooth inner bark of some tree, such as the birch, which supplies a fine silky substance, not at all unsuited for manuscripts.

MSS. on leaves. The large broad leaves of some varieties of the palm tree have also been used for manuscript purposes, more especially among the inhabitants of India and Ceylon. In early times the questions asked of the Oracle of the Pythian Apollo at Delphi were said to have been written on leaves of the laurel plant. Pali manuscripts in Ceylon are even now frequently written on palm-leaves; and we have the evidence of Pliny that this custom once existed among some of the ancient classical races: see *Hist. Nat.* XIII. 69, "Ante non fuisse chartarum usum, in palmarum foliis primo scriptitatum; deinde quarundam arborum libris. Postea publica monumenta plumbeis voluminibus, mox et privata linteis confici coepta aut ceris. Pugillarium enim usum fuisse etiam ante Trojana tempora invenimus apud Homerum." In this passage Pliny gives a list of all the chief materials that had been used for manuscripts in ancient times, the *leaves* and *bark of trees*, *plates of lead*, *linen cloth* and *waxed tablets*, he then goes on to describe at considerable length the methods of making paper from the pith of the papyrus plant; see page 22.

Greek libraries. Ancient libraries; among the Greeks and Romans of the historic period books do not appear to have been either rare or costly as they were during the greater part of the mediaeval period.

In the time of Alexander, the latter part of the fourth century B.C., large libraries had already been formed by wealthy lovers of literature, and in the second century B.C. the rival libraries of Ptolemy Epiphanes at Alexandria and of King Eumenes II. at Pergamus were said to have contained between them nearly a million volumes.

Roman libraries. Among the Romans of the Empire books were no less common. The owner of the above mentioned library at Herculaneum, consisting of nearly 1800 rolls or volumes, does not appear to have been a man of exceptional wealth; his house was small and his surroundings simple in character.

As early as the reign of Augustus, Rome possessed several large public libraries (*bibliothecae*). The first of these was instituted in 37 B.C. by Asinius Pollio both for Greek and Latin manuscripts. The second was the *Bibliotheca Octaviae* founded by Augustus in the Campus Martius in honour of his sister. The third was the magnificent double *library of Apollo Palatinus*, which Augustus built on the Palatine Hill. The fourth, also on the Palatine, the *Bibliotheca Tiberiana* was founded by Tiberius. The fifth was built by Vespasian as part of the group of buildings in his new *Forum Pacis*. The sixth and largest of all was the double library, for Greek and Latin books built by Trajan in his Forum close to the *Basilica Ulpia*. To some extent a classification of subjects was adopted in these great public libraries, one being mainly legal, another for ancient history, a third for state papers and modern records, but this classification appears to have been only partially adhered to. *The great libraries of Rome.*

In addition to these state libraries, Rome also possessed a large number of smaller "parish libraries" in the separate *vici*, and the total number, given in the *Regionary catalogues* as existing in the time of Constantine, is enormous; see Séraud, *Les livres dans l'antiquité*. *Parish libraries.*

With regard to the arrangement and fittings of Roman libraries, the usual method appears to have been this. Cupboards (*armaria*), fitted with shelves to receive the rolls or *codices* and closed by doors, were placed against the walls all round the room. These *armaria* were usually rather low, not more than from four to five feet in height, and on them were placed busts of famous authors; while the wall-space above the bookcases was decorated with similar portrait reliefs or paintings designed to fill panels or circular medallions. *Library fittings.*

Pliny (*Hist. Nat.* XXXV. 9), speaks of it being a new fashion in his time to adorn the walls of libraries with ideal portraits of ancient writers, such as Homer, executed in gold, silver or bronze relief. *Library decorations.*

The public library of Asinius Pollio was, Pliny says, decorated with portraits, but whether the great libraries of Pergamus and Alexandria were ornamented in this way, Pliny is unable to say. Magnificent medallion portraits in gold and silver were fixed round the walls of the two great libraries of Apollo on the Palatine Hill, and probably in the other still larger public libraries which were founded by subsequent Emperors.

Recent discovery. The ordinary private libraries of Rome were decorated in a similar way, but with reliefs of less costly materials. A very interesting example of this has recently been discovered and then destroyed on the Esquiline hill in Rome. The house in which this library was discovered was one of no very exceptional size or splendour. The *bibliotheca* itself consisted of a handsome room; the lower part of its walls, against which the *armaria* fitted, was left quite plain. Above that the walls were divided into square panels by small fluted pilasters, and in the centre of each space there was, or had *Authors' busts.* been, a medallion relief-portrait about two feet in diameter enclosed in a moulded frame. All this was executed in fine, hard marble-dust stucco (*opus albarium* or *marmoreum*).

The names of the authors whose portraits had filled the medallions were written in red upon the frames. Only one was legible—APOLLONIVS THYAN...No doubt the works of Apollonius of Thyana were kept in the *armarium* below the bust.

The library at Herculaneum, which contained the famous papyrus rolls, was a much smaller room. Besides the bookcases all round the walls, it had also an isolated *armarium* in the centre of the room; and this, no doubt, was a usual arrangement.

The room at Herculaneum was so small that there can only have been just enough space to walk between the central bookcase and the *armaria* ranged all round against the wall.

Closed bookcases. As the Comm. Lanciani has pointed out (*Ancient Rome*, p. 195), it is interesting to note that the ancient Roman method of arranging books in low, closed cupboards is still preserved in the great library of the Vatican in Rome; which is unlike most existing libraries in the fact that on first entering no one would guess that it was a library, not a single book being visible.

Of the ancient *armaria* themselves no example now

exists. They were of wood, and therefore, of course, perishable. But we may, I think, argue from analogy, that the doors of the cupboards were richly ornamented with painted decorations, thus forming an elaborate dado or *podium* below the row of portrait reliefs which occupied the upper part of the walls.

The principal quarter in Rome for the shops of booksellers (*bibliopolae* or *librarii*) appears to have been the *Argiletum*, which (in Imperial times) was an important street running into the Forum Romanum between the Curia and the Basilica Aemilia; see Mart. I. 3, 117[1]. *Booksellers' quarter.*

For ancient manuscripts or autograph works of famous authors large prices were often paid. Aristotle is said to have given three talents (about £750) for an autograph manuscript of Speusippus, and a manuscript of Virgil's second book of the *Aeneid*, thought to be the author's own copy, sold for twenty *aurei*, more than £20 in modern value; see Aul. Gell. III. 17, and II. 3.

But ordinary copies of newly published works, even by popular authors, appear to have been but little more expensive than books of this class are at the present day. The publisher and bookseller Tryphon could sell Martial's first book of *Epigrams* at a profit for two *denarii*—barely two shillings in modern value; see Mart. XIII. 3. It may seem strange that written manuscripts should not have been much more costly than printed books, but when one considers how they were produced the reason is evident. Atticus, the Sosii and other chief publishers of Rome owned a large number of slaves who were trained to be neat and rapid scribes. Fifty or a hundred of these slaves could write from the dictation of one reader, and thus a small edition of a new volume of Horace's *Odes* or Martial's *Epigrams* could be produced with great rapidity and at very small cost[2]. *Cost of new books.* *Slave scribes.*

Little capital would be required for the education of the

[1] The end of the Argiletum is shown in the plan of the Forum Romanum in Middleton. *Ancient Rome*, 1892, Vol. I.
[2] One reason of this was that even the most popular authors did not receive large sums for the copyright of their works.

20 ROMAN BOOKSELLERS. THE TECHNIQUE [CHAP. II.

slave-scribes, and when once they were taught, the cost of their labour would be little more than the small amount of food which was necessary to keep them alive and in working order.

Cicero (*Att.* II. 4) speaks of the publisher Atticus selling manuscripts produced in this way by slave labour on a large scale.

Librarii. The name *librarius* was given not only to the booksellers, but also to slave librarians, and to scribes, the latter being sometimes distinguished by the name *scriptores librarii*. *Librarii antiquarii* were writers who were specially skilled in copying ancient manuscripts. The word *scriba* commonly denotes a *secretary* rather than what we should now call a *scribe*.

In Athens a class of booksellers, βιβλιογράφοι, appears to have existed as early as the fifth century B.C.; see Poll. VII. 211. The name βιβλιοπῶλαι was subsequently used, and adopted by the Romans.

THE TECHNIQUE OF ANCIENT MANUSCRIPTS[1].

Parchment and vellum. Parchment. With regard to the preparation of parchment and other kinds of skin for writing on (*Pergamena* and *Membrana*) there is little to be said. The skins of many different animals have been used for this purpose both in classical and mediaeval times, especially skins of calves, sheep, goats and pigs. Unlike manuscripts on papyrus, parchment or vellum[2] manuscripts were usually covered with writing on both sides, since the ink does not show through from one side to the other, as it is liable to do on the more absorbent and spongy

[1] A good deal of what is said in this section with regard to the technique of classical manuscripts will apply also to manuscripts of the mediaeval period. Many of the processes had been inherited in an unbroken tradition from ancient times, and others were revived in the Middle Ages through a study of various classical writers on pigments and the like, especially Pliny and Vitruvius.

[2] The words *parchment* and *vellum* are used vaguely to imply many different kinds of skins. Strictly speaking *vellum* implies calf-skin, but the word is commonly used to denote the finer and smoother qualities of skin; the name *parchment* being given to the coarse varieties; see Peignot, *L'histoire du parchemin*, Paris, 1812.

papyrus paper. For this reason complete or partial erasures were much easier to execute on vellum than on papyrus. The writing was first sponged so as to remove the surface ink, and the traces that still remained were got rid of by rubbing the surface of the vellum with pumice stone. In some cases the manuscript was erased from the whole of a vellum codex or roll, and the cleaned surface then used to receive fresh writing. *Erasures.*

Palimpsests; manuscripts of this class, on twice-used vellum, were called *palimpsests* (παλίμψηστος); see Cic. *Fam.* vii. 18. Several important texts, such as the legal work of Gaius, have been recovered by laboriously deciphering the not wholly obliterated writing on these palimpsests. During the early mediaeval period, when classical learning was little valued, many a dull treatise of the schoolmen or other theological work of small interest was written over the obliterated text of some much earlier and more valuable classical author. *Palimpsests.*

In some cases it appears that papyrus manuscripts were made into palimpsests, but probably not very often, as it would be difficult to erase the ink on a roll of papyrus without seriously injuring the surface of the paper. *Papyrus MSS.*

Moreover as papyrus manuscripts were only written on one side of the paper, the back was free to receive new writing without any necessity to rub out the original text. The recently discovered treatise by Aristotle on the *Political Constitution of Athens* has some monetary accounts written on the back of the papyrus by some unphilosophical man of business not many years later than the date of the original treatise.

Papyrus paper. The ancient methods employed in the preparation of papyrus paper (*charta*) can be clearly made out by the evidence of existing examples aided by the minute but not wholly accurate description given by Pliny, *Hist. Nat.* XIII. 71 to 83. *Papyrus paper.*

The papyrus plant, the *Cyperus Papyrus* of Linnaeus, (Greek βύβλος) is a very tall, handsome variety of reed which grows in marshes and shallows along the sides of streams of

22   THE MANUFACTURE OF   [CHAP. II.

Papyrus plant. water. The plant has at the top a very graceful tufted bunch of foliage; its stem averages from three to four inches in diameter, and the total height of the plant is from ten to twelve feet.

It grows in many places in Syria, in the Euphrates valley and in Nubia. In Egypt itself it is now extinct, but it was abundant there in ancient times, especially in the Delta of the Nile.

The only spot in Europe where the papyrus plant grows in a wild state is near Syracuse in the little river Anapus, where it was probably introduced by the Arab conquerors in the eighth or ninth century A.D.

It grows here in great abundance and sometimes nearly blocks up the stream so that a boat can scarcely get along.

The stem of the papyrus consists of a soft, white, spongy or cellular pith surrounded by a thin, smooth, green rind. Papyrus paper ($\beta\iota\beta\lambda\iota a$ or $\chi\acute{a}\rho\tau\eta s$) was wholly made from the cellular pith. The method of manufacture was as follows.

Process of manufacture. The long stem of the plant was first cut up into convenient pieces of a foot or more in length; the pith in each piece was then very carefully and evenly cut with a sharp knife into thin slices. These slices were then laid side by side, their edges touching but not overlapping, on the smooth surface of a wooden table which was slightly inclined to let the superfluous sap run off, as it was squeezed out of the slices of pith by gentle blows from a smooth wooden mallet. When by repeated beating the layer of pith had been hammered down to a thinner substance, and a great deal of the sap had drained off, some fine paste made of wheat-flour was carefully brushed over the whole surface of the pith. A second layer of slices of pith, previously prepared by beating, was then laid crosswise on the first layer made adhesive by the paste, so that the slices in the second layer were at right angles to those of the first. The beating process was then repeated, the workmen being careful to get rid of all lumps or inequalities, and the beating was continued till the various slices of pith in the two layers were thoroughly united and amalgamated together.

For the best sort of papyrus these processes were repeated

a third and sometimes even a fourth time, the separate slices in each layer being cut much thinner than in the coarser sorts of paper which consisted of two layers only. The next process was to dry and press the paper; after which its surface was carefully smoothed and polished with an ivory burnisher[1]; its rough edges were trimmed, and it was then ready to be made up into sheets or rolls. There was nothing in the method of manufacture to limit strictly the size of the papyrus sheets (σελίδες, *paginae*) either in breadth or length; the workmen could lay side by side as many slices of the pith as he liked, and slices of great length might have been cut out of the long stem of the *papyrus*. Practically, however, it was found convenient to make the paper in rather small sheets; twelve to sixteen inches are the usual widths of papyrus manuscripts.

Use of many layers.

Sizes of papyrus.

The reason of this obviously was that it would have been impossible to cut slices of great length to the requisite thinness and evenness of substance, and so papyrus manuscripts are always made up of a large number of separate sheets carefully pasted together. This was very skilfully done by workmen who (in Pliny's time) were called *glutinatores;* cf. Cic. *Att.* IV. 4. The two adjacent edges of the sheets, which were to be joined together by lapping, were thinned down by careful rubbing to about half their original substance. The two laps were then brushed over with paste, accurately applied together, and the union was then completed by beating with the wooden mallet. When the pasted joint was dry it was rubbed and polished with the ivory burnisher till scarcely any mark of the joining remained. In this way long rolls were formed, often fifty feet or more in length; as a rule, however, excessive length for a single roll was inconvenient. Pliny mentions 20 sheets as being an ordinary limit. Thus, for example, in such works as Homer's *Iliad* or Virgil's *Aeneid*, each *book* would form a separate *volumen* or roll (Greek κύλινδρος or τόμος).

Union of the sheets.

Long rolls.

The invention of papyrus paper dates from an early period in the history of Egypt. Examples still exist which

---

[1] In some cases the paper was *sized*, before the final smoothing; but as a rule sufficient *size* was supplied by the flour used to paste the layers together.

are as early as 2300 B.C., and its manufacture was probably known long before that.

Papyrus used in Greece.

In later times Egyptian papyrus was an important article of export into many countries. An Attic inscription of the year 407 B.C. tells us what the cost of paper then was in Athens; two sheets (χάρται δύο) cost two drachmae and four obols, equal in modern value to about four shillings; see *C. I. A.* I. 324. The χάρται in this case probably mean, not a single page, but several sheets pasted together to form a roll.

Papyrus made in Rome.

In Pliny's time paper was made not only in Egypt but also in Rome and at other places in Italy[1]. The best kind was formerly called *Hieratica*, because it was used in Egypt for sacred hieroglyphic writing only. In later times this finest quality, in Rome at least, was called *Augusta*, and the second quality *Liviana*, from Livia the wife of Augustus. A coarse variety used for wrapping up parcels and the like was called "shop-paper," *emporetica*. Pliny also tells us that paper was manufactured of many different breadths, varying from about four to eighteen inches. The commonest width was about twelve inches; see Pliny, *Hist. Nat.* XIII. 71 to 83.

Old MSS. on papyrus.

In the last of these paragraphs Pliny mentions examples of old papyrus manuscripts existing in his time, such as manuscripts in the handwriting of Tiberius and Gaius Gracchus, which were nearly two centuries old. Manuscripts written by Cicero, Augustus and Virgil are, he says, still frequently to be seen.

With regard to the antiquity of paper Pliny's views are far from correct. He thinks paper was first made in Egypt in the time of Alexander the Great (*Hist. Nat.* XIII. 79), whereas, as is mentioned above, papyrus paper of fine quality was certainly made in Egypt nearly 2000 years before the time of Alexander, and probably much earlier.

The best kinds of papyrus paper are close in texture, with

---

[1] Some of the enormous ranges of store-houses for goods imported into Rome and landed on the Tiber quay were specially devoted to the use of paper warehouses, *horrea chartaria*; extensive remains of these have recently been discovered near Monte Testaccio; see Middleton, *Remains of Ancient Rome*, 1892, Vol. II. pp. 260—262.

CHAP. II.]   PAPER OF GOOD QUALITY.   25

a smooth surface, very pleasant to write upon with a reed *Paper of fine quality.*
pen, and adapted to receive miniature paintings of great
refinement and delicacy of touch. To prevent the ink
spreading or soaking into the paper, it was as a final process
sometimes soaked in size made of fish-bones or gum and
water, exactly as modern linen paper is sized. The colour of
the papyrus is a pale brown, very pleasant to the eye, and
excellent as a background to the painted decorations.

When it was first made, papyrus paper must have been *Fibrous texture.*
extremely durable and tough owing to its compound structure
with two or more fibrous layers placed cross-wise. The
parallel fibrous lines of the pith are very visible on the
surface of papyrus paper; and these regular lines served as a
guide to the scribe when writing, so that when papyrus was
used it was not necessary to cover the page with ruled lines
to keep the writing even, as had to be done when the
manuscript was on vellum.

In a papyrus manuscript the pages of writing are set side
by side, across the roll, with a small margin between each
page or column.

A small terra-cotta statuette[1] of about the fifth or fourth *Greek examples of papyrus rolls.*
century B.C. found at Salamis in Cyprus in 1890, shows a
Greek scribe writing on a long papyrus roll placed on a low
table before which he is sitting.

Among Greek vase paintings of the same date a not
uncommon subject is the poetess Sappho reading from a
papyrus roll. A fourth century vase with this subject in the
Central Museum in Athens shows Sappho holding a manuscript on which the following words are inscribed (supplying missing letters and correcting blunders)

ΘΕΟΙ ΗΕΡΙΩΝ ΕΠΕΩΝ ΕΡΧΟΜΑΙ
ΑΓΓΕΛΟΣ ΝΕΩΝ ΤΜΝΩΝ.

By the figure of Sappho is inscribed the beginning of her
name, ϟΑΠ in letters of archaistic form.

A very similar design occurs on a beautiful gem in the
British Museum (B.M. *Cat. of gems*, No. 556), which appears
to date from the latter part of the fifth century B.C. A very

[1] Now in the Fitzwilliam Museum.

26 PAPYRUS MANUSCRIPTS AND [CHAP. II.

Sappho reading. graceful female figure, probably meant for Sappho, is represented seated on a chair with high curved back. She is reading from a manuscript roll which she holds by the two rolled up ends, holding one in each hand.

This method of holding a papyrus manuscript is shown very clearly on a vase in the British Museum on which the same motive is painted. The lady (Sappho) holds the two rolled up portions of the manuscript, stretching tight the intermediate portion on which is the column of writing which she is reading.

As the reader progressed the paper was unrolled from the roll held in the right hand, and the part just read was rolled up in the left-hand roll. These Greek representations do not *Umbilicus or roller.* usually show any stick or roller for the manuscript to be rolled round; but in Roman times a wooden or ivory roller (ὄμφαλος, *umbilicus*) was used as the core of the roll; and the end of the long strip of papyrus by the last page or column of text was pasted on to it. The ends of the *umbilicus* were often fitted with a round knob or boss, which was decorated with gilding or colour. The edges of the papyrus roll were smoothed with pumice-stone (*pumice mundus*), and the whole manuscript was often provided with a vellum case, which was stained a bright colour, red, purple or yellow. Tibullus (*El.* III. i. 9) alludes to these ornamental methods.

Lutea sed niveum involvat membrana libellum.
Pumex et canas tondeat ante comas;
. . . .
Atque inter geminas pingantur cornua frontes.

The *frontes* are the edges of the roll, and the *cornua* are the projecting portions of the two wooden rollers.

Inscribed titles. The title of the manuscript was written on a ticket or slip of vellum, which hung down from the closed roll like the pendant seal of a mediaeval document. Thus when a number of manuscripts were piled on the shelf of an *armarium* the pendants hanging down from the ends of the rolls indicated plainly what the books were, without the necessity of pulling them from their place.

Small numbers of rolls, especially manuscripts which had

to be carried about, were often kept in round drum-like boxes (*capsae* or *scrinia*), with loop handles to carry them by.

Much of the beauty of an ancient manuscript depended on the use of red or purple ink for *headings, indices* and *marginal glosses*. As Pliny says (*Hist. Nat.* XXXIII. 122) *minium in voluminum quoque scriptura usurpatur*. *Coloured inks.*

The use of purple ink for the *index* is mentioned by Martial in his epigram *Ad librum suum* (III. 2) where he sums up the various methods of decoration which in his time were applied to manuscripts,

> *Cedro nunc licet ambules perunctus,*
> *Et frontis gemino decens honore*
> *Pictis luxurieris umbilicis;*
> *Et te purpura delicata velet,*
> *Et cocco rubeat superbus index.*

The oil of cedar wood, mentioned in the first of these lines, was smeared over the back of papyrus manuscripts to preserve them from book-worms. *Use of oil.*

The act of unrolling a manuscript to read it was called *explicare*, and when the reader had come to the end it was *opus explicitum*. In mediaeval times from the false analogy of the word (*hic*) *incipit*, a verb *explicit* was invented, and was often written at the end of *codices* to show that the manuscript was complete to the end, though, strictly speaking the word is only applicable to a *roll*.

The use of papyrus paper for manuscripts to some extent continued till mediaeval times. Papyrus manuscripts of the sixth and seventh century A.D. are not uncommon, and, long after vellum had superseded papyrus paper for the writing of books, short documents, such as letters, Papal deeds and the like, were still frequently written on papyrus. Papal *Briefs* on papyrus still exist which were written as late as the eleventh century. *Mediaeval use of papyrus.*

The *black ink* which was used for classical manuscripts was of the kind now known as "Indian" or more correctly "Chinese ink," which cannot be kept in a fluid state, but has to be rubbed up with water from day to day as it is required. One of the menial offices which Aeschines when a boy had to *Black ink.*

28 BLACK AND RED INK [CHAP. II.

Carbon ink. perform in his father's school was "rubbing the ink," τὸ μέλαν τρίβων; see Demos. *De Corona*, p. 313. This kind of ink (μέλαν or μελάνιον, *atramentum librarium*) simply consists of finely divided particles of carbon, mixed with gum or with size made by boiling down shreds of parchment. It was obtained by burning a resinous substance and collecting the soot on a cold flat surface, from which it could afterwards be scraped off. The soot had then to be very finely ground, mixed with a gummy medium and then moulded into shape and dried. The process is described by Pliny, *Hist. Nat.* XXXV. 41; and better still by Vitruvius, VII. 10.

Black pigment. A variety of this carbon pigment used for pictures on stucco by wall-painters was called *atramentum tectorium*, modern "lamp-black"; the only difference between this and writing ink was in the kind of glutinous medium used with it. Careful scribes probably prepared their own ink, as the writers of mediaeval manuscripts usually did. The common commercial black ink of about 300 A.D. was sold at a very cheap rate, as is recorded in an inscription containing part of Diocletian's famous edict which was found at Megalopolis and published by Mr Loring (*Jour. Hell. Stud.* Vol. XI., 1890, p. 318, line 46). Under the heading "Pens and ink," Περὶ καλάμων καὶ μελανίου, the price of ink, μελάνιον, is fixed at 12 small copper coins the pound.

Very great skill is required to prepare carbon ink of the finest quality. Though it is now largely manufactured in Europe, none but the Chinese can make ink of the best sort.

In some places sepia ink from the cuttle-fish was used in ancient times; see Persius, *Sat.* III. 12; and cf. Pliny, *Hist. Nat.* XI. 8, and XXXII. 141.

Red inks. The *red ink* used for ancient manuscripts was of three different kinds, namely red lead, vermilion or sulphuret of mercury, and red ochre. The ancient names for these red pigments were used very indiscriminately, μίλτος, *minium*, *cinnabaris* and *rubrica*. In some cases μίλτος certainly means the costly vermilion; and again the word is also used both for red lead and for the much cheaper red ochre. The latter appears to be always meant by the name μίλτος Σινώπις; see

Choisy, *Inscrip. Lebadeia*, p. 197. The Latin words *minium* and *rubrica* are used in the same vague way; see Vitruv. VII. 9; and Pliny, *Hist. Nat.* XXXV. 31 to 35.

In mediaeval manuscripts red ink (*rubrica*) was largely used not only for headings and glosses, but also in Service books for the ritual directions, which have hence taken the name of *rubrics*.

The purple ink (*coccus*), which Martial mentions in the passage quoted above at page 27, was made from the *kermes* beetle, which lives on the ilex trees of Greece and Asia Minor. This was one of the most important of the ancient dyes for woven stuffs and it was also used as a pigment by painters; see below, page 246. *Purple ink.*

The inkstands of ancient scribes were commonly made double, to hold both black and red ink. Many examples of these from Egypt and elsewhere still exist, and they are shown in many of the Pompeian wall-paintings. They usually are in the form of two bronze cylinders linked together, each with a lid which is attached by a little chain. Other inkstands are single, little round boxes of bronze, in shape like a large pill-box. Another method, specially common in ancient Egypt, was for the scribe to carry about his ink, both black and red, in a solid form; he then rubbed up with water just as much as he needed at the time. The box and palette mentioned below was made for this use of solid inks, except that the whole thing, handle and all, is made out of one piece of metal. *Double inkstands.*

The pens used by ancient writers of manuscripts were mainly some variety of reed (κάλαμος, *calamus* or *canna*), cut diagonally to a point like a modern quill pen. Great numbers of reed pens have been found in Egyptian tombs and also in Pompeii; they exactly resemble those still used in Egypt and in Oriental countries generally. *Reed pens.*

Metal pens were also used by Greek and Roman scribes. Examples both in silver and bronze have been found in Greece and in Italy, shaped very much like a modern steel pen[1]. *Metal pens.*

[1] A silver pen was found by Dr Waldstein in 1891 in the tomb of the Aristotle family at Chalcis.

30 PENS AND PEN-CASES. [CHAP. II.

Scribes' palettes.   In some cases manuscripts were written with a fine brush instead of a pen, especially the hieroglyphic manuscripts of ancient Egypt. Many combined scribes' palettes and brush cases have been found in Egyptian tombs. These are long slips of wood, partly hollowed to hold the brushes, and with two cup-like sinkings at one end for the writer to rub up his cakes of black and red ink.

In Egyptian manuscripts red ink is used much more copiously than either in Greek or Latin manuscripts. Very often the scribe writes his columns alternately in black and red for the sake of the decorative appearance of the page.

Pen-cases.   Egyptian pen-cases in the form of a bronze tube about $\frac{3}{4}$ inch in diameter and 10 inches long with a tightly fitting cap have frequently been found. The British Museum possesses good examples of these, and of the other writing implements here described.

Reed pens.   The above-mentioned passage in the *Edict of Diocletian* (see page 28) gives the prices of reed pens (κάλαμοι) of various qualities. The difference is very great between the best and the inferior kinds of pens; the best quality appears to have been made from the long single joint of a reed.

There is no evidence that quill pens were used in classical times, but it is difficult to believe that so natural an expedient never occurred to any ancient scribe, especially when the use of vellum for manuscripts came in; for papyrus paper the softer reed pen would be more convenient than a quill, and indeed for all the earlier sort of Greek and Latin writing in large *uncial* characters. It is only for the smaller *cursive* writing that a quill would be as suitable as a reed pen.

The inscription mentioned at p. 24 as giving the cost of paper in Athens in 407 B.C. is part of a record of the expenses of building the Erechtheum. It also mentions the purchase for 4 drachmae of 4 wooden writing-tablets, χάρται ἐωνήθησαν δύο, ἐς ἃς τὰ ἀντίγραφα ἐνεγράψαμεν ....┠┠|||| Σανίδες τέτταρες... ┠┠┠┠

CHAPTER III.

CLASSICAL ILLUMINATED MANUSCRIPTS.

THE mediaeval phrase *illuminated manuscript* means a manuscript which is "lighted up" with coloured decoration in the form of ornamental initial-letters or painted miniatures. Dante speaks of "The art which in Paris is called illuminating," *Illumination.*

......*quell' arte*
Che alluminare è chiamata in Parisi; Purg. XI. 80.

The important use that was made of red paint (*minium*) in the decoration of manuscripts led to the painter being called a *miniator*, whence the pictures that he executed in manuscripts were called *miniature* or *miniatures*. Finally the word *miniature* was extended in meaning to imply any painting on a *minute* scale[1]. Originally, however, it was only applied to the painted decorations of manuscripts. *Use of minium.*

The Egyptian manuscript "Books of the Dead" are very copiously illuminated with painted miniatures, both in the form of ornamental borders along the edge of the papyrus, and also with larger compositions which occupy the whole depth of the roll. *Egyptian miniatures.*

It is difficult to say to what extent illuminated manuscripts were known to the ancient Greeks, but they were certainly not uncommon in Rome towards the close of the Republic; and it may fairly be assumed that it was from the Greeks that the very inartistic Romans derived the custom of decorating manuscripts with painted miniatures.

[1] There is, of course, no etymological connection between the words *miniature* and *minute*; the latter being derived from the Latin *minutus, minus*.

32 ILLUMINATIONS IN CLASSICAL MANUSCRIPTS. [CHAP. III.

Illustrations in Roman MSS.

Pliny tells us (*Hist. Nat.* XXXV. 11) that a number of manuscripts in the library of M. Varro in the first century B.C. contained no less than 700 portraits of illustrious personages.

That the original manuscript of Vitruvius' work on *Architecture* was illustrated with explanatory pictures is shown by the frequent reference in the text to these lost illustrations which are mentioned as being at the end of the work; *e.g.* see III., *Praef.*, 4.

A manuscript written in letters of gold is mentioned by Suetonius (*Nero*, 10); this was a copy of Nero's own poem which was publicly read aloud to an audience on the Capitol, and was then deposited in the Temple of Jupiter Capitolinus.

Writing in gold.

Again, two centuries later the mother of Maximus, who was titular Caesar from 235 to 238 A.D., is said to have given him a manuscript of Homer's poems written in gold letters on purple vellum; see Jul. Capit., *Max. Vita.*

There is, in short, abundant evidence to show that illuminated manuscripts were common among the Romans of the Imperial period; and there is a very strong probability that manuscripts decorated with miniatures were no less frequent in the great libraries of the Ptolemies and of the Attalid kings, in fact throughout the Greek world from the time of Alexander the Great downwards, if not earlier still.

Greek miniatures.

Some notion of the great beauty of the illustrations in Greek manuscripts may perhaps be gathered from an examination of the masterly and delicately graceful drawings incised in outline which decorate the finest of the Greek bronze *cistae*. Nothing could surpass the perfect beauty of the outline engravings on the so-called *Ficoronian cista*, which is now preserved in the Museo del Collegio Romano in Rome. Part of this series representing scenes from the adventures of the Argonauts is shown on fig. 1.

Two sources of knowledge.

With regard to the general scheme of decoration in classical manuscripts, we have the evidence of a few existing examples dating from about the time of Constantine, and also a large number of copies of Roman manuscript-pictures of earlier date than the third century A.D., which are to be seen in various Italian and Byzantine manuscripts of the eleventh and twelfth centuries.

Fig. 1. Part of the drawing engraved on the bronze *cista* of Ficoroni, dating from the early part of the fourth century B.C. A beautiful example of Greek drawing.

The evidence derived from these two sources leads to the conclusion that as a rule the illuminations in classical manuscripts were treated as separate pictures, each surrounded with a simple painted frame, and not closely linked to the text in the characteristic mediaeval fashion. The mediaeval method, by often introducing miniature paintings within the boundary of large initial letters, and by surrounding the page with borders of foliage which grow out of the

Isolated pictures.

Mediaeval method. chief initials of the text, makes the decoration an essential part of the whole and creates a close union between the literary and the ornamental parts of the book, which is very unlike the usual ancient system of having a plainly written text with isolated miniature paintings introduced at intervals throughout the pages of the book.

Iliad of the 4th century. *Manuscript of the Iliad at Milan;* of all existing Greek or Latin manuscripts none gives a better notion of the style of illuminations used in manuscripts of the best Graeco-Roman period than the fragments of Homer's *Iliad* which are preserved in the Biblioteca Ambrogiana in Milan.

These fragments consist of fifty-eight miniature paintings, which have been cut out of a folio manuscript on vellum of Homer's *Iliad*, dating probably from the latter part of the fourth century A.D. The mutilator of this *codex* seems only to have cared to preserve the pictures, and the only portion of the text which still exists is about eight hundred not consecutive lines which happen to be written on the backs of the paintings. Great additional interest is given to this priceless fragment by the fact that the miniatures are much older in style than the date of the manuscript itself, and have evidently been copied from a much earlier Greek original.

Older Greek style. And more than that; these paintings take one back further still; their rhythmical composition, the dignity of their motives, the simplicity of the planes, and the general largeness of style which is specially noticeable in some of the miniatures representing fighting armies of gods and heroes, all suggest that we have here a record, weakened and debased though it may be, of some grand series of mural decorations on a large scale, dating possibly from the best period of Greek art.

As is naturally the case with copies of noble designs executed at a period of extreme decadence these paintings are very unequal in style, combining feebleness of touch and coarseness of detail with great spirit in the action of the figures and great dignity in the compositions, which have numerous figures crowded without confusion of line, thus suggesting large scale though the paintings are actually miniatures only five or six inches long. The treatment of gods and heroes, especially Zeus, Apollo, Achilles and others, has much that recalls fine Hellenic models. And some of the personifications, such as *Night* and the river *Scamander*, possess a gracefulness of pose and beauty of form which was far beyond the conception of any fourth century artist.

Hellenic models.

It should, however, be observed that a fine Hellenic origin is not suggested by all the fifty-eight pictures from this *Iliad*. Some of them are obviously of later and inferior style, with weak scattered compositions, very unlike the nobility and decorative completeness of the best among the miniatures.

With regard to the arrangement of these pictures, each is surrounded by a simple frame formed of bands of blue and red; in most cases the miniatures reach across the whole width of the page. The colouring is heavy, painted in opaque *tempera* pigments with an undue preponderance of *minium* or red lead. White lead, yellow, brown and red ochres are largely used, together with a variety of vegetable colours and the purple-red of the *kermes* beetle (*coccus*), but no gold is used, a bright yellow ochre being employed as a substitute[1].

Scheme of colour.

The costumes are partly ancient Greek and partly of later Roman fashion. A nimbus encircles each deity's head, and different colours are used to distinguish them. The nimbus of Zeus is purple, that of Venus is green; those of the other gods are mostly blue. To a large extent the backgrounds of the pictures are not painted, but the creamy white of the vellum is left exposed[2].

The Virgil of the Vatican; next in importance to the Ambrosian *Iliad*, among the existing examples of classical illuminated manuscripts, comes the manuscript of Virgil's poems (*Vat.* No. 3225) which is supposed to have been

The Vatican Virgil.

[1] Further details with regard to these pigments are given below, see pages 239 to 249.

[2] Reproductions of these miniatures were published by Cardinal Mai, *Picturae antiquissimae bellum Iliacum repraesentantes*, Milan, 1819. Far more accurate copies of some of the miniatures, but without colour, are given by *l'alaeo. Soc.*, Plates 39, 40, 50 and 51.

written in the third or more probably the fourth century
A.D. The text is written in large handsome capitals, well
formed except that all the cross lines are too short, T, for
example being written thus ⊤.

The whole manuscript, but especially the *Aeneid*, is decorated with pictures, fifty in all, each framed by a simple
border of coloured bands. The style of these miniatures
is very different and artistically very inferior to that of
the Ambrosian *Iliad*.

Miniatures of the 5th century.
The whole of the designs, in composition and drawing
and in the costumes of the figures, are those of the fourth
century. The details are coarse, the attitudes devoid of
spirit, and the figures clumsy. The backgrounds are painted
in and the colouring is dull in tone and heavy in texture, put
in with a considerable body of pigment (*impasto*). Gold, not
in leaf but as a fluid pigment, is largely used for high lights
on trees, mountains, roofs of buildings, and for the folds of
drapery, especially where the stuff is red or purple. The
male figures have flesh of a reddish-brown tint like many
of the Pompeian wall paintings; they wear short tunics
with cloaks thrown over the shoulders. Other figures wear
a long *dalmatica* or tunic, ornamented with two vertical
purple stripes, closely resembling the tunics which have
recently been found in such abundance in the late Roman
tombs of the Fayoum in Upper Egypt

Period of decadence.
On the whole the miniatures are neither graceful nor
highly decorative; they were executed at about the low
water mark of classical artistic decadence shortly before
the Byzantine revival under Justinian. Much that has been
written in their praise must be attributed to antiquarian
enthusiasm rather than to just criticism[1].

Before passing on to another class of manuscripts it should
be noted that there is in existence one manuscript of the
fourth or fifth century A.D. which is of special interest on

---

[1] Some fairly accurate reproductions of these miniatures were published by
Bartoli, *Antiquissimi Virgiliani Codicis fragmenta Bibl. Vat.*, Roma, 1741 and
1782. Examples from this and two other ancient but un-illuminated codices of
Virgil in the Vatican library are given by the *Palaeo. Soc.*, Plates 113 to 117.

CHAP. III.]   OF THE VATICAN VIRGIL.   37

account of its being ornamented, not only with miniature
pictures, but also with some decorative designs of a stiff

Fig. 2.   Miniature of classical design from a twelfth century *Psalter* in the
Vatican library.

conventional character. This is a Roman *Kalendar*, which forms part of a manuscript in the Imperial library in Vienna. The ornaments have but little decorative merit, but they are of interest as showing that the illuminations in classical manuscripts were not always confined to the subject pictures.

Copies of lost originals.

It has not as a rule been sufficiently noticed that the style of miniature paintings in manuscripts of a considerably earlier date than either the Ambrosian *Iliad* or the Vatican Virgil is very fairly represented in various manuscripts of the tenth to the twelfth century, the illuminators of which have evidently copied, as accurately as they were able, miniatures in manuscripts of the first or second century A.D.

The originals of these early Roman manuscripts do not now exist, and therefore the information as to their style and composition, which is given in the mediaeval copies, is of great interest.

Classical design.

A Greek twelfth century *Psalter* in the Vatican library (No. 381) has one special picture which is obviously a careful copy of a miniature painting of the first century A.D. or even earlier: see fig. 2. The subject is Orpheus seated on a rock playing to a circle of listening beasts together with two nymphs and a youthful Faun or shepherd. These figures are arranged so as to form a very graceful composition in a landscape with hills and trees. The figures are extremely graceful both in outline and in pose, showing a considerable trace of Greek influence. The whole design closely resembles in style some of the wall paintings in the so-called "House of Livia" on the Palatine Hill in Rome, of which fig. 3 shows the scene of Io watched by Argus, and those in the now destroyed villa which was discovered by the Tiber bank in the Farnesina Gardens[1],

Graeco-Roman design.

and many of the better class of paintings on the walls of the houses of Pompeii. Of the latter a good example is shown in fig. 4, a painting the design of which has much fine Hellenic feeling in the grace of its form and the simplicity of the composition.

[1] The chief of these paintings were cut off the walls of the villa, and are now placed in the Museo delle Terme in Rome. The painting shown in fig. 3 is still in situ; that given in fig. 4 is now in the Museum at Naples.

Fig. 3. Painting in the "House of Livia" on the Palatine Hill in Rome.

Orpheus made into David.

Returning now to the above mentioned *Psalter* of the Vatican, the scribe, probably a Greek monk, who in the twelfth century painted this miniature[1], converted it into quite a different subject, that of David playing on the harp, by the simple device of ticketing each figure with a newly devised name. Orpheus is called "David," one of the Nymphs who sits affectionately close to Orpheus, probably meant for his wife Eurydice, is labelled "Sophia", "wisdom"; while the other two figures are converted into local personifications to indicate the locality of the scene.

It is not often that a mediaeval copyist has thus preserved unaltered the composition of a whole subject of classical and pre-Christian date, but it is not uncommon to find single figures or parts of pictorial designs of equally early date among the illuminations of the ninth to the twelfth centuries.

As an example of this we may mention one painting in a Greek *Psalter* of the tenth century in the Paris library (*Bibl. Nat.* No. 139). This represents the Prophet Isaiah standing, gazing up to heaven, in a very beautiful landscape with trees growing from a richly flower-spangled sward. The somewhat stiff figure of the Prophet is Byzantine[2] rather than Classical in style, but the other two figures which are introduced are purely Graeco-Roman in design. On one side is a personification of Night (NTΞ), a very graceful standing female figure with part of her drapery floating in the wind, forming a sort of curved canopy over her head, such as is so often represented above the heads of goddesses or nymphs on the reliefs of fine Graeco-Roman sarcophagi.

Graeco-Roman personifications.

On the other side of the Prophet is a winged boy, like a youthful Eros, bearing a torch to symbolize the dawn.

The bold and very decorative, yet almost realistic treatment of the foliage of the trees and of the flowers which are

---

[1] See above, fig. 2.
[2] The term Byzantine as applied to art is commonly used to denote the style which was developed in the Eastern empire soon after Constantine had transferred the seat of government from Old to "New Rome," or Constantinople as it was also called instead of Byzantium, which was the ancient name.

Fig. 4. A Pompeian painting of Hellenic style, as an example of Greek drawing and composition.

Classical style.

sprinkled among the grass is purely classical in style, and the whole miniature shows that the tenth century illuminator had before him some very fine manuscript of early Imperial date. From this he has selected a picture which might by omissions and modifications be adapted to his subject; and for the figure of the Prophet he has fallen back on another less ancient original, but still one which must have been several centuries older than his own time.

This is the explanation of what at first seems so strange a union in the same painting of very graceful single figures by the side of others which are rigid and awkward; and again, great skill shown in the drawing of the individual figures combined with a feeble and clumsy arrangement of the whole composition.

Byzantine style.

Fig. 5 shows a miniature of very similar style representing the Prophet Ezechiel in the Valley of dry bones. It is taken from a manuscript of the *Sermons* of Saint Gregory Nazianzen, which was written for the Byzantine Emperor Basil who reigned from 867 to 886. This figure chiefly illustrates the Byzantine, not the Classical element in the miniatures of this mixed style of art, though there is also a clear trace of Graeco-Roman influence in the finely designed drapery of the Prophet.

The curious union of two utterly different styles is well exemplified in another of the miniatures in the last mentioned *Psalter*. Here David is represented like a Byzantine Emperor crowned and wearing the richly embroidered *toga picta*, and holding an open book. The figure might well pass for a representation of the Emperor Justinian, and the original painting was probably of that date, of the early part of the sixth century.

Graeco-Roman figures.

On each side of the Byzantine David is a female figure draped with most gracefully designed folds of pure Graeco-Roman style, a most striking contrast to the central figure. Who these ladies represented in the original manuscript it is impossible to say, but the painter who in the tenth century illuminated the *Psalter* called them *Wisdom* and *Prophecy*, writing by them the names *Sophia* and *Prophetia*.

Fig. 5. The Prophet Ezechiel from a Byzantine manuscript of the ninth century A.D.

Value of late copies.

Many other examples might be given to show that a truer notion of classical illuminated manuscripts of the best Graeco-Roman style can be gained from a study of the works of mediaeval copyists than from manuscripts which, though older, are of late and debased style like the famous illuminated Virgil of the Vatican[1].

After Rome had ceased to be the seat of government, Constantinople became the chief centre for the production of illuminated manuscripts[2], but nevertheless the older classical style of drawing to some extent did survive in Italy, though in a very debased form, down to the thirteenth century, when Cimabue and his pupil Giotto inaugurated the brilliant Renaissance of Italian painting.

Classical survival.

The *Gospels*, for example, which St Augustine is said to have brought with him to Britain in 597 A.D., have paintings, enthroned figures of the Evangelists, which in design and colour are purely of late Roman style, unchanged by the then wide-spread influence of Byzantine art.

[1] Several manuscripts of this class are described by H. Bordier, *Manuscrits Grecs de la Bibliothèque Nationale*, Paris, 1883.

[2] A great public library was founded by Constantine in New Rome and partially stocked by manuscripts transferred from the old Capital. This library was rapidly enlarged by his sons and successors, and it was rebuilt on a grander scale by the Emperor Zeno after the building had been injured by fire about the year 488 A.D.

CHAPTER IV.

Byzantine Manuscripts.

THE history of the origin, development and decay of the Byzantine style in manuscripts, as in other branches of art, is a long and strange one[1]. The origin of the Byzantine style dates from the time when Christianity had become the State religion, and when Constantine transferred the Capital of the World from Rome to Byzantium.

Byzantine style.

In Russia and other eastern portions of Europe the Byzantine style still exists, though in a sad state of decay, not as an antiquarian revival, but as the latest link in a chain of unbroken tradition, going back without interruption to the age of Constantine, the early part of the fourth century after Christ.

During the early years of the Eastern Empire, Constantinople, or "New Rome" as it was commonly called, became the chief world's centre for the practice of all kinds of arts and handicrafts. Owing to its central position, midway between the East and the West, the styles and technique of both met and were fused into a new stylistic development of the most remarkable kind. Western Europe, Asia Minor, Persia and Egypt all contributed elements both of design and of technical skill, which combined to create the new and for a while vigorously flourishing school of Byzantine art. The dull lifeless forms of Roman art in its extreme degradation

Many strains of influence.

[1] For a valuable account of Byzantine manuscripts, see Kondakoff, *Histoire de l'Art Byzantin*, Paris, 1886—1891.

were again quickened into new life and beauty in the hands of these Byzantine craftsmen, who became as it were the heirs and inheritors of the art and the technique of all the chief countries of antiquity.

Technical skill. In architecture, in mosaic work, in metal work of all kinds, in textile weaving, the craftsmen of New Rome reached the highest level of technical skill and decorative beauty. So also a new and brilliant school of manuscript illumination was soon formed, and Constantinople became for several centuries the chief centre for the production of manuscripts of all kinds.

The Oriental element in Byzantine art shows itself in a love of extreme splendour, the most copious use of gold and silver and of the brightest colours.

Murex purple. Manuscripts written in burnished gold, on vellum stained with the brilliant purple from the *murex* shell, were largely produced, especially for the private use of the Byzantine Emperors. This *murex* purple, produced with immense expenditure of labour, came to be considered the special mark of Imperial rank[1]. A golden inkstand containing purple ink was kept by a special official in waiting, and no one but the Emperor himself might, under heavy penalties, use for any purpose the purple ink; and the sumptuous gold and purple manuscripts were for a long time written only for Imperial use.

Gold and purple gospels. The principal class of manuscripts which were written either in part or wholly in this costly fashion were *Books of the Gospels;* and of these a good many magnificent examples still exist, dating not only from the early Byzantine period, but down to the ninth or tenth century. In these manuscripts the burnished gold and the brilliantly coloured pigments which are used for the illuminations are still as bright and fresh in appearance as ever, but the *murex* purple with which the vellum leaves were, not painted, but dyed, has usually lost much of its original splendour of colour.

---

[1] The title *Porphyro-genitus,* "Born in the purple," referred to the fact that Byzantine Empresses brought forth their children in a magnificent room lined with slabs of polished porphyry.

CHAP. IV.]   OF THE BYZANTINE STYLE.   47

Before describing the characteristics of Byzantine illuminated manuscripts it may be well to note that the Byzantine style is unique in the artistic history of the world from the manner in which it rapidly was crystallized into rigidly fixed forms, and then continued for century after century with marvellously little modification or development either in colour, drawing or composition.

Monotony of style.

This absence of any real living development was due to the fact that paintings of all kinds in the Eastern Church, from a colossal mural picture down to a manuscript miniature, were produced by ecclesiastics and for the Church, under a strictly applied series of hieratic rules.

The drawing, the pose, the colours of the drapery of every Saint, and the scheme of composition of all sacred figure subjects came gradually to be defined by ecclesiastic rules, which each painter was bound to obey. Thus it happens that during the many centuries which are covered by the Byzantine style of art, though there are periods of decay and revival of artistic skill, yet in style there is the most remarkable monotony. This makes it specially difficult to judge from internal evidence of the date of a Byzantine painting. In manuscripts the palaeographic, not the artistic evidence, is the best guide, aided of course by various small technical peculiarities, and also by the amount of skill and power of drawing which is displayed in the paintings.

Hieratic rules.

Long after the capture of Constantinople by the Ottoman Turks in 1453, the Byzantine style of painting survived; and even at the present day the monks of Mt Athos execute large wall paintings, which, as far as their style is concerned, might appear to be the work of many centuries ago. M. Didron found the monastic painters in one of the Mount Athos monasteries using a treatise called the 'Ερμηνεία τῆς ζωγραφικῆς, in which directions are given how every figure and subject is to be treated, and which describes the old traditional forms without any perceptible modification[1]. The proportions of the human form are laid down after the characteristic

Absence of change.

[1] A translation of this curious treatise was published by Didron and Durand, in their *Manuel d'iconographie chrétienne;* Paris, 1845.

slender Byzantine models, the complete body, for example, being nine heads in height.

5th century MS. of Genesis.

The earliest Byzantine manuscript which is now known to exist is a fragment of the *Book of Genesis*, now in the Imperial library of Vienna, which dates from the latter part of the fifth century. This fragment consists of twenty-four leaves of purple-dyed vellum, illuminated with miniatures on both sides. In the main the designs are feeble in composition and weak in drawing, belonging rather to the latest decadence of Roman classical art than to the yet undeveloped Byzantine style, which was soon to grow into great artistic spirit and strong decorative power, a completely new birth of aesthetic conceptions, the brilliance of which is the more striking from its following so closely on the degraded, lifeless, worn-out art of the Western Empire. In this manuscript of *Genesis* there is but little promise of the Renaissance that was so near

Weak drawing.

at hand. The drawing of each figure, though sometimes graceful in pose, is rather weak, and the painter has hardly aimed at anything like real composition; his figures merely stand in long rows, with little or nothing to group them together. Fig. 6 shows examples of two of the best miniatures, representing the story of the accusation of Joseph by Potiphar's wife. In every way this *Genesis* manuscript forms a striking contrast to the delicate beauty and strongly decorative feeling which are to be seen in a work of but a few years later, the famous *Dioscorides* of the Princess Juliana.

The Dioscorides of c. 500 A.D.

Among all the existing Byzantine manuscripts perhaps the most important for its remarkable beauty as well as its early date is this Greek *codex*[1] of Dioscorides' work on *Botany*, which is now in the Imperial library in Vienna[2], No. 5 in the Catalogue. The date of this manuscript can be fixed to about the year 500 A.D. by the record which it contains of its having been written and illuminated for the

---

[1] All manuscripts described in this book, from the Byzantine school onwards, may be understood to be in the *codex* form and written on *vellum*, unless they are otherwise described.

[2] Published by Lambecius, *Comment. sur la Bibl. de Vienne*, 1776, Vol. III.

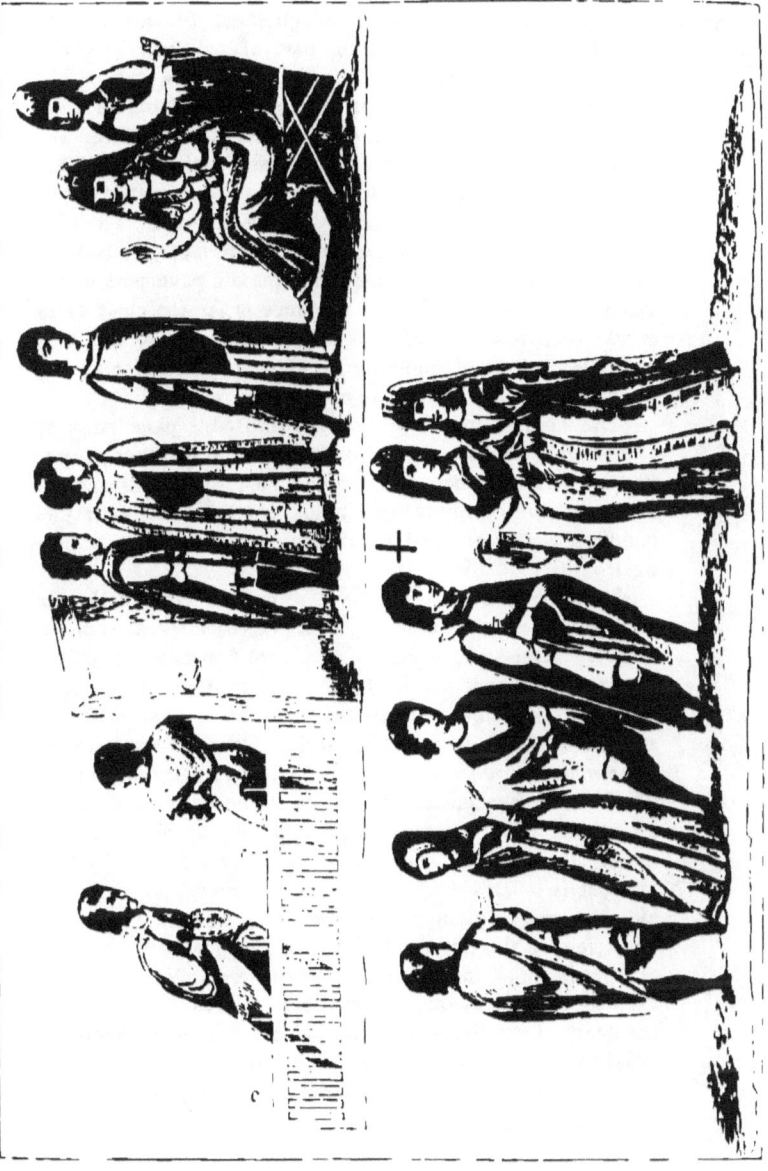

Fig. 6. Miniature from the Vienna manuscript of *Genesis*.

Dioscorides of Juliana. Princess Juliana Anicia, the daughter of Flavius Anicius Olybrius who was Emperor for part of the year 472, and his wife Galla Placidia : Juliana Anicia died in 527.

This beautiful manuscript, which was executed in Constantinople, contains five large and elaborate miniatures, and a great number of vignettes representing varieties of plants. The fifth of the large miniatures consists of a central group framed by two squares interlaced within a circle. The plait pattern on the bands which form the framework, and the whole design closely resemble a fine mosaic pavement of the second century A.D. The resemblance is far too close to be accidental; and indeed this manuscript is not the only example we have of miniature painters copying patterns and motives from mosaic floors of earlier date.

Portrait figure. The central group in this beautiful full page painting represents Juliana Anicia, for whom the manuscript was written, enthroned between standing allegorical female figures. Minutely painted figures of Cupids, engaged in a variety of handicrafts and arts, fill up the small spaces in the framework.

In these paintings we have a curious combination of different styles; the enthroned figure of the Princess is of the stiff Byzantine style, while the attendant figures and the little Cupids are almost purely classical in drawing. This manuscript forms a link between the classical or Graeco-Roman *Inferior paintings.* and the Christian or Byzantine style. Other paintings in the same manuscript are very inferior in design, partaking of the late Roman decadence, rather than of the better and earlier art of the above mentioned picture. Fig. 7 shows one of these. It represents Dioscorides seated on a sort of throne ; in front is a female figure *Euresis* (*Discovery*) presenting to him the magic plant *mandragora* (mandrake). The dying dog refers to the popular belief, given by Josephus, as to the manner in which the mandrake was gathered. When plucked from the ground the mandrake uttered a scream which caused the death of any living creature that heard it ; it was therefore usual to tie a dog to the plant and retire to a safe distance before calling it, and so causing the dog to drag the plant out

CHAP. IV.]   THE PRINCESS JULIANA.   51

of the ground. On hearing the scream the dog dropped down
dead. Cf. Shaks., *Romeo and Juliet*, IV. iii.

Fig. 7. Miniature from the manuscript of the work on *Botany* by Dioscorides, executed in Constantinople about 500 A.D.

The colours used in the *Dioscorides* of Juliana are very *Colours and gold.*
brilliant, especially the gorgeous ultramarine blue, and are
glossy in surface owing to the copious use of a gum medium.
Gold is very largely and skilfully used, especially to light up
and emphasize the chief folds of the drapery, a method which

4—2

is very widely used in Byzantine art, both in the colossal pictures of the wall-mosaics, and also in most of the finest class of illuminated manuscripts.

Cloisonné enamel.
In this use of gold, in thin delicate lines which strengthen the drawing, we have a very distinct copyism of another quite different art, that of the worker in enamelled gold, an art which was practised in Constantinople with wonderful taste and skill. The kind of enamel which was so often imitated by the manuscript illuminator is now called cloisonné enamel from the thin slips of gold or *cloisons* which separate one colour from another, and mark out the chief lines of the design. So closely did many of the illuminators copy designs in this cloisonné that very often one sees manuscript miniatures which look at first sight as if they were actual pieces of enamel. In other ways too the art of the goldsmith had considerable influence on Byzantine illuminations; and the designs of the mosaic-worker and the miniaturist acted and reacted upon each other, so that we sometimes see an elaborate painting in a book which looks like a design for a wall-mosaic; or again the gorgeous glass mosaics with gold grounds on the vaults and walls of Byzantine churches frequently look like magnified leaves cut out of some gorgeously illuminated manuscript.

The pure Byzantine style.
It was only for a short period that manuscripts were executed at Constantinople which, in their miniatures, were links between the classical and the Byzantine style. Thus we find that the famous Greek manuscript of *Cosmas Indopleustes* in the Vatican library (No. 699) is of the pure and fully developed Byzantine style, with its formal attitudes, its rigid drapery, its lengthy proportions of figure, and stiff monotonous schemes of composition, such as grew to be accepted as the one sacred style, and as such has been preserved by the Eastern Church down to the present century.

This manuscript of Cosmas is certainly a work of Justinian's time, the first half of the sixth century A.D., though it has usually been attributed to the ninth century; it really is but little later than the Dioscorides of Juliana, and yet it has but

CHAP. IV.] EARLY PAINTING OF THE CRUCIFIXION. 53

little trace of the older classical style, either in drawing, composition or colour[1].

The Laurentian library in Florence possesses a manuscript of the *Gospels* which, though poor as a work of art, has several points of special interest. A contemporary note in the *codex* records that it was written in the year 586 by the Priest Rabula in the Monastery of St John at Zagba in Mesopotamia.

Its illuminations are weak in drawing, coarse in execution and harsh in colouring, but one of them, representing the Crucifixion of our Lord between the two thieves, is noticeable as being the earliest known example of this subject. The primitive Christian Church avoided scenes representing Christ's Death and Passion, preferring to suggest them only by means of types and symbols taken from Old Testament History.

Early crucifixion.

This and other subsequent paintings of the Crucifixion treat the subject in a very conventional way, and it is not till about the thirteenth century that we find the Death of Christ represented with anything like realism.

In the *Gospels* of the Priest Rabula, Christ is represented crowned with gold, not with thorns; He wears a long tunic of Imperial purple reaching to the feet. The arms are stretched out horizontally, an impossible attitude for a crucified person, and four nails are represented piercing the hands and both feet separately.

It appears to have been the gloomy Oriental influence that gradually introduced scenes of martyrdom, with horrors of every description into Christian art, which originally had been imbued with a far healthier and more cheerful spirit, a survival from the wholesome classical treatment of death and the grave. Hell with its revolting horrors and hideous demons was an invention of a still later and intellectually more degraded period.

Oriental influence.

Evangeliaria or manuscripts of the Gospels. One of the most important classes of Byzantine manuscripts, and the

MSS. of the Gospels.

[1] Copies of some of the miniatures in the Vatican *Cosmas* are given by N. Kondakoff, *Histoire de l'Art Byzantin*, Paris, 1886, Vol. I. pp. 142 to 152.

one of which the most magnificent examples now exist are the *Books of the Gospels* already mentioned at page 46 as being occasionally, either wholly or in part, written in letters of gold on leaves of purple-dyed vellum.

These Imperially magnificent manuscripts are usually decorated with five full page paintings, placed at the beginning of the codex. These five pictures represent the four Evangelists, each enthroned like a Byzantine Emperor under an arched canopy supported on Corinthian columns of marble or porphyry. Each Evangelist sits holding in his hand the manuscript of his *Gospel;* or, in some cases, he is represented writing it. In the earlier manuscripts, St John is correctly represented as an aged white-bearded man, but in later times St John was always depicted as a beardless youth, even in illuminations which represent him writing his Gospel in the Island of Patmos, as at the beginning of the fifteenth century *Books of Hours*. Next comes the fifth miniature representing "Christ in Majesty," usually enthroned within an oval or vesica-shaped aureole; He sits on a rainbow, and at His feet is a globe to represent the earth, or in some cases a small figure of *Tellus* or Atlas with the same symbolical meaning.

Other highly decorated pages in these Byzantine *Gospels* are those which contain the "Canons" of Bishop Eusebius, a set of ten tables giving lists of parallel passages in the four Gospels. These tables are usually framed by columns supporting a semicircular arch, richly decorated with architectural and floral ornaments in gold and colours. Frequently birds, especially doves and peacocks, are introduced in the spandrels over the arches; they are often arranged in pairs drinking out of a central vase or chalice—a motive which occurs very often among the reliefs on the sarcophagi and marble screens of early Byzantine Churches both in Italy and in the East[1]. These birds appear to be purely ornamental, in spite of the many attempts that have been made to discover symbolic meanings in them. Other birds, such as cocks, quails and partridges, are commonly used in these

[1] St Mark's in Venice and the churches of Ravenna and Constantinople are full of examples of this design.

decorative illuminations, and this class of ornament was probably derived from Persia, under the Sasanian Dynasty, when decorative art and skilful handicrafts flourished to a very remarkable extent[1].

Sasanian style.

Among the most sumptuous and beautiful illuminations which occur in these Byzantine *Gospels* are the headings and beginnings of books written in very large golden capitals, so that six or seven letters frequently occupy the whole page. These letters are painted over a richly decorated background covered with floreated ornament, and the whole is framed in an elaborate border, all glowing with the most brilliant colours, and lighted up by burnished gold of the highest decorative beauty[2].

These sumptuous *Evangeliaria*, or *Textus* as they were often called, soon came to be something more than merely a magnificent book. They developed into one of the most important pieces of furniture belonging to the High Altar in all important Cathedral and Abbey churches[3]. Throughout the whole mediaeval period every rich church possessed one of these magnificently written *Textus* or *Books of the Gospels* bound in costly covers of gold or silver thickly studded with jewels. This *Textus* was placed on the High Altar before the celebration of Mass, during which it was used for the reading of the Gospel.

Textus for the High Altar.

The jewel-studded covers had on one side a representation

[1] This Sasanian art was an inheritance from ancient Babylon and Assyria, and was the progenitor of what in later times has been called Arab art, though the quite inartistic Arabs appear to have derived it from the Persians whom they conquered and forcibly converted to the Moslem Faith.

[2] The mere gold of even the finest Byzantine manuscripts is never as sumptuous or as highly burnished as that in manuscripts of the fourteenth century, owing to its being usually applied as a fluid pigment, or at least not over the best kind of highly raised ground or *mordant*, which is described below at p. 234.

[3] In early times and indeed throughout the whole mediaeval period very few objects of any kind were placed upon the High Altar even in the most magnificently furnished churches. In addition to the chalice and paten, and the *Textus*, the only ornaments usually allowed were a small crucifix and two candlesticks. The modern system of crowding the *mensa* of the altar with many candles and flowers did not come in till after the Reformation.

In the fourteenth and fifteenth centuries the *Pax* was usually a separate thing, of more convenient size and weight than the heavy, gold-covered *Textus*.

Textus used as a Pax. of Christ's crucifixion, executed in enamel or else in gold relief, and the book was used to serve the purpose of a *Pax*, being handed round among the ministers of the Altar for the ceremonial kiss of peace, which in primitive times had been exchanged among the members of the congregation themselves. One of the most magnificent examples of these *Textus* is the one now in the possession of Lord Ashburnham, the covers of which are among the most important and beautiful examples of the early English goldsmith's and jeweller's art which now exist[1].

The Textus at Durham. An interesting description of the *Textus* which, till the Reformation, belonged to the High Altar of Durham Cathedral, is given in the *Rites and Monuments of Durham* written in 1593 by a survivor from the suppressed and plundered Abbey[2], who in his old age wrote down his recollections of the former glories of the Church. He writes, "the Gospeller[3] did carrye a marvelous FAIRE BOOKE, which had the Epistles and Gospels in it, and did lay it on the Altar, the which booke had on the outside of the coveringe the picture of our Saviour Christ, all of silver, of goldsmith's worke, all parcell gilt, verye fine to behould; which booke did serve for the PAX in the Masse."

These *Textus* were not unfrequently written wholly in gold on purple stained vellum, not only during the earliest and best period of Byzantine art but also occasionally by the illuminators of the age of Charles the Great.

Weak drawing of the figure. Returning now to the general question of the style of Byzantine art, it should be observed that, though little knowledge of the human form is shown by the miniaturists, yet they were able to produce highly dignified compositions, very strong in decorative effect. Study of the nude form was strictly prohibited by the Church; and the beauty of the human figure was regarded as a snare and a danger to minds

---

[1] Fine coloured plates of this wonderful *Textus*-cover were published in 1888 by the Society of Antiquaries in their *Vetusta Monumenta*.
[2] Published in 1844 by the Surtees Society of Durham.
[3] The "Gospeller" was the officiating Deacon; the Sub-deacon being called the "Epistoller."

CHAP. IV.]   UNREAL FIGURE PAINTING.   57

which should be fixed upon the imaginary glories of another world. What grace and dignity there is in Byzantine figure painting depends chiefly on the skilful treatment of the drapery with simple folds modelled in gracefully curving lines.

The utmost splendour of gold and colour is lavished on this drapery, and on the backgrounds, border-frames and other accessories, while the colouring of the flesh, in faces, hands and feet, is commonly unpleasant; with, in many cases, an excessive use of green in the shadows, which gives an unhealthy look to the faces. This copious use of green in flesh tints is especially apparent in the later Byzantine paintings, and again in the Italian imitations of Byzantine art. Even paintings by Cimabue and some of his followers, in the second half of the thirteenth century, are disfigured by the flesh in shadow being largely painted with *terra verde*[1]. *Livid flesh colour.*

The monastic bigotry, which prohibited study either of the living model or of the beauties of classical sculpture, tended to foster a strongly conventional element in Art, which for certain decorative purposes was of the highest possible value. Anything like realism is quite unsuited both for colossal mural frescoes or mosaics and for miniature paintings in an illuminated manuscript. *Monastic bigotry.*

Thus, for example, the existing mosaics on the west front of St Mark's Basilica in Venice[2], which were copied from noble paintings by Titian and Tintoretto, are immeasurably inferior to the earlier mosaics with stiff, hieratic forms designed after Byzantine models, as for example the mosaics in the Apse of SS. Cosmas and Damian in Rome, executed for Pope Felix IV. 526 to 530; see fig. 8. *Fine early mosaics.*

So, again, the skilfully drawn and modelled figures in a manuscript executed by Giulio Clovio in the sixteenth

[1] The remarkable artistic advance which was made by Giotto is to be seen not only in his improved and more realistic drawing, but also in his freedom from the long-established abuse of green in his flesh painting, for which he substituted a warmer and healthier tint.

[2] Of the original mosaics on the west façade of Saint Mark's only one remains of the original highly decorative twelfth century mosaics. The rest, shown in Gentile Bellini's picture of Saint Mark's, have all been replaced by later mosaics. Inside the church, happily, the old mosaics still, in most places, exist; see p. 61.

century are not worthy to be compared, for true decorative beauty and fitness, with the flat, rigid forms, full of dignity and

Fig. 8. Mosaic of the sixth century in the apse of the church of SS. Cosmas and Damian in Rome.

simple, rhythmical beauty which we find in any Byzantine manuscript of a good period[1].

Limitations of Byzantine Art.

It should, however, be remarked that in Byzantine art this conventional treatment of the human form is carried too far, and therefore, splendid as a fine Byzantine manuscript usually is, it falls far short of the almost perfect beauty that may be seen in Anglo-Norman and French illuminated manuscripts of the thirteenth and fourteenth centuries, such marvels of beauty, for example, as French manuscripts of the *Apocalypse* executed in the first half of the fourteenth century in Northern France; see below, page 118.

Till the eighth century, Byzantine art, both in manuscripts

[1] See page 202 for an account of Giulio Clovio.

CHAP. IV.] ICONOCLAST SCHISM. 59

and in other branches of art, continued to advance in technical skill, though little change or development of style took place. In the eighth century the iconoclast schism, fostered by the Emperor Leo III. the Isaurian, an uncultured and ignorant soldier who began by issuing an edict against image-worship in the year 726 A.D., gave a blow to Byzantine art which brought about a very serious decadence during the ninth and tenth centuries, more especially in Constantinople, which up to that time had been one of the chief literary and artistic centres of the Christian world.

Edict against statues.

Pictures of all kinds, as well as statues, were destroyed by the iconoclast fanatics, and the cause of learning suffered almost as much as did the arts of painting and sculpture.

One result of this schismatic outbreak was that Constantinople ceased to be one of the chief centres for the production of beautiful illuminated manuscripts, and various Frankish cities, such as Aix-la-Chapelle and Tours, took its place under the enlightened patronage of Charles the Great the Emperor of the West, who, in the second half of the ninth century, by the aid of the famous Northumbrian scholar and scribe Alcuin of York, brought about a wonderful revival of literature and of the illuminator's art in various cities and monasteries within the Western Empire.

Frankish MSS.

At the end of the eleventh century Byzantine art, practised in its original home, had reached the lowest possible level. Thus, for example, a manuscript of some of the works of St Chrysostom (Paris, *Bibl. Nat. Coislin.*, 79) contains miniatures the figures in which are mere sack-like bundles with little or no suggestion of the human form. The whole skill of the artist has been expended on the painting of the elaborate patterns on the dresses; drawing and composition he has not even attempted.

Byzantine decadence.

Fig. 9 shows a miniature from this manuscript, representing the Greek Emperor enthroned between four courtiers, and two allegorical figures of *Truth* and *Justice*. The Emperor is Nicephoros Botaniates, who reigned from 1078 to 1081. An equally striking example of the degradation of Byzantine art in Germany is illustrated on page 78.

Fig. 9. Miniature from a Byzantine manuscript of the eleventh century; a remarkable example of artistic decadence.

After this period of decay during the tenth and eleventh centuries, Byzantine art began to revive, largely under the influence of the West; the original life and spirit had, however, passed away, and the subsequent history of Byzantine art is one of dull monotony and growing feebleness, the inevitable result of a continuing copying and recopying of older models.

Want of life in Byzantine Art.

It is rather as a modifying influence on the art of the West that Byzantine painting continued to possess real importance. As a distinct and isolated school, Constantinople fell into the background at the time of the iconoclasts and never again came to the front as an artistic centre of real importance[1].

[1] Mr M. R. James has pointed out to me an interesting example of similar designs being used by illuminators of manuscripts and by mosaic-workers. The designs of the miniatures in a fifth or sixth century manuscript of *Genesis* in the British Museum (*Otho*, B, vi) are in many cases identical with those of the twelfth and thirteenth century mosaics in Saint Mark's at Venice; see Tikkanen, *Genesisbilder*, Berlin.

CHAPTER V.

Manuscripts of the Carolingian Period.

The Age of Charles the Great. THE age of Charles the Great and his successors. Charles the Great, who was elected King of the Franks in 768 and in the year 800 became Emperor of the West, did much to foster all branches of art—architecture, bronze-founding, goldsmith's work, and more especially the art of writing and illuminating manuscripts. The Imperial Capital, Aix-la-Chapelle (Aachen), became a busy centre for arts and crafts of all kinds, and various monasteries throughout the Frankish kingdom became schools of manuscript illumination of a very high order of excellence.

Alcuin of York. It was specially with the aid of a famous English scholar and manuscript writer, Alcuin of York[1], that Charles the Great brought about so remarkable a revival both of letters and of the illuminator's art, and created what may be called the Anglo-Carolingian school of manuscripts. From 796 till his death in 804 Alcuin was Abbot of the Benedictine monastery of St Martin at Tours; and there he carried out various literary works for Charles the Great, and superintended the production of a large number of richly illuminated manuscripts. Alcuin's most important literary work was the revision of the Latin text of the Bible, the *Vulgate*, which

---

[1] Alcuin, when Dean of York, was sent by Offa, king of Mercia, about 782, as an envoy to Charles the Great. A large number of manuscripts were written under his guidance and influence, not only in Tours, but also at Soissons, Metz, Fulda, and in other Benedictine monasteries.

CHAP. V.]   THE SCHOOL OF ALCUIN.   63

since Saint Jerome's time had become seriously corrupted. The British Museum possesses (*Add. Manuscripts*, No. 10546) a magnificently illuminated copy of the *Vulgate* as revised by Alcuin, which, there is every reason to believe, is the actual manuscript which was prepared for Charles the Great either by Alcuin himself or under his immediate supervision. This splendid manuscript is a large folio in delicate and beautifully formed *minuscule* characters, with the beginnings of chapters in fine *uncials;* it is written in two columns on the purest vellum. The miniature paintings in this manuscript show the united influence of various schools of manuscript art. The figure subjects are mainly classical in style, with fine architectural backgrounds of Roman style, drawn with unusual elaboration and accuracy, and even with fairly correct perspective. The initial letters and all the conventional ornaments show the Northern artistic strain which

The Gospels of Alcuin.

Fig. 10. An initial P. of the Celtic-Carolingian type, of the school of Alcuin of York.

64 THE NORTHUMBRIAN SCHOOL. [CHAP. V.

Northum-brian influence. Alcuin himself introduced from York. Delicate and complicated interlaced patterns, such as were first used in the wonderful sixth and seventh century manuscripts of the Celtic monks, are freely introduced into the borders and large capitals.

In Alcuin's time Northumbria and especially York was one of the chief centres in the world, for the production of manuscripts, and the Dean of York naturally introduced into France the style and influence of his native school, which had

Fig. 11. An initial B. of the Celtic-Carolingian type.

grown out of a combination of two very different styles, that of Rome, as introduced by St Augustine, and the Celtic style which the monks of Ireland and Lindisfarne had brought to such marvellous perfection in the seventh century. *Celtic influence.*

Fig. 10 shows an initial of the Celtic-Carolingian type, with a goldsmith's pattern on the shaft of the *P*, and a bird of Oriental type forming the loop; and fig. 11 gives a large initial *B* in which the Oriental element is very strong, cf. fig. 13, page 68.

The Carolingian class of manuscripts in this way combined many different strains of influence—native Frankish, Classical, Oriental and English, all modified by the Byzantine love for gorgeous colours, shining gold and silver, and purple-dyed vellum. A considerable number of manuscripts were written in the reign of Charles the Great in letters of gold on purple vellum like those prepared in earlier times for the Byzantine Emperors. A manuscript *Book of the Gospels* of this magnificent class was given by Pope Leo X. to Henry VIII. of England in return for the presentation copy of his work against Luther, entitled *Assertio Septem Sacramentorum*, which the king had sent in 1521 to the Pope as a proof of his allegiance to the Catholic Faith and the Holy See. This magnificent *Textus* afterwards came into the Hamilton collection through Mr Beckford of Fonthill, and was subsequently bought by Mr Quaritch[1]. *Henry VIII's Gospels.*

As was the case with the earlier Byzantine manuscripts, the most magnificent books produced in the Carolingian period were this kind of *Evangeliaria* or *Books of the Gospels*. Though differing in the details of their ornamentation, these later *Gospels* are decorated with the same set of miniature subjects that occur in the Byzantine Gospels. The library of Paris possesses a fine typical example of this (*Bibl. Nat. Nouv. Acq. Lat.* 1993), a richly decorated and signed *Evangeliarium*, *Carolingian Gospels.*

[1] It is priced in Mr Quaritch's catalogue of 1890 at £2500. This manuscript was probably written at Tours in the school of Alcuin of York; see Wattenbach, *Die mit Gold auf Purpur geschriebenen Evangelienhandschriften der Hamilton'schen Bibliothek*, Berlin, 1889.

Fig. 12. Miniature of Christ in Majesty from a manuscript of the school of Alcuin, written for Charles the Great.

CHAP. V.] CELTIC AND ORIENTAL INFLUENCE.   67

which was written for Charles the Great in 781 by the scribe *Gospels of Godesscalc.*
and illuminator Godesscalc. Every page is sumptuously
ornamented with large initials and a border in brilliant
burnished gold, and silver, and bright colours; and there are
also six full-page miniatures, the first four representing the
four Evangelists enthroned in the usual way. The fifth has a
painting of *Christ in Majesty* with one hand holding a book,
the other raised in blessing; see fig. 12. The sixth miniature represents the Fountain of Life. In all these paintings
the backgrounds are very rich and decorative, with a greater
variety and more fancifully designed ornament than is to be
found in Byzantine manuscripts of a similar class, owing, of
course, to the introduction of the many different elements of
design which were combined with great taste and skill by the
Carolingian illuminators.

In this and many other manuscripts of the same class a *Oriental influence.*
very distinct Semitic or Persian strain of influence can be
traced in much of the rich conventional ornament. Very
beautiful and highly decorative forms and patterns were
derived from Oriental sources[1], owing to the active import
into France and Germany of fine Persian carpets and textile
stuffs from Moslem looms in Syria, Sicily (especially Palermo)
and from other parts of the Arab world; all these textiles
were designed with consummate taste and skill both in colour
and drawing.

Fig. 13 shows a fine specimen of woven silk from the *Sicilian silk cope.*
Arab looms of Syria. It was used as an Imperial cope or
mantle by various German Emperors; in the centre is a
palm-tree, and on each side a lion devouring a camel, treated
in a very decorative and masterly manner. The form of the
conventional foliage on the lions' bodies is imitated in many
manuscript illuminations, as, for example, in the ornaments of
the initial *B* shown in fig. 11, page 64.

One important characteristic of the Carolingian manuscripts is their extreme splendour. The freely used burnished
gold is often made more magnificent by the contrast of no

[1] See for example the beautiful patterns of the woven hangings behind the
enthroned figure of Christ shown on fig. 12; cf. also page 84.

5—2

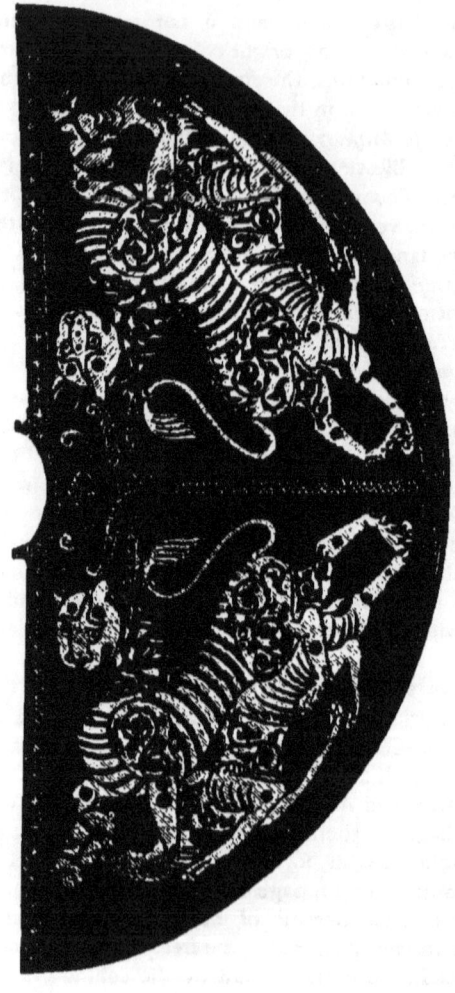

Fig. 13. A cope made of silk from the loom of an Oriental weaver.

CHAP. V.]   CAROLINGIAN MINIATURES.   69

less brilliant silver. Purple-stained vellum was largely used, *Splendour of MSS.* and all the pigments are of the most gorgeous hues that great technical skill could produce. And yet in spite of all this magnificence of shining metals and bright colours the effect is never harsh or gaudy, owing to the taste and judgment shown by the illuminators in the way they broke up their colours, avoiding large unrelieved masses, and in the arrangement of the colours so as to give a general effect of harmony in spite of the great chromatic force of the separate parts.

The somewhat realistic way of representing the Evangelists as aged white-haired men, which occurs in Byzantine manuscripts, in the Carolingian *Gospels* is replaced by a more conventional treatment, and thus they are as a rule represented as youthful, beardless men of an idealized type. The general *Technical methods.* treatment of the figure is flat, with little or no light and shade or modelling of any kind. The drapery is represented by strong, dark lines applied over a flatly laid wash of pigment. The painter first drew in his outlines with a fine brush dipped in red, and then filled in the intermediate spaces with a wash of colour mixed with a large proportion of gummy medium, so that a very glossy, lustrous surface was produced. The folds of the drapery and the rest of the internal drawing of the figures were put in after the application of the flat ground colour. This method very much resembles the process of the early Greek vase-painters. In order to give richness of effect by the use of a thick body of colour the illuminator commonly applied his flat tints in two or even three distinct washes, a method which is recommended by Theophilus[1] and other early writers on the technique of illumination.

Another *Book of the Gospels* which belonged to Charles *Gospels at Vienna.* the Great, now preserved in the Imperial Treasury at Vienna, is decidedly inferior as a work of art to the Paris manuscript mentioned above. In it the influence of the enfeebled Roman style is much stronger; the detail is far less refined and decorative, in spite of a copious use of burnished gold. This inferiority is due mainly to the absence of that Northumbrian

[1] Theophilus, *Schedula diversarum Artium*, I. 34; this work is frequently quoted in Chapter XV.

influence, to which the best Carolingian manuscripts owe so much of their beauty.

Successors of Charles. **Manuscripts of the later Carolingian school.** Under Charles the Great's successors the art of illuminating manuscripts continued to flourish, and, in the ninth century, under his grandsons Lothair and Charles the Bald, reached the climax of its development. During this century decorative splendour of a very high order was reached, in spite of there being very little advance in the power of rendering the human form. Gold, silver, ultramarine and brilliant pigments of all kinds were skilfully used; the subjects for miniatures became more varied, and detail was more delicate and highly finished[1].

Portrait figures. Portraits of the kings are often introduced at the beginning of books of this period, a fashion which in later times was extended to other than royal patrons of art and learning. A great number of places, chiefly Benedictine monasteries in France, became active centres for the production of fine illuminated manuscripts. Among them some of the principal places were Paris, St Denis, Rheims, Verdun, Fontanelle, and the two Abbeys of St Martin at Tours and Metz.

Fig. 14 shows a miniature from a manuscript of the *Gospels* in the Paris library representing King Lothair enthroned between two guards. This manuscript was written about the year 845 in the monastery of St Martin at Metz. In this picture a strong classical influence is apparent; the illuminator must have been familiar with manuscripts written in Rome or elsewhere in Italy.

Celtic influence. Some of the finest manuscripts of this period show a strongly marked Northern influence, imitated from the old Celtic illuminations of Ireland and Lindisfarne. Less gold is used in this class of manuscripts; and the intricate interlaced patterns of the Celtic monks are used with much skill and great beauty of effect. The figures of Christ and the Evangelists are sometimes hardly human in form, but are worked up into a kind of conventional scroll-pattern, just as they are in the older Celtic illuminations. The Paris library possesses

[1] See Janitschek, *Die künstlerische Ausstattung des Ada-Evangeliars und die Karolingische Buchmalerei*; fol. Leipzig, 1889.

Fig. 14. King Lothair enthroned; a miniature from a manuscript of about the year 845 A.D.

two manuscripts of the *Gospels*, which are good examples of this revived Celtic style (*Bibl. Nat. Lat.* Nos. 257 and 8849). The borders and initial letters in these manuscripts are remarkable for their intricate delicacy of design, and for their rich colour, tastefully arranged; while the figure drawing is of the purely ornamental scroll type.

Classical school of St Gall. In the ninth century the Benedictine monastery of St Gallen in Switzerland, which had formerly produced manuscripts of a purely Celtic type, now developed a very strange school of miniature art[1]. The pictures in these St Gallen manuscripts have figure subjects drawn in outline and then faintly coloured with transparent washes, very like the Anglo-Saxon (classical) style of illumination during the ninth and tenth centuries. These rather weak drawings, which have but little decorative value, show the influence of the Roman school of illuminators, who still mainly adhered to the old debased form of classical art, modified by some observation and even careful study of the actual life and movement which the painters saw around them. In this curious class of manuscripts, though the figure subjects are devoid of much vigour and artistic force, yet the decorative details of the initials and borders are extremely fine, full of invention and delicacy of detail. Fig. 15 shows a pen drawing from a St Gallen manuscript of the ninth century, the magnificent *Psalterium aureum*[2]; it represents David going forth to battle.

Studies from life. With regard to studies from the life, either of men or animals, it should be remembered that an artist is always biased by tradition and association to a degree which is now very difficult to realise. Even when looking at the same object two painters of different race and education might receive very different impressions on their retina. Thus in the very interesting sketch-book of Villard de Honecourt, a French sculptor and architect of the thirteenth century, there are studies of men, lions and other animals, which he has noted as being from the life; and yet these drawings look to

---

[1] See Weidmann, *Geschichte der Bibliothek von St Gallen*, 8vo, St Gall, 1841.

[2] See J. R. Rahn, *Das Psalterium Aureum von St Gallen, ein Beitrag zur Geschichte der Karolingischen Miniaturmalerei*, folio, St Gall, 1878.

CHAP. V.]   ATTEMPTS AT REALISM.   73

us like the purely imaginative conceptions of a heraldic draughtsman, in spite of the fact that Villard certainly

Fig. 15. Illumination in pen outline, from a manuscript written in the ninth century at St Gallen. It represents David riding out against his enemies.

represented them as faithfully as he was able, putting down on his vellum the subjective visual and mental impression that he had received[1].

In the same way a modern Japanese artist evidently sees the nobler animals, such as men and horses, in a very subjec-

[1] An excellent edition with 72 facsimiles of Villard de Honecourt's *Album* or sketch-book was produced by Professor Willis, London, 1859; it is superior to the French edition issued by J. B. Lassus, Paris, 1858.

Figs. 16 and 17. Subject countries doing homage to the Emperor Otho II; from a manuscript of the *Gospels*.

tive and distorted manner, whereas when he is dealing with fishes, reptiles, plants and the like he is able to depict them with the most wonderful grace, accuracy and realistic spirit.

Personal equation. For this reason in examining an illuminated manuscript, or other early work of art, to discover what use the artist has made of actual study from nature, one should always take into account the influences which made him see each natural object in a special, personal way, and we must not argue that because the drawing now looks very unreal that it may not possibly have been as careful and accurate a study from life as the painter's eye and hand could produce.

Byzantine influence. During the later Carolingian period there was a marked revival of Byzantine influence, which did not tend to delay the advancing decadence[1]. Figs. 16 and 17 show a very striking example of this, a two-page miniature from a magnificent purple and gold manuscript of *the Gospels*, which was executed for the Emperor Otho II., and is now in the Munich library. On the right-hand page is the Emperor enthroned holding the long sceptre and the orb, with an archbishop and some armed courtiers beside him. On the opposite page, personifications of *Rome, Gaul, Germany* and *Slavonia* are doing homage and offering gifts. The whole motive and design is borrowed from a much earlier Byzantine work, such as the mosaics of Justinian's time (c. 530 A.D.) in the churches of Ravenna.

Classical influence. Fig. 18 from another fine manuscript of *the Gospels* is far nobler in style; here the influence is rather classical than Byzantine. The figure illustrates one of the usual four miniatures of the Evangelists, Saint Mark dipping his pen into the ink. The Saint is robed in the *alb, dalmatic* with two stripes, *chasuble* and *pall* as being Archbishop of Alexandria. The figure is very dignified, and is evidently copied from a much earlier Italian *Textus*, such as that which Saint Augustine received from Pope Gregory or brought from Italy to Canterbury.

[1] See L. Delisle, *L'Evangéliaire d'Arras et la calligraphie Franco-Saxonne du IXme siècle*, 8vo, Paris, 1888.

Fig. 18. Miniature of the Evangelist St Mark; from a manuscript of the *Gospels*.

78   THE LATER CAROLINGIAN SCHOOL.   [CHAP. V.

Later Emperors.   Throughout the tenth century, and especially under the patronage of the three Emperor Othos and Henry the Fowler, fine and richly decorative manuscripts continued to be produced, with little change in the style of ornament employed. After a long period of great artistic brilliance and wonderful fertility of production the Carolingian style of illumination came to an end when Charles the Great's Empire was (in France) divided among various Feudal Lords. Then a serious decadence of art set in, and lasted till the beginning of a most magnificent artistic revival in the twelfth century.

To a large extent the illuminations of French manuscripts during the latter part of the eleventh century consisted of

Fig. 19. Miniature of the Crucifixion from a German manuscript of the eleventh century; showing extreme artistic decadence.

rude pen drawings with no washes of colour. The subsequent history of the illuminator's art in France is discussed below, see page 126.

Fig. 19 gives an example of the extreme artistic decadence that in many places followed the brilliant Carolingian period. This miniature of the Crucifixion is copied from a German early eleventh century manuscript, now at Berlin. The ludicrous ugliness of the drawing is not atoned for by any decorative beauty of colour; the whole miniature is dark and heavy in tone, with yellow and green flesh-tints of the most cadaverous hues.

Extreme decadence.

CHAPTER VI.

THE CELTIC SCHOOL OF MANUSCRIPTS.

ONE of the most extraordinary artistic developments that ever took place in the history of the world has been the Celtic Monastic School of Art which in the seventh century reached its highest aesthetic and technical climax, more especially in the production of exquisitely minute gold jewellery and no less minute and richly illuminated manuscripts.

The Irish Church. The Christian Church in the east of Ireland dated from an earlier period than the establishment of Christianity in England[1]. It was founded about the year 430 A.D., and the monks of Ireland, owing to their remote position, were able for a long period to develope peacefully their artistic skill, undisturbed by such successive foreign invasions as those which for so many years kept Britain in a constant tumult of war and massacre.

Celtic goldsmiths. Thus it happened that by the middle or latter part of the seventh century the Celtic monks of Ireland had learned to produce goldsmiths' work and manuscript illuminations with such marvellous taste and skill as has never been surpassed by any age or country in the world[2]. Not even the finest Greek or Etruscan jewellery, enriched with enamels and

---

[1] Earlier that is than the conversion of the Saxon conquerors; to some extent a Romano-British Church had been established in Britain during the period of Roman domination, but this native Church appears to have been almost wholly eradicated by the Saxon Conquest.

[2] Celtic manuscripts of all periods are well illustrated by Westwood, *Miniatures and Ornaments of Anglo-Saxon and Irish Manuscripts*, London, 1868; see also Westwood, *Palaeographia Sacra Pictoria*, 1843—5, and the companion volume, *Illuminated Illustrations of the Bible*, 1846.

studded with gems, can be said to surpass the amazing perfection shown in such a masterpiece of the goldsmith's art as the so-called "Tara brooch"[1] in the Museum of the Royal Irish Academy. As a rule the skill of these Irish goldsmiths was devoted to the service of the Church in the manufacture of such objects as croziers, morses (or cope-brooches), shrines, chalices, textus-covers, receptacles for Bishops' bells, and other pieces of ecclesiastical furniture.

Gold jewellery.

These precious objects are decorated by a variety of technical processes, such as applied filagree, repoussé or beaten reliefs, enamels, both *champlevé* and *cloisonné*, and inlay of precious stones, especially the carbuncle in minute slices, set in delicate gold *cloisons* and backed with shining gold-leaf. All these and other decorative processes were employed with unrivalled skill by the monastic goldsmiths of eastern Ireland, a fact which it is important to notice, since nearly all the methods and styles of ornament which occur in the Irish illuminated manuscripts of the same period are clearly derived from prototypes in gold jewelled work. It is in fact often possible to trace in a fine Irish manuscript of the class we are now concerned with, ornamental patterns of several quite distinct classes, one being derived from the patterns of spiral or plaited form produced by soldering delicate gold wire on to plain surfaces of gold, another being copied from gold *champlevé* enamels, and a third no less clearly derived from the inlaid rectangular bits of carbuncle framed in delicate gold strips or *cloisons*.

Technical processes.

This strongly marked influence of the technique of one art on the designs of another is due to the fact that the arts both of the goldsmith and the manuscript illuminator were carried on side by side in the same monastery or group of monastic dwellings[2], and in some cases we have written

Influence on illuminations.

[1] Tara was the ancient inland capital of Ireland before Dublin was founded by the Viking pirates.

[2] The Irish monasteries of this date appear, frequently at least, to have consisted of a group of a dozen or more separate wooden huts or stone "bee-hive" cells, with one small central chapel of rectangular plan; the whole being enclosed within a wooden fence or a stone circuit wall, in which there was only one door of approach; see *Arch. Jour.* XV. p. 1 seq.

evidence that the scribe who wrote and illuminated an elaborate manuscript and the goldsmith who wrought and jewelled its gold cover were one and the same person[1].

The Book of Kells. It was in the second half of the seventh century that the Celtic art of Eastern Ireland reached its highest point of perfection. To this period belongs the famous *Book of Kells*, now in the library of Trinity College, Dublin, which was probably written between 680 and 700, and for many years was, with its jewelled gold covers, the principal treasure of the cathedral church at Kells[2]. This church had been founded by Saint Columba, and so in old times this marvellous manuscript was usually known as "the Great Gospels of Saint Columba."

Perfect workmanship. No words can describe the intricate delicacy of the ornamentation of this book, lavishly decorated as it is with all the different varieties of pattern mentioned above, the most remarkable among them being the ingeniously intricate patterns formed by interlaced and knotted lines of colour, plaited in and out, with such amazingly complicated lines of interlacement that one cannot look at the page without astonishment at the combined taste, patience, unfaltering certainty of touch and imaginative ingenuity of the artist. The wonderful minuteness of the work, examined through a microscope, fills one with wonder at the apparently superhuman eyesight of the scribe.

Complex interlacings. With regard to the intricate interlaced ornaments in which (with the aid of a lens) each line can be followed out in its windings and never found to break off or lead to an impossible loop of knotting, it is evident that the artist must have enjoyed, not only an aesthetic pleasure in the invention of his pattern, but must also have had a distinct intellectual

[1] For example, in an early Cashel *Kalendar* the monk Dagaeus, who died in 586, is recorded to have been both a goldsmith (*aurifex*) and an illuminator of manuscripts. Westwood, *Miniatures in Irish Manuscripts*, gives a number of excellent coloured reproductions of illuminations of this school and also of the Anglo-Celtic school of Northumbria.

[2] It was formerly believed that this manuscript had once belonged to Saint Columba, who lived from 521 to 597, but it is shown by the internal evidence of its style to be a century later than Saint Columba's time.

enjoyment in his work, such as a skilful mathematician feels in the working out of a complicated geometrical problem."

The combined skill of eye and hand shown in the minute plaits of the *Book of Kells* places it among the most wonderful examples of human workmanship that the world has ever produced. By the aid of a microscope Mr Westwood counted in the space of one inch no less than 158 interlacements of bands or ribands, each composed of a strip of white bordered on both sides with a black line.

Microscopic intricacy.

Giraldus Cambrensis, who visited Ireland in 1185 as secretary to Prince John, writes in the most enthusiastic language of the splendour of a similar manuscript of the *Gospels* which he saw in Kildare Cathedral. It shows, he says, superhuman skill, worthy of angels' hands, and he was lost in wondering admiration at the sight.

One class of ornament in the *Book of Kells* and in other manuscripts of this class consists of bands or diapers formed with step-like lines enclosing small spaces of brilliant colour. It is this class of pattern which is derived from the *cloisonné* inlay with bits of transparent carbuncle used in gold jewellery. Other ornaments consist of various spiral forms derived from the application of gold wire to flat surfaces of gold, a class of pattern which appears to have come, as it were, naturally to the gold-workers of many different periods and countries. Many of these spiral designs in the Irish manuscripts are almost identical with forms which occur so frequently among the gold ornaments of the Greek "Mycenean period," one among many examples in the art history of the world, which show the remarkable sameness of invention in the human mind at a certain stage of development whatever the time or the place may be[1].

Copies of jewellery.

Primitive spiral patterns.

It should moreover be noticed that this close imitation of metal-work is not limited to the separate details of the manuscripts. The main lines and divisions of the decoration on whole pages are accurately copied from the enamelled and jewelled gold or silver covers in which these precious *Gospels* were bound. Thus, the same design might appear in delicate

[1] See Westwood, *Irish Manuscripts*, Plate 9.

goldsmiths' work on the covers of a *Textus*, and also might be seen represented by the illuminator in brilliant colours on a page within.

Trumpet pattern.
One form of ornament, which occurs very frequently in the Irish manuscripts, is what is often called "the trumpet pattern" from its supposed resemblance to a curved metal trumpet. This kind of spiral ornament is used not only in the Celtic manuscripts and goldsmiths' work, but also on bronze shields and other pieces of metal-work on a large scale. This special ornament is not peculiar to the Irish, but was commonly used by the Celtic tribes of Britain from a very early date.

Arab influence.
United with these purely native types of ornament, we find in these Celtic manuscripts one curious class of foreign ornament derived from the patterns on imported pieces of textile stuffs woven in Arab looms[1]. Among many strange forms of serpents, dragons and other monsters of northern origin, other animals, such as lions, eagles and swans, occur which resemble closely those represented with such perfect conventional skill on the rich silk stuffs and early Oriental carpets woven in Syria, in the Arab towns of Sicily and in other Moslem centres. These beautiful stuffs were imported largely into Northern Europe for ecclesiastical purposes, such as for the vestments of priests or to form wrappings round some sacred reliquary[2].

The human form.
Though these Celtic manuscripts show such marvellous dexterity of touch and unerring firmness of line in every minute and complicated pattern, yet the monastic artist appears to have been absolutely incapable of representing the human form.

The figures of Christ and the Saints, which sometimes do occur in these manuscripts, are treated in a purely ornamental and (in its stricter sense) conventional way; the hair and beard, for example, are worked up into scrolls or spiral

[1] See fig. 13 on page 67.
[2] When the grave of Saint Cuthbert in Durham Cathedral was opened in 1827, it was found that the Saint's body had been wrapped in rich Siculo-Arab silk of the eleventh century at the time when his body was moved, in 1104 A.D. See Raine, *St Cuthbert*, Durham, 1828, p. 183 seq.

ornaments, and the draperies are merely masses of varied colour, with little or no resemblance to the folds of a dress.

Colours without gold.

The pigments used by the Celtic monks are very varied and of the most brilliant tints, prepared with such skill that after more than a thousand years they seem as fresh and bright as ever.

Among these pigments is included the fine *murex* purple which the Irish monks used occasionally to stain sheets of vellum like those in the *Golden Gospels* of the Byzantines. We are told by the Venerable Bede that the Irish monks had learnt how to extract this beautiful dye from a variety of the *murex* shell-fish which is not uncommon on both shores of the Irish Channel. Splendid as they are in colour, there is one curious feature in the early Irish manuscripts of the finest class, such as the *Book of Kells;* that is, that no gold or silver either in the form of leaf or as a fluid pigment is used. This seems specially strange when we remember the close connection there was between the arts of the goldsmith and of the illuminator of manuscripts among the Irish artists.

Celtic art in Britain.

In later times, when the Celtic style of illumination was transplanted to England, gold was to some extent introduced, but in the finest Irish manuscripts of the best period, the latter half of the seventh century, gold is completely absent. Nevertheless, so great was the decorative genius of these Irish monks that, even without burnished gold and silver, their illuminated pages quite equal, not only in artistic beauty, but even in mere splendour of effect, any illuminations that have ever been produced.

The Book of Durrow.

In addition to the *Book of Kells* another manuscript of similar style and date and of almost equal splendour should be mentioned, the *Book of Durrow*[1], which, like the *Book of Kells*, was also known as the "Gospels of Saint Columba," who is said to have left behind him, at his death in 597, no less than three hundred manuscripts written with his own hand. It is not impossible that the *Book of Durrow* is one of these, as it bears some signs of being earlier in date than the *Book of Kells*.

[1] Library of Trinity College, Dublin, manuscripts A, iv. 5.

86 CELTIC ART IN SCOTLAND [CHAP. VI.

Monks of Iona.

From Ireland the art of illuminating manuscripts was carried by monkish colonists to the Western coasts of Scotland, and especially to the Island of Iona, where a monastery had been founded by Saint Columba in the latter part of the sixth century[1]. Great numbers of manuscripts resembling in style the *Book of Kells* were produced in Iona; and offshoots from the monastery of Iona, established at various places on the mainland, became similar centres for the writing of richly decorated manuscripts. No less than thirteen monasteries in Scotland and twelve in England were founded by Irish monks from the mother settlement in Iona. In fact the whole of Britain seems to have owed its Christianity, during the Anglo-Saxon period, to the Irish missionaries from Iona, with the important exception of the kingdom of Kent, which was occupied by the Roman mission of Saint Augustine.

Celtic missionaries.

In the year 635, at the request of Oswald King of Northumbria, the Scottish king sent an Irish monk from Iona, named Aidan, to preach Christianity to the Northumbrian worshippers of Thor and Odin. Aidan selected the little island of Lindisfarne as the head-quarters of his missionary church, which, at first consisting mainly of a few Irish monks from Iona, rapidly grew in size and importance. In a few years, Saint Aidan, Bishop and Abbot of Lindisfarne, was able to establish a number of monastic houses throughout the Northumbrian Kingdom, and his own Abbey of Lindisfarne became one of the chief centres of Northern Europe for the production of fine illuminated manuscripts of the Celtic type.

After the death of Saint Aidan other Irish monks succeeded him as Bishop of Lindisfarne, and the school of manuscript illumination continued to flourish.

Gospels of St Cuthbert.

One of the most beautiful existing examples of the Lindisfarne branch of the Irish school of miniature work is the famous "Book of the Gospels of Saint Cuthbert[2]" as it is

[1] See Jamieson, *History of the Ancient Culdees of Iona*; Edinburgh, 1811.
[2] Saint Cuthbert was a monk of Irish descent, at first a member of the Celtic monastery of Melrose, and afterwards sixth Bishop of Lindisfarne from 685 to 688. In later times his gold, gem-studded shrine in Durham Cathedral was one of the most magnificent and costly in the world; see *Rites and Monuments of Durham*, Surtees Soc., 1842, pp. 3 and 4.

called, now in the British Museum (*Cotton manuscripts, Nero*, D. IV). The history of this manuscript is a very curious one; it was written some years after Saint Cuthbert's death in 688, not during his lifetime as was formerly believed. Eadfrith, a monk of Lindisfarne in Saint Cuthbert's time, and subsequently eighth Bishop of Lindisfarne (698 to 721), was the writer of these *Gospels*, "in honour of God and of Saint Cuthbert," as he records in a note. The illuminations were added by the monk Aethelwold, afterwards ninth Bishop of Lindisfarne, and the elaborate gold, gem-studded cover of this magnificent *textus* was the work of a third monk of the same Abbey named Bilfrith.

Gospels of St Cuthbert.

In the ninth century the Viking pirates were constantly harrying the shores of Northumbria; more than once the Abbey of Lindisfarne was plundered and many of the monks were slain, till at last, in the year 878, the small remnant who had escaped the cruelty of the Northmen decided to leave Lindisfarne and seek a new settlement in the original home of the founders of Lindisfarne, the eastern coast of Ireland. In 878 the survivors set off, carrying with them the body of Saint Cuthbert, and the magnificent manuscript of the *Gospels*, which was the chief treasure of their Abbey, and which had been successfully hidden in Saint Cuthbert's grave at the time of the invasion of the Northmen. The monks crossed to the western shore of Northumbria, and there took ship for Ireland. A great storm, however, arose; their boat shipped a heavy sea which washed overboard the precious Gospels of Saint Cuthbert, which had been carefully packed in a wooden box. Eventually the little ship was driven back, and finally was stranded on the Northumbrian shore. Soon after reaching the land the fugitive monks, wandering sadly along the beach, found, to their great joy, the lost box with its precious manuscript thrown up by the waves and lying on dry land. According to the chronicle of Symeon[1] (chapter xxvii.), the brilliant illuminations were quite uninjured by the sea-water; this is not literally the case; some of the pages are a good

Viking piracy.

Travels of the Gospels.

[1] The works of Symeon Dunelmensis were published by the Surtees Society in 1868.

deal stained, but wonderfully little injured considering what the book has gone through.

Minster of Durham.
When after many wanderings the successors of the exiles from Lindisfarne found, in 995, a final resting-place for the body of Saint Cuthbert in the Minster which they founded at Durham, the manuscript of the Gospels was laid on the coffin of the Saint. There it remained till 1104, when Saint Cuthbert's body was exhumed, and soon after it was sent back to Lindisfarne, where a Benedictine monastery had been founded in 1093 by some monks from Durham on the site of Saint Cuthbert's ruined Abbey.

There it was safely preserved till the dissolution of the monasteries under Henry VIII. The gold covers were then stripped off and melted, but the still more precious manuscript escaped destruction; it was subsequently acquired by Sir Robert Cotton, and is now one of the chief manuscript treasures of the British Museum.

Anglo-Celtic school.
In point of style the "Gospels of Saint Cuthbert" are a characteristic example of the Irish school of illumination, modified by transplantation to English soil. The intermediate stage in Iona and other monasteries of western Scotland seems to have introduced no change of style into the primitive Irish method of ornament. Whether produced in eastern Ireland or in western Scotland the manuscripts were the work of the same Celtic race, the Scots, who, at first inhabiting the north-east of Ireland, passed over to the not very distant shores of northern Britain to which these Irish settlers gave the name Scotland.

When however the Irish monks passed from Iona to Northumbria the case was different; they were surrounded with a new set of artistic influences mainly owing to the introduction into Northumbria of fine Byzantine and Italian manuscripts. The result of this was that though the Lindisfarne manuscripts continued to be decorated with exactly the same class of patterns that had been used in the *Book of Kells* and other Irish manuscripts for initials, borders and the like, yet in the treatment of the human figure a very distinct advance was made. Thus in Saint Cuthbert's *Gospels* the seated figures of the Evangelists are drawn with much dignity of form and with some attempt at truth in the pose, the proportions and in the disposition of the folds of the drapery. The monk Aethelwold who painted these miniatures must have had before him some fine manuscripts of the Gospels probably both of Byzantine and Italian style.

Improved drawing.

The whole result is a very splendid one, the *Gospels* of Saint Cuthbert in richness of invention and minute intricacy of pattern almost equal the *Book of Kells;* while the figure subjects, instead of being grotesque masses of ornament, are paintings with much beauty of line as well as extreme splendour of colour. Another modification is the introduction of gold and silver leaf, which are wholly wanting in the *Book of Kells* and the other finest purely Irish manuscripts.

Use of metal leaf.

Other typical examples of this combined Celtic and English style are the magnificent *Gospels* in the Imperial library in St Petersburg, and a manuscript of the Commentary on the Psalms by Cassiodorus now in the Chapter library at Durham. This latter manuscript, which dates from the eighth century, is traditionally said to have been written by Bede himself. The illuminations in this manuscript are specially rich with interlaced patterns, dragon monsters and diapers of the most minute scale, all purely Celtic in style, and all showing with special clearness their derivation from originals in goldsmiths' work. Not only the distinctly metallic motives of ornament are faithfully copied, but even the manner in which the gold-workers built up their elaborate manuscript covers by the insertion of separate little plates of gold filagree and enamel side by side on a large plate or matrix is exactly reproduced by the illuminator. As in the case of the Lindisfarne *Gospels*, the figures of the Psalmist which are introduced are very superior to any figures which occur in the purely Irish manuscripts, showing the distinct influence of Italian manuscripts of debased classical style.

MS. of Bede.

Italian influence.

Another very interesting example of the Anglo-Celtic school of illumination, with fine initials and a painting of an eagle of the characteristic Northern type, is in the possession of Corpus Christi College, Cambridge; No. CXCVII.

90 THE CORPUS AND LAMBETH GOSPELS. [CHAP. VI.

The Corpus Gospels.

This is an imperfect manuscript of the *Gospels* containing only the Gospels of Saint Luke and Saint John. The decorative borders and initials have the interlaced Irish class of ornament. This interesting manuscript was (in the sixteenth century) in the library of Archbishop Parker, who inserted a note stating that it was one of the manuscripts which were sent by Pope Gregory to Saint Augustine. The actual date of the manuscript is probably not earlier than the eighth century, in spite of the ancient appearance of the figure painting. An earlier copy of the *Gospels* in the same library has full page miniatures of the two Evangelists of purely classical style, surrounded with architectural framework of debased Roman form, very little modified from similar Roman miniatures of the fifth century A.D.

Returning for the moment to the Irish school of Celtic art, it should be observed that richly illuminated manuscripts continued to be produced in Ireland till the ninth and tenth centuries, but these later manuscripts, fine as they are, do not equal in beauty the *Book of Kells* and other works of the seventh and eighth century. The Book of the *Gospels of MacDurnan*[1], who was Archbishop of Armagh from 885 to 927, is a good example of the later school of Irish art, in which the figures of the Evangelists are no less grotesque than those in the earlier manuscripts, while the interlaced and diapered patterns of the borders and initials are inferior in minute delicacy of execution to such masterpieces as the *Book of Kells*; see fig. 20.

Gospels of Mac- Durnan.

Book of Deer.

Another still stronger proof of artistic decadence among the Celtic illuminators of this period is afforded by the *Book of Deer*[2] in the Cambridge University library. This is a small octavo copy of the *Latin Gospels* after the Itala version[3]. In style it is a mere shadow of the glories of early Irish art,

[1] Now in the Archbishop of Canterbury's library at Lambeth.

[2] The *Book of Deer* was first brought to light by Mr Henry Bradshaw, and has been published by the Spalding Club, Ed. John Stuart, Edinburgh, 1869. The Monastery at Deer in Aberdeenshire was founded by Saint Columba as a branch house from Iona.

[3] The so-called *Itala* version is the older Latin translation of the Bible, which existed previous to the recension of Saint Jerome.

CHAP. VI.] THE BOOK OF DEER. 91

with comparatively coarse and feebly coloured decorative

Fig. 20. Miniature from the *Gospels* of MacDurnan of the ninth century.

patterns. It appears to have been written in Scotland by an Irish scribe during the ninth century[1].

[1] A very interesting *Psalter* of similar style and date is preserved in the library of St John's College, Cambridge; its ornaments are of the unmixed Celtic style, broad in treatment without any of the marvellous minuteness of the *Book of Kells* and the *Book of Durrow*.

Gospels of MacRegol. One of the finest of the manuscripts of the later Irish type is the Book of *the Gospels of MacRegol* in the Bodleian library (D. 24. No. 3946) executed in the ninth century. The ornaments and the very conventional figures of the Evangelists are of the purely Irish type, unmodified by any imitation of the superior figure drawing in Byzantine and Italian miniatures[1].

Gospels of St Chad. The manuscript *Gospels of Saint Chad* in the Chapter library of Lichfield Cathedral is another example of the Irish school and of the same date as the last-mentioned book. It is named after Ceadda or Chad who, in the seventh century, was the first Bishop of Lichfield, nearly two hundred years before the date of this manuscript of the *Gospels*[2].

During the most flourishing period of Celtic art in Ireland its influence was by no means limited to the Northumbrian school of illuminators. The Irish types of ornament were adopted by the scribes of Canterbury and other places in the South of England; and on the Continent of Europe Celtic art was widely spread by Irish missionaries such as Saint Columbanus, and by the founding of Irish monasteries during the sixth century in various countries, as, for example, at Bobbio in Northern Italy, at St Gallen in Switzerland, at Wurtzburg in Germany, and at Luxeuil in France. In these and in other places Irish monastic illuminators worked hard at the production of manuscripts and spread the Celtic style of ornament over a large area of Western Europe. The library of St Gallen possesses a number of richly illuminated manuscripts of the later Irish type, exactly similar in style to those which during the eighth and ninth centuries were produced in the monasteries of Ireland and Scotland[3].

Celtic school on the Continent.

The result of this spread of Celtic influence was that borders, initial letters and similar ornaments of pure Irish

---

[1] See Westwood, *Irish Manuscripts*, Pl. 16.
[2] This is one of many examples of Books being called after some earlier Saint who was connected with the monastery where the manuscript was written; for example the Gospels of Saint Augustine in the Corpus library at Cambridge, the Gospels of Saint Cuthbert, and the Gospels of Saint Columba, are all later than the dates of the Saints they are called after.
[3] See Weidmann, *Geschichte der Bibliothek von St Gallen*; St Gall, 1841.

style were used in many manuscripts in which the figures of Saints were designed after an equally pure Italian or debased classic style. A good example of this is the so-called *Psalter of Saint Augustine*[1] (Brit. Mus. *Cotton manuscripts Vesp.* A. i) which for many centuries belonged to the Cathedral of Canterbury. This is a manuscript of the eighth century; one of its chief miniature paintings represents David enthroned, playing on a harp with a group of attendant musicians and two dancing figures round his throne. These figures are purely Italian in style, of the debased Roman School; but the arched frame which borders the picture is filled in with ornament of the Irish metal type, closely similar in style, except that gold and silver are largely used, to those in the *Book of Kells*, though inferior in minute delicacy of execution. It is of course very possible that the illuminations in this *Psalter* are the work of two hands, the figures being painted by an Italian illuminator and the borders by an English or Irish monk.

Psalter of St Augustine.

In later times, especially during the ninth century, the Celtic art of Ireland appears to have been largely introduced into Scandinavia by means of the Viking pirates who harried the whole circuit of the shores of Britain and Ireland, and finally in the ninth century established a Norse Kingdom in eastern Ireland with the newly founded Dublin as its capital[2]. The Norsemen were far from being a literary race and it was not in the form of manuscript illuminations that Irish art was introduced into Norway and Denmark, but rather in the rich gold and silver jewellery with which the Viking chiefs adorned themselves, and also on a larger scale in the magnificently decorative reliefs which were carved on the wooden planks which formed the frames or architraves of the doors of the Scandinavian wooden churches in the eleventh

Scandinavian art.

[1] This manuscript was formerly believed to have been once in the possession of Saint Augustine, but it is clearly a good deal later in date than his time.

[2] Eventually there were three Norse kingdoms in Ireland, the capitals of which were Dublin, Waterford and Limerick; and the three chief ports of Ireland, Dublin, Cork and Belfast were all founded by the Viking invaders; see C. F. Keary's valuable work, *The Vikings in Western Christendom*, London, 1891, pp. 165 to 185.

and twelfth centuries, after the worship of the Thunderer had been replaced by the Faith of the White Christ.

Lindisfarne, Iona and the other chief Irish monasteries suffered again and again from the inroads of the Vikings, who found rich and easily won plunder in the form of gold and silver chalices, reliquaries and book-covers in the treasuries of the monastic churches undefended by any except unarmed and peaceful monks.

The Golden Gospels of Stockholm. One curious record of Viking plunder is preserved in the Royal library of Stockholm. This is a very magnificent manuscript Book of the *Gospels* of the eighth century, commonly known as the *Codex aureus* of Stockholm. It is mostly written with alternate leaves of purple vellum, the text on which is in golden letters. In general style and in the splendour of its ornaments it closely resembles the Lindisfarne "*Gospels of Saint Cuthbert,*" described above at page 88, and most probably, like the latter, was also written in the monastery of Lindisfarne. The interlaced ornaments of the Irish type are marvels of beauty, while the dignified drawing of the enthroned figures of the four Evangelists shows clearly the influence of Continental manuscript art. In this case the Celtic or English illuminator must have had before him a copy of the *Gospels* not of the Italian but of the Byzantine style, since the Evangelists and other figures in the book which are represented in the act of benediction do so in the Oriental not in the Latin fashion[1].

Viking robbers. On the margin of the first page of Saint Matthew's Gospel an interesting note has been written about the year 850 by the owner of the Gospels, an English Ealdorman named Aelfred; this note records that the manuscript had been stolen by Norse robbers and that Aelfred had purchased it from them for a sum in pure gold in order that the sacred book might be rescued from heathen hands. Aelfred then presented it to the Cathedral Church of Canterbury, and new gold covers appear then to have been made for this *Textus*, as there is another note in a ninth century hand

[1] The blessing in the Greek Church is given by raising three fingers; in the Western Church two fingers and the thumb are used.

requesting the prayers of the Church for three goldsmiths, probably those who replaced the original gold covers which the Viking pirates had torn off[1].

Returning now to the manuscripts of the Celtic Church in Northumbria, in order to understand the gradual introduction into Northern England of the Italian or classical style of painting it is necessary to remember the struggle which took place during the seventh century between the adherents of the older Celtic Church and those who supported the Papal claims for supremacy throughout Britain.

The two Churches in Britain.

On the one hand the See of Canterbury, founded by the Roman Saint Augustine, claimed jurisdiction in the north as well as in the south of Britain, in opposition to the Celtic Abbot of Iona, who was then the real Metropolitan of the Church in the north of England.

Wilfrid of York and Benedict Biscop of Jarrow spent many years in a series of embassies, between 670 and 690, backward and forward between Northumbria and Rome striving to introduce the Papal authority, by the aid of imported books, relics and craftsmen skilled in building stone churches in place of the simple wooden structures which at that time were the only ecclesiastical buildings in Northumbria[2]. Very large numbers of illuminated manuscripts were brought to England during the many journeys of Wilfrid and Benedict Biscop; and important libraries were created at York and at Jarrow which led to these places becoming literary and artistic centres of great and European importance.

Long struggle.

In the end, after many failures, Wilfrid, Archbishop[3] of York, was successful in bringing Northumbria under the supremacy of Canterbury and Rome. In 664 a great Council was held at Whitby in the presence of the Northumbrian King Oswiu. Bishop Colman, the successor of Saint Aidan at Lindisfarne, represented the Celtic Church and the authority of Saint Columba, while Wilfrid appeared to support the authority

Synod of Whitby.

[1] See Westwood, *Miniatures of Irish Manuscripts*, London, 1868, Pl. 1. and 11.

[2] The points of difference between the Roman and Celtic Churches were very trivial, the chief being the date for the celebration of Easter and the shape of the monastic tonsure.

[3] See *note* 2 on page 97.

of Saint Peter and the Bishop of Rome. After hearing that Saint Peter possessed the keys of Heaven and Hell, while Saint Columba could claim no such marvellous power, King Oswiu decided in favour of the Roman Supremacy. This decision, though based on such fanciful grounds, was a fortunate one for the English Church, since, in the main, learning, culture and established order generally were on the side of the Italian Church.

Defeat of the Celtic party.

The practical result of this Roman victory at the Synod of Whitby in 664 was that a classical influence gradually extended itself in all the English centres for the production of illuminated manuscripts. It has already been noted that the splendid manuscripts of Lindisfarne and other Northumbrian monasteries, though of Celtic origin, show a distinct Roman influence in the improvement of the drawing of their figures of Saints. By degrees the Irish element in the illuminations grew less and less; though the interlaced patterns and fantastic dragon and serpent forms lasted for many centuries in all the chief countries of western Europe and form an important decorative element till the thirteenth century[1].

Baeda of Durham.

One of the chief schools of English manuscript illumination, that of the Benedictine Abbey at Durham, was raised to a position of European importance by the Northumbrian monk Baeda, afterwards called the Venerable Bede, who was born in 673, a few years after the Synod of Whitby.

As the author of a great *Ecclesiastical History of the English Nation*, Baeda ranks as the Father of English History; he did much to foster the study of ancient classical authors, was himself a skilful writer of manuscripts, and made the Abbey of Jarrow, where he lived till his death in 735, an active centre for the production of richly illuminated manuscripts of many different literary classes.

Northumbrian school.

In the eighth century the schools of illumination in the Abbeys of Jarrow, Wearmouth and York in Northumbria, and of Canterbury and Winchester in the south were among

[1] This very decorative class of ornament not only survived till the thirteenth century but was again revived in Italy at the close of the fifteenth century; see below, page 193.

CHAP. VI.] ENGLISH SCHOOL OF ILLUMINATION. 97

the most active and artistically important in the world[1]. In these schools of miniature painting was gradually created a special English style of illumination, partly formed out of a combination of two very different styles, that of the Irish Celtic illuminators and that of the Italian classical scribes.

Celtic and Classic styles.

This English School of illumination, which had been partially developed before the close of the tenth century, became, for real artistic merit, the first and most important in the whole of Europe, and for a considerable period continued to occupy this foremost position[2].

[1] It is mentioned above, see page 62, how Alcuin of York in the reign of Charles the Great created the Anglo-Carolingian style of illumination by introducing in the eighth century into the kingdom of the Franks manuscripts and manuscript illuminators from the monasteries of Northumbria.

[2] Canon G. F. Browne tells me that it is very doubtful whether Wilfrid ever received the *pall* from Rome. It may therefore be more correct to speak of him as Bishop rather than Archbishop of York.

CHAPTER VII.

THE ANGLO-SAXON SCHOOL OF MANUSCRIPTS[1].

Danish invasions.

THE ninth century in England was one of great turmoil and misery, on account of the fearful havoc wrought by the Danish Northmen throughout the whole length and breadth of the land. In Northumbria the thriving literary and artistic school which had been raised to such preeminence by Baeda was utterly blotted out from existence by the invading Danes; and when at last King Alfred, who reigned from 871 to 901, secured an interval of peace he was obliged to seek instructors in the art of manuscript illumination from the Frankish kings.

Time of King Alfred.

In this way the wave of influence flowed back again from France to England. In Charles the Great's time the Carolingian school of manuscripts had been largely influenced by the Celtic style, which Alcuin of York introduced from Northumbria, and now the later art of Anglo-Saxon England received back from France the forms of ornament and the technical skill which in Northumbria itself had become extinct.

Alfred was an enthusiastic patron of literature and art, especially the art of manuscript illumination, and before long a new school of manuscript art was created in many of the

---

[1] The word "Anglo-Saxon" is a convenient one to use, and is supported by various ancient authorities; for example in a manuscript *Benedictional* (in the library of Corpus College, Cambridge) England is called "Regnum Anglo-Saxonum," and the English king is entitled "Rex Anglorum vel Saxonum."

CHAP. VII.] BENEDICTIONAL OF AETHELWOLD. 99

Benedictine monasteries of England and especially among the monks of the royal city of Winchester, which in the tenth century produced works of extraordinary beauty and decorative force.

As an example of this we may mention the famous *Benedictional* of Aethelwold, who was Bishop of Winchester from 963 to 984[1]. The writer of this sumptuously decorated manuscript was Bishop Aethelwold's chaplain, a monk named Godemann, who afterwards, about the year 970, became Abbot of Thorney. Unlike the manuscripts of earlier date in which the illuminated pictures are usually few in number, this *Benedictional* contains no less than thirty full page miniatures, mostly consisting of scenes from the life of Christ. Each picture is framed by an elaborate border, richly decorated in gold and brilliant colours, with conventional leaf-work of classical style. The drawing of the figures is dignified, and the drapery is usually well conceived and treated in a bold, decorative way, showing much artistic skill on the part of the illuminator.

Benedictional of Aethelwold.

Fig. 21 shows one of the miniatures, representing the Ascension; the colouring is extremely beautiful and harmonious, enhanced by a skilful use of burnished gold.

Though the figures and especially the delicately modelled faces have a character of their own, peculiarly English in feeling, yet in the general style of the miniatures, and in their elaborate borders there are very distinct signs of a strong Carolingian influence, owing, no doubt, to the introduction of Frankish illuminators and the purchase of Carolingian manuscripts during the reign of Alfred the Great, more than half a century before the date of this manuscript.

Foreign influence.

There is, for example, much similarity of style in the miniatures of this *Benedictional* and those in a Carolingian

[1] This splendid manuscript is in the possession of the Duke of Devonshire; a good description of it, with engravings of all its miniatures, is published in *Archaeologia*, Vol. XXIV. 1832, pp. 1 to 117, and a coloured copy of one of the miniatures is given by Westwood, *Irish Manuscripts*, Plate 45.

The library of Trinity College, Cambridge, possesses a book of the *Gospels* which in style is very similar to the *Benedictional* of Aethelwold.

Fig. 21. Miniature from the *Benedictional* of Aethelwold; written and illuminated by a monastic scribe at Winchester.

CHAP. VII.] THE WINCHESTER SCHOOL. 101

manuscript of *the Gospels* written for King Lothaire in the monastery of St Martin at Metz soon after 843[1]; see above fig. 14, p. 71.

Another very fine example of the Winchester school of illumination is the manuscript *Charter* which King Edgar granted to the new minster at Winchester in 966. The first page consists of a large miniature, painted in gold and brilliant colours on a purple-stained leaf of vellum[2], with Christ in Majesty supported by four angels in the upper part of the picture, and, below, standing figures of the B. V. Mary and Saint Peter, with King Edgar in the middle offering his charter to Christ. The whole picture is very skilfully designed so as to fill the whole page in the most decorative way, and it is framed in a border with richly devised conventional leaf-forms.

Winchester Charter.

In artistic power this tenth century Winchester school of illuminators appears, for a while at least, to have been foremost in the world. Both in delicacy of touch and in richness of decorative effect the productions of this school are superior to those of any contemporary Continental country.

Saint Dunstan, the great ecclesiastical statesman of the ninth century, created another school of illumination in the Benedictine Abbey of Glastonbury. Dunstan himself was no mean artist, as may be seen from a fine drawing of Christ, which he executed[3]; the Saint has represented himself as a small monkish figure prostrate at the feet of Christ. At the top of the page is inscribed in a twelfth century hand, "Pictura et scriptura hujus pagine subtus visa est de propria manu sancti Dunstani."

St Dunstan as an artist.

During the tenth century a large number of illuminated manuscripts were executed in the southern parts of England, the miniatures in which are very unlike and, as decoration, very inferior to the manuscripts of the Anglo-Carolingian

[1] The Gospels of Lothaire are in Paris, *Bibl. Nat. Lat.* 266.
[2] This is one of the latest examples of the use of vellum dyed with the *murex* purple; the purple grounds occasionally used in fifteenth century manuscripts are usually produced by laying on a coat of opaque purple pigment.
[3] Now preserved in the Bodleian library at Oxford.

style, as represented by the magnificent *Benedictional* of
Aethelwold. This class of illumination consists of drawings,
often with a large number of small figures, executed with a
pen in red, blue and brown outline. The drawing of these
figures is very mannered, the heads are small, the attitudes
awkward, and the draperies are represented in numerous
small, fluttering folds, drawn with an apparently shaky line,
as if the artist had lacked firmness of hand. This, however,
is a mere mannerism, as wherever he wished for a steady
line, as, for example, in the drawing of the faces, the artist has
drawn with the utmost decision and firmness of touch. The
costumes of these curious outline drawings, the architectural
accessories and other details, all show clearly the influence of
the very debased forms of classical Roman art, which still
survived among the manuscript illuminations of Italy[1]. This
degraded form of classical art was far from being a good
model for the Anglo-Saxon illuminator to imitate, and the
blue and red outline miniatures are very inferior to the
sumptuous Anglo-Carolingian manuscripts which were being
produced at Winchester by contemporary illuminators.

In the eleventh century Anglo-Saxon miniatures in
coloured outline improved greatly in beauty of form and
in gracefulness of pose; till at the beginning of the twelfth
century extremely fine miniatures of this class were produced.
A very beautiful example of this is a long vellum roll
illuminated with eighteen circular miniatures, mostly drawn
with a pen in dark brown ink. These outline miniatures
represent scenes from the life of Saint Guthlac, the Hermit of
Crowland. The series begins with a drawing of the youthful
Guthlac receiving the tonsure from Hedda, Bishop of Winchester (676 to 705), in the presence of the Abbess Ebba and
two nuns. The whole composition is very skilfully arranged
to fill the circular medallion, and there is great dignity and
even delicate beauty in the separate figures. The precision of

[1] The celebrated "Utrecht Psalter" is the best known example of a fine
manuscript of this date with outline drawings of the revived classical style.
Some northern influence is shown in the interlaced ornaments of the large initials.
Facsimiles of some pages have been published by W. G. Birch, London, 1876.

CHAP. VII.]   LIFE OF SAINT GUTHLAC.   103

touch shown in the drawing is most admirable, recalling the *Beauty of* perfect purity of line seen in the finest vase-paintings of the *line.* Greeks, in which, as in these miniatures, the greatest amount of effect is produced with the fewest possible touches. A few flat washes are introduced into the backgrounds, but all the principal part of the miniatures is executed with this pure outline.

There are no grounds for the suggestion that these medallion drawings were intended as designs for stained glass. There is much similarity of style in stained glass paintings and manuscript illuminations during the twelfth to the fourteenth century in England, just as in the early Byzantine manuscripts the same design serves for a miniature painting and a colossal wall-mosaic. The same simplicity of drawing and flatness of composition were preserved in both classes of art, and there is nothing exceptional in the fact that these miniatures of Saint Guthlac might have served as excellent motives for a glass-painter[1].

The *Pontifical* of Saint Dunstan (Brit. Mus. *Cott. Claud.* *Pontifical* A. 3), executed in the early part of the eleventh century, is a *of St* magnificent example of decorative art, both in its noble *Dunstan.* designs and richness of colour. Though no gold is used, the greatest splendour of effect is produced, especially in a large miniature representing Saint Gregory enthroned under an elaborate architectural canopy, with prostrate figures at his feet of Archbishop Dunstan and the Benedictine scribe of this beautiful manuscript; see Westwood, *Irish Manuscripts,* Pl. 50.

The beauty of the best English manuscripts of the twelfth *Byzantine* century is a remarkable contrast to the once splendid *decadence.* Byzantine school of illumination, which by this time had sadly degenerated from its former vigorous splendour, and had become weak in drawing, clumsy in pose and inharmonious in colour. The English school on the other hand, all through the twelfth century, was making rapid advances towards a

[1] This beautiful roll is now in the British Museum, *Harl.,* Roll Y, 6; two of the miniatures are photographically illustrated by Birch and Jenner, *Early Drawings and Illuminations,* London, 1879, p. 142.

perfection both of design and technique which culminated in the Anglo-Norman style of the latter part of the thirteenth century, which for beauty of all kinds remained for a long time quite without rival in any European country.

Canute a patron of art.
To return to the Anglo-Saxon school of manuscripts in the eleventh century, it should be observed that the Danish King Canute, unlike his destructive predecessors, did all that he could to encourage literature and art in England. With a view to fostering the production of fine illuminated manuscripts he introduced into this country, and especially into the royal and monastic libraries of Winchester, a large number of Roman manuscripts with the usual illuminations of the debased classic type. This, no doubt, helped to encourage the production of miniatures in outline such as those in the *Utrecht Psalter*[1]. Another variety of Anglo-Saxon manuscript illumination, executed during the first half of the eleventh century, consists first of all of a pen drawing in brown outline; to which subsequently the artist added with a brush narrow bands of blue or red laid on in a thin wash as a sort of edging to the brown outlines, apparently with the object of giving roundness to the drawing[2].

Feeble colouring.

This class of illumination is, however, very inferior in beauty and decorative splendour to the finest works of the monks of Winchester and Glastonbury, in which solid colour in great variety of tint is used, as, for example in the above-mentioned *Benedictional* of Aethelwold and the *Pontifical* of Saint Dunstan.

[1] This *Psalter*, which is now in the public library at Utrecht, may possibly be one of the very manuscripts which Canute brought from abroad. It was certainly in England for many centuries before it passed into the possession of Sir Robert Cotton, from whose library it must have been stolen, else it would have passed into the library of the British Museum along with the rest of the great Cotton collection of manuscripts.

The *Utrecht Psalter* has been thought to be the work of an Anglo-Saxon artist, but, most probably, it is the work of a French scribe, though the miniatures are mainly of the debased classical style of Rome, and the character of the writing is even more distinctly classical, differing very little in fact from that of the fourth century Virgil of the Vatican written several centuries earlier.

[2] Good examples of this curious style of miniature are to be seen in a manuscript in the British Museum, *Cotton, Tib.* C. vi.

CHAP. VII.]   THE NORMAN INVASION.   105

The Norman conquest of England in 1066 soon put an end to the Anglo-Saxon school of illumination, with its weak imitations of the debased classical style of Italy. In place of this the magnificent Anglo-Norman schools of miniature painting were developed on both sides of the British Channel. England and Normandy became one country, and as long as this union lasted manuscripts of precisely similar character were produced both in Normandy and in England, as is described in the following Chapter.

The Anglo-Norman school.

CHAPTER VIII.

THE ANGLO-NORMAN SCHOOL OF MANUSCRIPTS.

THE twelfth century in England and Northern France was a period of rapid artistic development in almost all branches of the arts, from a miniature illumination to a great Cathedral or Abbey church.

The Norman invasion. With regard, however, to the art of illuminated manuscripts and other branches of art in England it should be observed that though the conquered English and the Norman conquerors with remarkable rapidity were amalgamated with great solidarity into one united people[1], yet for a long period after the Conquest it was distinctly the Norman element that took the lead in all matters of art and literature. The Bishops, Abbots and Priors of the great English ecclesiastical foundations were for a long period wholly or in the main men of the Norman race, and thus (intellectually) the native English took a lower place, and did far less to advance the arts of England than did the Normans who formed the upper and *Robert of Gloucester.* more cultivated class. As Robert of Gloucester the Benedictine monkish Chronicler of the thirteenth century says,

𝔒𝔣 𝔱𝔥𝔢 𝔑𝔬𝔯𝔪𝔞𝔫𝔫𝔢𝔰 𝔟𝔢𝔱𝔥 𝔱𝔥𝔶𝔰 𝔥𝔢𝔶 𝔪𝔢𝔫, 𝔱𝔥𝔞𝔱 𝔟𝔢𝔱𝔥 𝔬𝔣 𝔱𝔥𝔶𝔰 𝔩𝔬𝔫𝔡, 𝔄𝔫𝔡 𝔱𝔥𝔢 𝔩𝔬𝔴𝔢 𝔪𝔢𝔫 𝔬𝔣 𝔖𝔞𝔵𝔬𝔫𝔰, 𝔞𝔰 𝔶𝔢𝔥 𝔲𝔫𝔡𝔢𝔯𝔰𝔱𝔬𝔫𝔡𝔢[2].

[1] Indeed it was not very long before the tables were turned and Normandy was reconquered by an English army under a king, who, though of Norman blood, was distinctly an English king. The victory of Henry I. over Robert, Duke of Normandy, at Tenchebray in 1105, went far to wipe out any feeling on the part of the English that they were a nation under the rule of a conqueror.

[2] *Chronicles* of Robert of Gloucester, Hearne's edition, 1724 (reprinted in 1810), Vol. I. p. 363.

CHAP. VIII.]   THE ANGLO-NORMAN SCHOOL.   107

In the eleventh century building in stone on a large scale for military and ecclesiastical purposes had been introduced into England by the Normans in place of the frail wooden structures of the Anglo-Saxons. Towards the close of the twelfth century the Gothic style of architecture, with its pointed arches and quadripartite vaults, was brought to England by the Cistercian monks of northern France, and soon spread far and wide throughout the kingdom.

Architectural growth.

The artists of this century began to study the human form, its pose and movement, and also in their drapery learnt to depict gracefully designed folds with much truth and with a keen sense of beauty[1].

Manuscripts of various classes were now richly illuminated with many varied series of picture subjects, and the old hieratic canons of Byzantine conservatism were soon completely thrown aside. In the ornaments of the Anglo-Norman manuscripts of the twelfth century rich foliage is used made of conventionalized forms which recall the old acanthus leaf, the half expanded fronds of various ferns and other plants, all used with great taste in their arrangement, and wonderful life and spirit in every line and curve of the design. Older Celtic motives are also used; ingeniously devised interlaced work of straps and bands, plaited together in complicated knots, and terminating frequently in strange forms of serpents, dragons and other grotesque monsters[2]. These ornaments are strongly decorative both in form and colour, and, though delicately painted, are treated somewhat broadly, very unlike the microscopic minuteness of the earlier Irish and Anglo-Celtic school.

Anglo-Norman school.

At this time a large number of very magnificently illuminated *Psalters* were produced; and the use of gold leaf both for the backgrounds of pictures and in combination with brilliant pigments began to come into more frequent use. A fine typical example of English manuscript art at the

Illuminated Psalters.

---

[1] An interesting example of this revived study from the life is afforded by the Sketch-book of Villard de Honecourt, which is mentioned above at page 72.

[2] See below, page 193, on the revival of this class of ornament in Italy in the second half of the fifteenth century.

close of the twelfth century is to be seen in the so-called *Huntingfield Psalter*, which was executed, probably in some monastic house in Yorkshire, a little before 1200 A.D.[1] It contains 68 miniatures of very fine style, delicately painted on backgrounds partially of gold; the subjects are taken from both the Old and the New Testament, beginning with the Creation of the World. The general style of the illuminations in this *Psalter* is more exclusively English in character and less Norman than is usual in manuscripts of this date.

Martyrdom of St Thomas. The book is interesting as containing one of the earliest representations of the Martyrdom of Thomas à Becket, who subsequently became so popular a Saint in England and Normandy. In this case the painting is not quite of the same date as the bulk of the manuscript, but it evidently was added not many years after Becket's death, which occurred in 1170; Saint Thomas was canonized only two years later[2].

One of the earliest representations of this subject is a miniature painted by Matthew Paris on the border of a page of his *Greater Chronicle* in the library of Corpus Christi College, Cambridge, No. xxvi.

Though I have used the phrase "Anglo-Norman" to denote the school of manuscript illumination which, from the twelfth to the fourteenth century, existed on both sides of the Channel, it should be observed that manuscripts of a similar type to those of Normandy were produced in many places far to the south, and indeed almost throughout the whole *The Angevin kingdom.* dominions of the Angevin kings, including the whole western half of France down to Gascony and the Pyrenees. The fact is that to a great degree all forms of Norman art extended throughout the whole Angevin dominions, so that, for example, we find a Cathedral as far south as Bayonne (not far from the Spanish frontier) resembling closely both in

---

[1] This beautiful manuscript is now in the possession of Mr Quaritch, who prices it at £800 in his catalogue of December, 1891. It appears once to have belonged to Sir Roger Huntingfield, who died about 1337 A.D.

[2] It is noticeable that even the earliest miniatures of Saint Thomas' death represent him in Mass vestments, officiating at the High Altar, whereas he was really killed late in the afternoon, and on the north side of the church.

CHAP. VIII.] THE PERFECTION OF ENGLISH ART. 109

general design and details of mouldings and carving the ecclesiastical architecture of Canterbury and Caen.

English art at its highest period of development. The thirteenth century was the culminating period of Anglo-Norman art of all kinds; and indeed for a brief period England occupied the foremost position in the world with regard to nearly all the principal branches of the fine arts. *English art in the XIIIth century.*

The early years of the thirteenth century were a time of war and tumult, little favourable to artistic advance, but during the long reign of Henry III., which lasted from 1216 to 1272, progress of the most remarkable kind was made. The King himself was an enthusiastic patron of all the arts, ranging from manuscript illumination to the construction of such a fabric as Westminster Abbey; and the lesser arts of life, such as weaving, embroidery, metal work, together with stained glass, mural painting and other forms of decoration, were all brought in England to a wonderful pitch of perfection between 1250 and 1300. *Henry III. as an art patron.*

Immense sums were spent by the King in improving and decorating his Palaces and Manor Houses all over the kingdom with an amount of refinement and splendour that had hitherto been unknown. Many interesting contemporary documents still exist giving the expenses of the many works which Henry III. carried out. He spent large sums on fitting the windows with glass casements, laying down floors of "painted tiles," and in panelling the walls with wainscot which was richly decorated with painting in gold and colours. Large mural paintings were executed by a whole army of painters on the walls of the chief rooms; and decorative art both for domestic and ecclesiastical purposes was in England brought to a pitch of perfection far beyond that of any continental country. *Houses of Henry III.*

The chief works of Henry III. were the building of a magnificent Palace at Westminster in place of the ruder structure of the earlier Norman kings; the reconstruction of Westminster Abbey, and the providing for the body of Edward the Confessor a great shrine of pure gold, richly studded with jewels of enormous value. A long and interest- *Chief works of Henry III.*

Wall-paintings at Westminster.

ing series of accounts of these and other lavish expenditures of money still exist in the Record Office[1].

A magnificent series of wall-paintings, with subjects from sacred and profane history and from the Apocryphal books of the Old Testament, were executed by various artists, both monks and laymen, on the walls of the chief rooms in the new Palace of Westminster. In style these paintings were very like the miniatures in an illuminated manuscript of the time; they were simply designed, flat in treatment, and executed with the most minute and delicate detail. Great richness of effect was produced by the use of wooden stamps with which delicate diapers and other patterns were stamped over the backgrounds of the pictures on the thin coat of *gesso* which covered the stone wall. These minutely executed reliefs were then thickly gilt, forming rich gold backgrounds, such as are so commonly used in the manuscripts of the Anglo-Norman school; see fig. 23, p. 130.

Paintings copied from MSS.

The close connection between these magnificent wall paintings and the illuminated miniatures in manuscripts is borne witness to by an interesting record that, in the year 1250, the King ordered Richard de Sanford, Master of the Knights Templars, to lend an illuminated manuscript in French of "*The Gestes of Antioch and the History of the Crusades*" to the painter Edward of Westminster, so that he might copy the miniatures, using the designs to paint the walls of "the Queen's low room in the new Palace of Westminster" with a series of historical pictures. From these paintings of "the Gestes of Antioch" the Queen's room was thenceforth known as "the Antioch chamber[2]".

---

[1] See *Vetusta Monumenta*, Vol. VI. pp. 1 to 37, and Plates 26 to 39; illustrations are given here of "the Painted Chamber" and its decorations before the fire of 1834, and a number of interesting extracts are quoted from the accounts now preserved in the Record Office.

[2] *The Gestes of Antioch* probably means the capture of Antioch in 1098 under the Crusader leaders Tancred and Godfrey of Bouillon. In the same way the "Jerusalem" and "Jericho chambers" in the house of the Abbot of Westminster were so called from the paintings on their walls. The curious "archaism" of these paintings, with figures of knights in the armour of the eleventh century, is explained below; see page 118.

CHAP. VIII.]   OF WESTMINSTER PALACE.   111

The largest of the halls in the Westminster Palace, decorated with a marvellous series of exquisitely finished paintings, was known as "the Painted Chamber" *par excellence* from its great size and the immense number of pictures which covered its walls. The system of decoration adopted in the thirteenth century was not to paint large pictures in a large hall, but simply to multiply the number of small ones, keeping the figures as delicate in execution and small in scale as if the room had been of the most limited dimensions.   *The Painted Chamber.*

This had the effect of enormously adding to the apparent scale of the room, a great contrast to the method of decoration which was employed in later times of decadence, when large halls were dwarfed and rendered insignificant by covering the walls with figures of colossal size. The sixteenth century tapestry in the great hall at Hampton Court is a striking example of the way in which gigantic figures may destroy the scale of an interior.

The great beauty and extreme minuteness of the work can be seen in some few damaged fragments, now in the British Museum, which were not completely destroyed when the Royal Palace of Westminster, the seat of the two Houses of Parliament, was burnt in 1834.   *Existing fragments.*

In the second half of the thirteenth century, during the reigns of Henry III. and Edward I., the painting of England was unrivalled by that of any other country[1]. Even in Italy, Cimabue and his assistants were still labouring in the fetters of Byzantine conventionalism, and produced no works which for jewel-like beauty of colour and grace of form were quite equal to the paintings of England under Edward I.

In sculpture too England was no less pre-eminent; no continental works of the time are equal in combined dignity and beauty, both of the heads and of the drapery, to the bronze effigies of Henry III. and Queen Eleanor of Castile on the north side of Edward the Confessor's Chapel at Westminster. These noble examples of bronze sculpture   *English sculpture.*

[1] See, for example, that wonderful frontal, covered with miniature paintings, from the High Altar of Westminster Abbey, which is now preserved in the south ambulatory of the Sanctuary.

William Torell. were the work of the goldsmith citizen of London William Torell, who executed them by the beautiful *cire perdue* process with the utmost technical skill[1]; see page 232 on their gilding, which was executed by the old "mercury process."

The Fitz-Othos. One of the chief English families of the thirteenth century, among whom the practice of various arts was hereditary, was named Otho or Fitz-Otho. Various members of this family were goldsmiths, manuscript illuminators, cutters of dies for coins and makers of official seals, as well as painters of mural decorations. The elaborate gold shrine of the Confessor, one of the most costly works of the Middle Ages, was made by the Otho family. The great royal seals of more than one king were their handiwork, and it should be observed that the seals of England, not only of the thirteenth century but almost throughout the mediaeval period, were far the most beautiful in the world, both for splendour and elaboration of design, and for exquisite minuteness of detail.

English needle-work. Another minor branch of art, in which England during the thirteenth century far surpassed the rest of the world, was the art of embroidering delicate pictures in silk, especially for ecclesiastical vestments. The most famous embroidered vestments now preserved in various places in Italy are the handiwork of English embroiderers between the years 1250 and 1300, though their authorship is not as a rule recognized by their present possessors[2]. The embroidered miniatures on these marvellous pieces of needlework resemble closely in style the illuminations in fine Anglo-Norman manuscripts of the thirteenth century, and in many cases have obviously been copied from manuscript miniatures.

[1] Various attempts have been made to show that Torell was an Italian, and that the painted retable at Westminster was the work of a foreign artist, but there is not the slightest foundation for either of these theories.

[2] As examples of this I may mention the famous "Lateran Cope" in Rome, the "Piccolomini Cope" at Pienza, and two others of similar date and style in the Museums of Florence and Bologna. On many occasions we find that the Popes of this period, on sending the Pall to a newly elected English Archbishop, suggested that they would like in return embroidered vestments of English work, *opus Anglicanum*. It should be observed that in almost all published works on the subject the above mentioned copes are wrongly described as being of Italian workmanship.

CHAP. VIII.] MANUSCRIPTS OF THE VULGATE.

There is, in short, ample evidence to show that the Anglo-Norman art of the thirteenth century, in almost all branches, and more especially on English soil, had reached a higher pitch of perfection, aesthetic and technical, than had been then attained by any other country in the world. In the fourteenth and fifteenth centuries, owing largely to the Black Death and the protracted Wars of the Roses, the arts of England fell into the background, but it should not be forgotten that there was one period, from about 1260 to 1300 or 1320, when England occupied the foremost place in the artistic history of the world. *Decay of English art.*

With regard to the Anglo-Norman manuscripts of the thirteenth and early part of the fourteenth century, the most remarkable class, both for beauty of execution and for the extraordinary number that were produced, consists of copies of the *Vulgate*, richly decorated with a large number of initial letters containing minute miniatures of figure subjects[1].

These Bibles vary in size from large quartos or folios down to the most minute *codex* with writing of microscopic character. In the latter it appears to have been the special aim of the scribe to get the whole of the *Vulgate*, including the *Apocrypha*, the *Prologue of St Jerome*, and an explanatory *list of Hebrew names*, into the smallest possible space. The thinnest uterine vellum of the finest quality is used[2], the text is frequently much contracted, and the characters are of almost microscopic size[3]. In these smallest Bibles the initials are mostly ornamented with conventional leaves and grotesque dragon monsters; but in the larger manuscripts the initials at *MS. Bibles.*

---

[1] Both before and after this period manuscripts of the *Vulgate* were comparatively rare, but between 1250 and about 1330 many thousands of manuscript Bibles must have been produced, all closely similar in style, design, choice of subject and character of writing. There is no other large class of manuscripts in which such remarkable uniformity of style is to be seen.

[2] As an example of the wonderful thinness of this uterine vellum, I may mention a Bible of about 1260 in my own possession which consists of 646 leaves, and yet measures barely an inch and a half in thickness. In spite of its extreme thinness this vellum is sufficiently opaque to prevent the writing on one side from showing through to the other.

[3] For example a Bible of this class in the Cambridge University library, dating from about 1280, has from thirteen to seventeen lines to an inch!

Historiated Bibles. the beginning of every book, about 82 in number, are illuminated with a miniature picture of the most exquisite workmanship, a perfect model of beauty and refined skill. The drawing of the faces and hair is specially beautiful, being executed with a fine, crisp line with the most precise and delicate touch, worthy of a Greek artist of the best period. The drawing of the hair and beard of the male figures is most masterly, with waving curls full of grace and spirit, in spite of the extreme minuteness of the scale.

Method of execution. The miniatures of this school are executed in the following manner: first of all a slight outline is lightly sketched with a lead or silver point; the main masses are then put in with flat, solid colour; the internal drawing of the folds of the drapery, the hair and features and the like, are then added with a delicate pointed brush, capable of drawing the finest possible line; and finally some shading is added to give roundness to the forms, especially of the drapery, a broader touch being used for this, unlike the first drawing of the details, which is executed with a thin, though boldly applied line. As a rule the portions which are in shadow are put in with a pure pigment; the high lights being represented with white, and the half lights with a mixture of white and the same pigment that is used for the dark shadows. By this somewhat conventional system of colouring, the local colour is never lost, and the whole effect is highly decorative, and far more suitable for painting on such a minute scale than a more realistic system of colour would have been[1].

Bible of Mainerius. One of the larger and more magnificent manuscripts of this class, in the library of Ste Géneviéve in Paris, is a historiated *Vulgate* in three large volumes, which is of special interest from the fact that it is signed by its scribe, a monk named Mainerius of the Benedictine Abbey of Canterbury.

Most of these Bibles and other sacred manuscripts of this

---

[1] This method of painting the shadows in pure colour, and using the same pigment mixed with white for the rest, was employed on a large scale by many of the Sienese painters in the fourteenth century, and by the Florentine Fra Angelico in the fifteenth. Fra Angelico's earliest works were manuscript illuminations, executed about the year 1407 in the Dominican Convent at Fiesole.

CHAP. VIII.]   UNITY OF STYLE.   115

period appear to have been written and illuminated in the great Benedictine Abbeys of England and Normandy. On this side of the Channel York, Norwich, Bury St Edmunds, Winchester, St Albans, and Canterbury were specially famed for their schools of illumination[1]. And probably some work of the kind was done in every Benedictine House[2].

Benedictine scribes.

The unity of a great monastic Order like that of St Benedict, and the fact that monks were often transferred from a monastery in one country to one of the same Order in another country, had an important influence on the artistic development of mediaeval Europe.

This unity of feeling was of course encouraged by the existence of a common language (Latin) among all the ecclesiastics of Western Europe; and to a great extent the old traditions of a great Western Empire, uniting various races under one system of government, survived in the organization of the Catholic Church.

Monastic unity.

This unity of life, of custom and of thought, which was so striking a feature of the monastic system, was, to a great extent, the cause why we find a simultaneous change of artistic style taking place at several far distant centres of production[3]. Hence also it is usually impossible, from the style of illumination in an Anglo-Norman manuscript of the thirteenth century, to judge whether it was executed in Normandy or in England.

One extremely magnificent class of illumination of this date and school, specially used for *Psalters, Missals* and other Service-books, has the background behind the figures formed of an unbroken sheet of burnished gold of the most sumptuously decorative effect.

Backgrounds of sheet gold.

[1] The Bodleian library (*Douce*, 366) possesses a specially beautiful manuscript *Psalter*, which belonged to Robert of Ormsby, a monk of Norwich Abbey.

[2] In all periods the Benedictines were the chief monastic scribes and miniaturists; the Mother House at Monte Cassino was one of the chief centres in Italy for the production of manuscripts, and wherever the Benedictines settled they brought with them the art of manuscript illumination; see page 211.

[3] This is specially noticeable in the development of the architectural styles; not only general forms, but details of mouldings and the like seem to spring up all over England almost simultaneously.

8—2

Chequer backgrounds.

In the fourteenth century the plain gold background was mostly superseded by delicate diapers of lozenge and chessboard form, with alternating squares of gold and blue or red, very rich and beautiful in effect, and sometimes of extreme minuteness of scale, so that each lozenge or square of the diaper is not larger than an ordinary pin's head. In France these diapered patterns were used with great frequency, and their use survived in some cases till the early part of the fifteenth century.

Scroll patterns.

Another form of background, used in Anglo-Norman miniatures, consists of delicate scroll patterns or outlined diapers put in with a fine brush and with fluid gold over a ground of flat opaque colour. Gold scroll-work of this kind on a *pink* ground is specially characteristic of miniatures painted in England during the fourteenth and first half of the fifteenth century.

Architectural backgrounds.

A fourth style of background, used in miniature pictures of this date, consists of architectural forms, which frequently enshrine the whole miniature, with background, frame, and canopy in one rich architectural composition. This is often painted in gold, with details in firm, dark lines, and, though conventionally treated, gives not unfrequently a representation of an exquisitely beautiful Gothic structure[1].

Realistic backgrounds.

Last of all come the realistic backgrounds, with pictorial effects of distance and aerial perspective, often very skilful and even beautiful in effect, but not so strongly decorative or so perfectly suited to manuscript illumination as the more conventional backgrounds of an earlier date.

These realistic surroundings began to be introduced in the fourteenth century, but are more especially characteristic of the fifteenth century. In the sixteenth century, when the illumination of manuscripts had ceased to be a real living art, though painfully and skilfully practised by such masters of technique as Giulio Clovio and various Italian and French painters, the pictorial character of the backgrounds was carried to an excessive degree of elaboration and decadence.

[1] See below, fig. 25, page 133.

CHAP. VIII.] ILLUMINATED PSALTERS. 117

Among the most magnificent of the Anglo-Norman manuscripts of the thirteenth century are copies of the Psalter. One in the library of the Society of Antiquaries in Burlington House is of extraordinary beauty for the delicate and complicated patterns of interlaced scroll-work which fill its large initials. The first letter *B* of the beginning of the Psalms (*Beatus vir* etc.) is in this and some other illuminated *Psalters* of the same class, of such size and elaboration that it occupies most of the first page. Among its ingeniously devised interlaced ornaments various little animals, rabbits, squirrels and others are playing—marvels of minute and delicate painting. Round the border which frames the whole are ten minute medallion pictures, some of them representing musicians playing on various instruments, one of which is a kind of barrel organ, called an *organistrum*, worked by two players. This magnificent manuscript dates from about the middle of the thirteenth century.

Psalter at Burlington House.

Another still more beautiful *Psalter* in the British Museum, called from its former owner *Archbishop Tenison's Psalter*, was illuminated for Queen Eleanor of Castile, the wife of Edward I., about the year 1284. It was intended as a marriage gift for their third son Alphonso, who, however, died in August 1284, a few days after the signing of his marriage contract. The manuscript was for this reason unfortunately left unfinished, and was afterwards completed by a very inferior illuminator. The letter *B* on the first page is filled by an exquisite miniature of the Royal Psalmist; and in the lower part of the border is the slaying by an infantile David, of Goliath, represented as a gigantic knight in chain armour. At intervals round the border are minute but very accurately painted birds of various kinds, including the gull, kingfisher, woodpecker, linnet, crane and goldfinch. In places where the text does not reach to the end of the line the space is filled up by a narrow band of ornament in gold and colours, occupying the same space that a complete line of words would have done. This method of avoiding any blank spaces in the page, and making the whole surface one unbroken mass of beauty was employed in the finest manu-

The Tenison Psalter.

scripts of this and of other classes, especially the manuscripts of France and Flanders.

Tenison Psalter.
The *Tenison Psalter* appears to have been written and illuminated in the Monastic House of the Blackfriars in London; it is quite one of the noblest existing examples of English art during the thirteenth century, and is unsurpassed in beauty and skilful technique by the manuscripts of any age or country[1].

MSS. of the Apocalypse.
Manuscripts of the Apocalypse. The Anglo-Norman and French manuscripts of the *Apocalypse*, executed during the fourteenth century, are on the whole the most beautiful class of illuminated manuscripts that the world has ever produced[2].

For combined decorative splendour, exquisite grace of drawing, and poetry of sentiment they are quite unrivalled. During several years before and after 1300 a considerable number of these copiously illustrated manuscripts of the *Apocalypse* seem to have been produced with a certain uniformity of style and design, which shows that, as in the case of the historiated Bibles, one model must have been copied and passed on from hand to hand through the *Scriptoria* of many different Monastic Houses.

Perfect beauty.
No words can adequately express the refined and poetical beauty of these miniatures of Apocalyptic scenes, glowing with the utmost splendour of burnished gold, ultramarine and other brilliant pigments. The whole figures of the angels, their beautiful serene faces, their exquisitely pencilled wings with feathers of bright colours, the simple dignified folds of their drapery, all are executed with the most wonderful certainty of touch and the highest possible sense of romantic beauty.

The accessories are hardly less beautiful; the Gothic arches and pinnacles of the New Jerusalem, the vine plants and other trees and flowers, designed with a perfect balance between decorative conventionalism and realistic truth, and

---

[1] The first pages of the two last-mentioned *Psalters* are illustrated by Shaw, *The Art of Illumination*, London, 1870, pp. 17 to 23.

[2] An example of the most marvellous beauty and perfection was presented by Lady Sadleir to Trinity College library in Cambridge.

last of all the sumptuous backgrounds covered with delicate diapers or scroll-work in gold and blue and crimson, all unite the whole composition into one perfect harmony, like a mosaic of gleaming gems, fixed in a matrix of pure, shining gold.

Nothing perhaps could better exemplify the gulf that separates the artistic productions of this feverish, steam-driven nineteenth century from the serene glories of the art of bygone days than a comparison of such a book as the Trinity *Apocalypse* with that masterpiece of commercial art called "the Victoria Psalter," which, printed in a steam-press on machine-made paper, illuminated by chromolithography, and bound in a machine-embossed leather cover, produces a total effect which cannot adequately be described in polite language[1].

Machine-made art.

The later English manuscripts. In the fourteenth century a more distinctly English style of illumination began to branch off from the Anglo-Norman style. Something like separate schools of painting gradually grew up in the great Benedictine Monasteries, such as those at St Albans, Norwich, Glastonbury and Bury Saint Edmunds.

English Monasteries.

The type of face represented in English miniatures from about the middle of the fourteenth century onwards is rather different from the French type with its long oval face and pointed nose[2]. In English manuscripts the faces are rounder and plumper, and the backgrounds are very frequently formed

---

[1] The *Victoria Psalter* is however frequently described in booksellers' catalogues, not only in polite, but in enthusiastic language. As an example I may quote the following,

THE BEAUTIFUL VICTORIA PSALTER:

PSALMS of David illuminated by OWEN JONES, *beautifully printed in large type, on thin cardboards, on* 104 *pages, each of which is surrounded by* SUMPTUOUS BORDERS *in* GOLD *and* COLOURS, *with the* CAPITALS ILLUMINATED, *and some of the pages consisting of large and most beautifully illuminated texts*, columbier 4to. *elegantly bound in morocco, the sides elaborately carved, leathern joints, and gilt edges* (A VERY HANDSOME VOLUME), £4. 10s.   n. d.

[2] These same characteristics of face are very noticeable in the beautiful carved ivory diptychs and statuettes of the Virgin and Child made during the fourteenth century in France and England.

by gold scroll-work over a peculiar pink, made by a mixture of red lead with a large proportion of white.

The Black Death. On the whole the style of figure painting in English manuscripts deteriorated very distinctly after the ravages caused by the Black Death in the middle of the fourteenth century; that is to say the average of excellence became lower; and, especially in the fifteenth century, a good deal of very coarse and inferior manuscript illumination was produced. On the other hand there were some illuminators in England whose work is not surpassed by that of any contemporary French or Flemish artist.

Outline drawings. One very beautiful class of English illumination, executed about the middle of the fourteenth century, has very small and delicate figures, drawn in firm outline with a pen and brown ink; relief is then given to the figures by the partial application of transparent washes of delicate colour, producing an effect of great beauty and refinement. *The Poyntz Book of Hours* in the Fitzwilliam Library has no less than 292 miniature paintings of this very beautiful style. The book was written for a friend and companion of the Black Prince about the year 1350. Its delicate paintings have unfortunately, in many places, been coarsely touched up with gold and colours by a later hand.

Lectionary of Sifer Was. A very fine characteristic example of English art towards the close of the fourteenth century is preserved in the British Museum (*Harl. Manuscripts* 7026). This is a noble folio manuscript *Lectionary*[1], unfortunately imperfect, which was written and illuminated by a monk named Sifer Was for Lord Lovel of Tichmersh, who died in 1408; it was presented by him to the Cathedral church of Salisbury, as is recorded by a note which asks for prayers for the donor's soul. The text is written in a magnificent large Gothic hand, such as was imitated by the printers of early *Missals*[2] and *Psalters*. On the first page is a large, beautifully painted miniature representing the scribe

[1] A *lectionary* contained the *Gospels* and *Epistles* arranged for use at the celebration of Mass.
[2] Especially for the Canon of the Mass. The famous *Mentz Psalter* of 1459 is printed in characters of this size and style; see below, page 149.

Sifer Was presenting the manuscript to Lord Lovel. The figures are large in scale, and the heads are carefully executed portraits, evidently painted with great eiconic skill. Each page of the text has a richly decorative border with conventional foliage of the characteristically bold English type. Figures of angels are introduced at the sides, and an exquisitely minute little painting is placed at the top, by the initial letter of the page.

The English foliated borders and capitals in manuscripts of this type are very bold and decorative in effect, with a simple form of leaf with few serrations, twining in most graceful curves and broadly painted in blue and red with very good effect, even in many manuscripts where the execution is not of the most refined kind. A variety of what is commonly known as "the pine-apple design"[1] is frequently introduced into these very effective pieces of ornament. *English foliage.*

It should be noticed that the first growth of portrait painting in Western Europe seems to have arisen out of this custom of introducing portrait figures of patrons and donors at the beginning of important manuscripts. In French and Burgundian manuscripts especially we find many very interesting portraits of Kings and Princes together with those of the authors or the illuminators of richly decorated manuscripts. *Portrait figures.*

Donors' portraits are also commonly introduced into votive altar-pieces, usually in the form of small kneeling figures. As time went on these figures of donors gradually became more important in scale and position. Thus, for example, the magnificent altar-piece in the Brera Gallery in Milan, painted by Piero della Francesca about the year 1480[2], has, in the most conspicuous place in the foreground, a kneeling figure of the donor, Duke Federigo da Montefeltro *Altar-pieces.*

---

[1] The pine-apple was not known in Europe before the discovery of America, and this very decorative form, which occurs so largely on the fine woven velvets of Florence and Northern Italy, was probably suggested by the artichoke plant, largely assisted by the decorative invention of the designer.

[2] In the Brera Catalogue this very beautiful painting is wrongly ascribed to Fra Carnovale, a pupil of Piero della Francesca.

of Urbino, which is actually larger in scale than the chief figures of the picture—the Madonna and attendant angels. During the fourteenth century, both in altar-pictures and in manuscript illuminations, the portraits of living people are treated in a more subordinate way.

A fine example of portraiture in a manuscript is to be seen in the *Epistre au Roy Richard II. d'Angleterre* (Brit. Mus. *Royal Manuscripts* 20 B. vi) written by a Hermit of the Celestin Order in Paris. The upper half of the first page is occupied by an exquisite miniature of Richard II. on his throne, surrounded by courtiers, accepting the bound copy of the manuscript from the monastic author, who kneels on one knee, presenting his book with one hand, while in the other he holds a sacred banner embroidered with the Agnus Dei. The background is of the sumptuous chess-board pattern in gold, blue and red, and the whole page is surrounded with the so-called ivy-leaf border.

Portrait of Richard II.

The *Shrewsbury manuscript*, containing a collection of chivalrous *Romances* (Brit. Mus. *Royal Manuscripts* 15 E vi), has another beautiful example of miniature portraiture. The first painting represents John Talbot, Earl of Shrewsbury, for whom this interesting manuscript was illuminated, kneeling to present the book to Queen Margaret of Anjou on the occasion of her marriage with Henry VI. The King and Queen are represented side by side on a double throne, and around is a group of courtier attendants. The kneeling figure of Earl Talbot is interesting for its costume ; the mantle which the Earl wears is powdered (semée) with small garters embroidered in gold ; an early but now obsolete form of state robe worn by Knights of the Order of the Garter. Both these manuscripts, though executed for English patrons, are of French workmanship.

Portraits of Henry VI. and his Queen.

Some of the most magnificent manuscripts of the fifteenth century and earlier were, like Lord Lovel's *Lectionary*, illuminated at the cost of some wealthy layman for the purpose of presentation to a Cathedral or Abbey Church. In return for the gift the Church often agreed to keep a yearly *obiit* or annual Mass for the donor's soul, which in England was called "the year's mind"; and this kind of gift thus often served to provide a "Chantry" of a limited kind.

One of the finest examples of English manuscript art in the fourteenth century is a *Psalter* commonly known as "Queen Mary's Prayer-book". This exquisite manuscript, which is in the British Museum, contains, before the *Psalter*, a large number of miniatures of Biblical scenes executed in outline, treated with delicate washes of transparent colour. The *Psalter* is illuminated in quite a different style, with brilliant gold and colours in all the miniatures and borders, which are painted with wonderful delicacy of touch, unsurpassed by the best French work. A *Bestiary* is introduced into the margins of the *Psalter;* and at the end there are beautiful paintings of New Testament scenes. The date of this book is c. 1330; in 1553 it was given to Queen Mary.

Queen Mary's Prayer-book.

Another English manuscript of special interest both for its text and its beautiful illuminations is a copy in the British Museum of Dan Lydgate's *Life of Saint Edmund*, which was written and illuminated in 1433 by a Monk in the Benedictine Monastery at Bury Saint Edmunds; it is an early and very beautiful example of a manuscript in the Vulgar tongue. In style the illuminated borders are not unlike those in "Queen Mary's Prayer-book."

MSS. of Dan Lydgate.

Another very similar manuscript both in date and style was sold at the Perkins sale, in June, 1873, for £1320[1]. This is a magnificently illuminated folio of "The Siege of Troye compiled by Dann John Lydgate, Monke of Bury"; it contains seventy miniature paintings, chiefly of battle scenes, in which the combatants wear armour of the first half of the fifteenth century. The illuminated borders are of the boldly decorative English type mentioned above, and the miniatures are large in scale, in many cases extending across the whole width of the page with its double column of text.

In England the introduction of the art of printing in 1477

[1] This very important English manuscript was bought by Mr Quaritch and priced at £1600 in his catalogue, No. 291, 1873. It was written in or soon after 1420 when Lydgate completed writing his work; it may possibly have been written and illuminated by the author himself.

Woodcut initials. seems to have brought the illuminator's art to an end more quickly than was the case in Continental countries. Caxton's later books have printed initials[1], instead of blank spaces left for the illuminator, as in most of the early printed books of Germany, France and Italy; and English book-buyers appear to have been soon satisfied with simple illustrations in the form of rather rudely executed woodcuts.

The subjects represented in English miniatures are for the most part the same as those in contemporary French manuscripts; but the martyrdom of Saint Thomas of Canterbury occurs more frequently in English than in any continental manuscripts[2]. Almost immediately after the event in 1170 this scene began to be represented; see above, page 108.

St George and the Dragon. Another specially English subject is Saint George, who was at first the Crusaders' Patron and then the national Saint of England. He is usually represented as a Knight on horseback slaying the dragon with a lance. This subject did not come into popular use till the fourteenth century[3].

Both in England and in France, during the fourteenth and fifteenth centuries, manuscript *Chronicles* and *Histories* of both ancient and modern times formed a large and important class of manuscripts; and these were usually copiously illustrated with miniatures. The *Chronicles* of Sir John Froissart was justly a very favourite book on both sides of the Channel[4], and many richly illuminated manuscripts of it still exist; see below, page 139.

---

[1] Caxton appears to have begun to use woodcut initials in the year 1484 or 1485, but most Continental printers continued to use hand-painted capitals many years later than that.

[2] This scene and the name of Saint Thomas, wherever it occurs, are frequently obliterated in English manuscripts. This was done by the special order of Henry VIII., who, after his quarrel with the Pope, appears to have regarded Thomas à Becket as a sort of personal enemy.

[3] See page 187 for a fine Italian example of this subject. It is interesting to note that the popular legend of Saint George and the dragon is simply a mediaeval version of the old classical myth of Perseus and Andromeda. In the more genuine Oriental lives of Saint George this episode is not introduced.

[4] It should be remembered that Norman-French continued to be the Court language of England till late in the fifteenth century, and for certain legal purposes even later. Its use still survives in the Law-Courts of Quebec and Montreal.

The British Museum possesses a magnificent manuscript of the *Chronicles of England* in seven large folio volumes, which were compiled and written at the command of Edward IV. The miniatures which decorate this sumptuous work are partly Anglo-Norman and partly Flemish, in the style of the school of the Van Eycks at Bruges.

MS. Chronicles.

One favourite form of *Chronicle*, giving an abstract of the whole World's history, was in the shape of a long parchment roll, illuminated with miniatures in the form of circular medallions. Some of these great rolls were written and illuminated by English miniaturists, but they appear not to have been as common in England as they were in France ; see below, page 139. On these rolls the writing usually continues down the strip, not at right angles to the long sides, as on classical papyrus rolls.

CHAPTER IX.

FRENCH MANUSCRIPTS.

Psalter of St Louis.

DURING the thirteenth century "the art of illumination as it is called in Paris"[1] flourished under the Saintly King Louis IX. (1215—1270) as much as it did in England under Henry III. Manuscripts of most exquisite beauty and refinement were produced in Paris, in style little different from those of the Anglo-Norman school. One of the most beautiful and historically interesting is a *Psalter* (Paris, *Bibl. Nat.*) which is said to have been written for St Louis about 1260. This is a large folio, copiously illustrated with sacred subjects minutely painted on a ground of burnished gold enriched by tooling. Many of the miniatures are framed in a beautiful architectural composition of cusped arches, with delicate open tracery supported by slender columns.

Perfect finish.

Fig. 22 gives the bare design of one of the historiated initials in this lovely manuscript, the capital *B* at the beginning of the Psalms. In the upper part is the scene of David watching Bathsheba bathing; and below is a kneeling figure of the king adoring Christ in Majesty. No reproduction can give any notion of the exquisitely delicate painting, or of the splendour of its burnished gold and colours. The historical scenes from the Old Testament have, after the usual fashion of the time, the Hebrew warriors and their enemies represented as mediaeval knights in armour.

It should, however, be observed that in this and many

---

[1] Dante, *Purg.* XI. 80; see above, p. 31.

Fig. 22. A page from the *Psalter* of Saint Louis, written about the year 1260, by a French scribe.

Archaism of detail. other French and English miniatures of the time the ancient warriors are represented not in the armour of the actual date of the execution of the manuscript, but with the dress and arms of a couple of generations earlier. The monastic artists were not skilled archaeologists, but they wished to suggest that the scene they were painting was one that had happened long ago, and therefore they introduced what was probably the oldest armour they were acquainted with—that of their grandfathers' or great-grandfathers' time. This is an important point, as in many cases a wrong judgment has been formed as to the date of a manuscript from the mistaken supposition that contemporary dress and armour were represented in it.

It is just the same with the thirteenth century art of England. Paintings executed for Henry III. in his Palace at Westminster had representations of knights in the armour of William the Conqueror's time or a little later. In later times, especially in the fifteenth century, this *naïve* form of archaeology was given up, and the heroes of ancient and sacred history are represented exactly like kings and warriors of the artist's own time.

MS. Bibles. The historiated Bibles of Paris in the thirteenth century were equal in beauty and very similar in style to those of the Anglo-Norman miniaturists, but they do not appear to have been produced in such immense quantities as they were in the more northern monasteries.

In the fifteenth century the influence of the Church tended to check the study of the Bible on the part of the laity, and very few manuscripts of the Bible were then written. Their place was to some extent taken by the *Books of Hours*, enormous numbers of which were produced in France and the Netherlands, all through the fifteenth century; see page 141.

French illuminated Manuscripts of the XIVth and XVth centuries. To this class belong a great many of the magnificent manuscripts of *the Apocalypse* which have been described under the head of Anglo-Norman manuscripts. No hard and fast line can be drawn between the manuscript styles of Normandy and the northern provinces of France.

In the fourteenth century Paris and Saint Denis were important centres for the production of manuscripts of the most highly finished kind. Historiated Bibles, both in Latin and in French, continued to be produced in great number till past the middle of the fourteenth century. Some of these French translations, executed as late as 1370, are what may be called archaistic in style; that is to say, the subjects selected and the method of their treatment and execution continued to be almost the same as that of the historiated *Vulgates* of France and Normandy at the beginning of the century. The miniatures are very minute in scale, and are often painted on backgrounds of the brilliant chess-board and other diapers in red, blue and gold. Though extremely decorative and beautiful, the miniatures of this class are not quite equal to those of the thirteenth century Bibles, either in vigour of drawing or in delicacy of touch.

Archaism of style.

On the whole, in the fourteenth century, the French schools of illumination were the finest in the world, and the manuscripts of Northern France were the most sumptuously decorated of all. One specially beautiful style of ornament was introduced early in the century and lasted with little modification for more than a hundred years. This was the method of writing on a wide margined page, and then covering the broad marginal space by delicate flowing scrolls or curves of foliage, leaves and small blossoms of various shapes being used, but more especially one form of triple-pointed leaf which is known commonly as the "ivy" or "thorn-leaf pattern." Brilliant effect is given to these rich borders by forming some of the leaves in burnished gold; and variety is given to the foliage by the introduction of minutely painted birds of many kinds, song-birds, game-birds and others, treated with much graceful realism[1].

The ivy pattern.

Fig. 28 shows part of a border from a manuscript of this class, a *Book of Hours* executed for the Duke de Berri; the

[1] In the magnificent English embroideries of the thirteenth century, such as the Lateran and Pienza copes, mentioned at page 112, we see birds of exactly similar style and kinds introduced among the scroll-work of the grounds and borders.

130

Fig. 23. Miniature representing King Conrad of Bohemia, with an attendant, hawking; from a manuscript of the fourteenth century, showing the influence of French art.

CHAP. IX.]   THE FINEST PERIOD.   131

typical pointed "ivy-leaves" grow from each of the quatrefoils which are introduced to hold the arms and initials of the owner. It comes from the same manuscript as the illumination shown in fig. 25.

These elaborate borders are usually made to grow out of the ornaments of the illuminated initials in the text, and thus a sense of unity is given to the whole page, the decorations of which thus become, not an adjunct, but an essential part of the text. *Decorative unity.*

Fig. 24 shows a miniature from a French manuscript of this magnificent class, the *Treasure-Book* of the Abbey of Origny in Picardy, executed about 1312 for the Abbess Héloise. It contains fifty-four large miniatures of scenes from the life and martyrdom of Saint Benedicta. The shaded part of the border is of the richest burnished gold, and the whole effect is magnificently decorative.

The scene represented is the murder of the Saint, whose soul is being borne up to Heaven by two Angels, held in the usual conventional loop of drapery.

As an example of this class of illumination we may mention the famous *Book of Hours* of the Duke of Anjou (Paris, Bibl. Nat.) illuminated about the year 1380. Every page has a rich and delicate border covered with the ivy foliage[1], and enlivened by exquisitely painted birds, such as the goldfinch, the thrush, the linnet, the jay, the quail, the sparrow-hawk and many others; and at the top of the page, at the beginning of each division of the *Horae*, is a miniature picture of most perfect grace and beauty, the decorative value of which is enhanced by a background, either of gold diaper, or else of delicate scroll-work in light blue painted over a ground of deep ultramarine. *Horae of the Duc d'Anjou.*

Enormous prices were frequently paid by wealthy patrons for sumptuously illuminated manuscripts, especially in the fifteenth century for *Books of Hours*.

[1] The phrase *ivy pattern* is a convenient one to use, as it expresses a very common and well-defined type of ornament, but the leaf is too conventionally treated to be recognized as that of the ivy or any other plant: and the pattern is varied with blossoms of different forms and colours.

9—2

Fig. 24. Scene of the martyrdom of Saint Benedicta from a *Martyrology* of about 1312.

The Paris library possesses (*Bibl. Nat.* Lat. 919) a very magnificent manuscript *Horae*, which was painted for the Duc de Berri at the beginning of the century by a French miniaturist named Jaquemart de Odin. At the Duke's death this *Book of Hours* was valued at no less than four thousand livres Tournois, equal in modern value to quite two thousand pounds. It is mentioned thus in the inventory of the Duke's personal property, *item, unes tres belles heures tres richement enluminees et hystoriees de la main de Jaquemart de Odin....* Like all books of this class, specially painted for a distinguished person, the arms and badges of the owner are introduced among the foliated ornaments of the borders of many pages; as the inventory states, *par les quarrefors des feuilles en plusieurs lieux faictes des armes et devises*[1].

Horae of the Duc de Berri.

Fig. 25 shows part of a page from this lovely book, with a miniature of the Birth of the Virgin, painted by Jaquemart de Odin, within a beautiful architectural framing of the finest style.

Space will not allow any attempt to describe even in outline the many splendid classes of illuminated manuscripts which were produced by the French artists of the fourteenth and fifteenth centuries. A few notable points only can be briefly mentioned.

One special beauty of French illumination of this date is due to the exquisite treatment of architectural frames and backgrounds which are used to enshrine the whole picture. The loveliest Gothic forms are introduced, with the most delicate detail of tracery, pinnacles, canopy-work, shafts and arches, all being frequently executed in gold with subtle transparent shading to give an effect of relief. From the technical point of view these manuscripts reach the highest pitch of perfection; the burnished gold is thick and solid in appearance, and is convex in surface so as to catch high lights, and look, not like gold leaf, but like actual plates of the purest and most polished gold[2]. The pigments are of the

Architectural framing.

[1] See Laborde, *Les Ducs de Bourgogne*, Vol. II. p. 1, and note to p. 121.
[2] The manner in which this splendid effect is produced is described below, see page 234.

Fig. 25. Miniature of the birth of the Virgin painted by the illuminator Jacquemart de Odin for the Duc de Berri. The border is of the characteristic French and Franco-Flemish style; see fig. 28 on page 146.

CHAP. IX.]   COPIOUS ILLUSTRATION.   135

most brilliant colours, so skilfully prepared and applied that they are able to defy the power of time to change their hue or even dim their splendour.

Another noticeable point about the French and Franco-Flemish illumination is the manner in which certain modes of decoration survived with very little alteration for more than a century. Thus we find the blue, red and gold diapers used for backgrounds, and the ivy-leaf pattern and its varieties[1], which had been fully developed before the middle of the fourteenth century, still surviving in manuscripts of the second half of the fifteenth century, and continuing in use till the growing decadence of taste caused them to be superseded by borders and backgrounds painted in a naturalistic rather than a decorative manner[2]. *Survival of style.*

The Franco-Flemish manuscripts of the fifteenth century were in some cases remarkable for the amazing amount of laborious illumination and the enormous number of miniatures which they contain. Some of these, which were executed for Royal or Princely patrons and liberal paymasters, engaged the incessant labour of the illuminator for many years. In these cases he was usually paid a regular salary, and so was relieved from the incentive to hasty work which caused so much inferior illumination to be produced in the fifteenth century. *Costly Horae.*

One of the most famous examples of this lavish expenditure of time on one book is the *Breviary* of the Duke of Bedford, who, was Regent of France from 1422 to 1435[3]. This wonderful manuscript, in addition to countless elaborate initials, and borders round every page, contains more than 2500 miniature paintings, all delicately and richly executed in burnished gold and brilliant colours, with backgrounds, in many cases, of the fourteenth century type, with chess-board *The Bedford Breviary.*

[1] Shown, for example, in fig. 25, page 134.
[2] The border from the Grimani Breviary shown on page 168, is an example, though a very beautiful one, of this decadence of taste.
[3] Now in Paris, *Bibl. Nat. Lat.* 17, 294. John, Duke of Bedford, was a son of Henry IV.; he married in 1423 Anne, daughter of the Duke of Burgundy. Very fine portraits of the Duke and Duchess of Bedford occur in the *Bedford Missal* mentioned below.

patterns and other diapers of the most elaborate and sumptuous kind. The figures are of the finest Franco-Flemish style, showing the influence of the Van Eycks, who were then becoming the most skilful painters, technically at least, in the world.

The Bedford Missal. Another no less famous manuscript is the *Bedford Missal* in the British Museum, which was painted for the Duke of Bedford, and was presented by his wife to Henry VI. of England, when he was crowned King of France in Paris in the year 1430. The *Bedford Missal* contains no less than fifty-nine large miniatures and about a thousand smaller ones, not counting initials and borders. One point of special interest about this gorgeous manuscript is that the illuminations have evidently been executed by at least three different miniaturists, who represent three different schools, the Parisian-French, the Franco-Flemish and the English.

MSS. by various hands. It is by no means uncommon to find the work of several different illuminators in one manuscript. Naturally, when a wealthy patron ordered a magnificent book, he was not always willing to wait several years for its completion, as must have been necessary when the whole of a sumptuous manuscript was the work of one man.

Again, it was not an uncommon thing for unfinished manuscripts to be sent to Bruges, Ghent and other centres of the illuminator's art from various distant towns and countries, especially from France, Italy and Spain, in order that they might be decorated with borders and miniatures by one of the Flemish miniaturists.

In some cases it was only the miniature subjects which were left blank; so that we have the text with the illuminated borders and initials executed in the style of one country, while the miniatures are of another quite different school.

Moreover, we find from the Guild records of Bruges that a certain number of Italian and Spanish scribes had taken up their residence in Bruges, and become members of the Guild of Saint John and Saint Luke, so that some manuscripts actually written in Flanders have a text which in style is Italian or Spanish.

CHAP. IX.] ILLUMINATIONS IN GRISAILLE. 137

Various other combinations of style occur not unfrequently. Many English manuscripts, for example, have miniature paintings which are French or Flemish in style, united with bold decorative borders of the most thoroughly English type.

Manuscripts in Grisaille. In addition to the illuminations glowing with gold and colour of jewel-like brilliance, a peculiar class of miniature painting came into use in France during the fourteenth century and to some extent lasted till the close of the fifteenth. This was a system of almost monochromatic painting in delicate bluish grey tints with high lights touched in with white or fluid gold; this is called painting in *grisaille* or *camaieu-gris*[1]; it frequently suggests the appearance of an onyx *cameo* or other delicate relief.

MSS. in Grisaille.

The earliest examples of *grisaille*, dating from the first half of the fourteenth century, sometimes have grounds of the brilliant gold, red and blue diapers, the figures themselves being painted in *grisaille*; but in its fully developed form no accessories of colour are used, and no burnished gold is introduced, only the *mat*, glossless fluid gold being used in some cases for the high lights.

Some of the miniatures of this class are extremely beautiful for the delicacy of their modelling and the great refinement of the design, and are evidently the work of artists of the highest class. This system of illumination, being unaided by the splendours of shining gold and bright colours, requires a rather special delicacy of treatment, and was of course quite unsuited for the cheap and gaudy manuscripts which were mere commercial products. In some cases the *grisaille* pictures are clearly the work of a different hand from the rest of the book, and thus we sometimes see them combined with richly illuminated initials and ivy-leaf borders of the usual gorgeously coloured type.

Delicacy of Grisaille.

In some late manuscripts the *grisaille* miniatures are distinctly intended to imitate actual bas-reliefs, and are

[1] The Italians call it *chiaro-scuro* or "light and shade" painting; its use in manuscripts may have been suggested by the *grisaille* stained glass windows which were introduced by the Cistercian monks, whose Rule prohibited the use of brightly coloured figure subjects either in their windows, on their walls, or in their books.

painted with deceptive effects of roundness. This led to the introduction into manuscript ornaments of imitations of classical reliefs of gilt bronze or veined marbles, such as occur so often in the very sculpturesque paintings of the great Paduan, Andrea Mantegna.

Secular MSS. Till the early part of the fourteenth century the art of the illuminator had been mostly devoted to books on sacred subjects, but at this time manuscripts of *Chronicles*, accounts of travel, *Romances* and other secular works, often in the vulgar tongue, were largely written and illuminated in the most sumptuous way, especially for the royal personages of France and Burgundy.

Philip the Bold of Burgundy, who died in 1404, was an enthusiastic patron of literature and of the miniaturist's art; as was also Charles V. of France (1337-1380). A typical example of this school of manuscripts is a magnificent folio, formerly in the Perkins collection[1], of *Les cent Histoires de Troye*, a composition in prose and verse written by Christina of Pisa[2] about 1390. This magnificent volume contains one hundred and fifteen delicately executed miniatures, the first of which represents Christina presenting her book to Philip of Burgundy.

Interesting details. These miniatures and others of the same class are very interesting for their accurate representations of contemporary life and customs. The costumes, the internal fittings and furniture of rooms, views in the streets and in the country, feasts, tournaments, the king amidst his courtiers, scenes in the Court of Justice, and countless other subjects are represented with much minuteness of detail and great realistic truth. We have in fact in the miniatures of this class of manuscripts the first beginning of an early school of *genre* painting, which in its poetic feeling and sense of real beauty ranks far higher than the ignoble realism of the later Dutch painters.

[1] It was sold for £650 at the Perkins sale in June, 1873.
[2] Christina was one of the most famous authors of her time; she produced thirteen different works; one of which, *The Fayts of Armes and Chivalry*, was translated and printed by Caxton about a century after it was written, in 1489.

One rather abnormal class of manuscript, which belongs *MS.*
both to this period and the following (the fifteenth) century, *Chronicles.*
consists of French or Latin *Chronicles of the World* beginning
with the Creation and reaching down to recent times, written
and illuminated with numerous miniature paintings on great
rolls of parchment, often measuring from fifty to sixty feet
in length. These are usually rather coarse in execution.

Sir John Froissart's *Chronicles*, and their continuation from
the year 1400 by Enguerrand de Monstrelet, were favourite
manuscripts for sumptuous illumination among the courtier
class both of France and England.

Among the many illuminated books of travel which were *MS.*
produced during the latter part of the fourteenth and the *travels.*
fifteenth centuries one noble example in the Paris library
may be selected as a typical example. This is a large folio
manuscript entitled *Les Merveilles du Monde*, containing
accounts in French of the travels of Sir John Mandeville,
Marco Polo and others. This manuscript was written about
the year 1412 for the Duke of Burgundy and was given by
him to his uncle the Duc de Berri. Its numerous miniatures
are very delicate and graceful, of elaborate pictorial style,
with views of landscapes and carefully painted buildings,
street scenes and other realistic backgrounds to the figure
subjects, all executed with great patience and much artistic
feeling. The richly illuminated borders to the text are filled
with elaborate foliage, in which real and conventional forms
are mingled with fine decorative results.

In the fourteenth century the growing love for national *MS.*
poetry and the more widely spread ability to read and write, *poems.*
which in previous centuries had been mostly confined to
ecclesiastics, led to the production of a large number of
illuminated manuscripts of works such as the *Quest of the
Holy Grail*, including the whole series of the *Chansons de
Geste* with the Lancelot and Arturian romances, the *Roman
de la Rose*, one of the most popular productions of the
fourteenth century, and a whole class of *Fabliaux* or short
stories in verse dealing with subjects of chivalrous and romantic character.

140   SECULAR SCRIBES AND   [CHAP. IX.

Romances based on ancient history and mythology, such as *Les cent Histoires de Troye* written by Christina of Pisa[1] about 1390—1395, became very popular among the knightly courtiers of the Rulers of France and Burgundy[2].

In manuscripts of this class the miniature illuminations play a very important part, and give great scope to the fancy and skill of the illuminator.

Italian influence. In southern France the style of manuscript illumination differed a good deal from that of the northern provinces. During the fourteenth century there was a considerable strain of Italian influence, partly due to the establishment of the Papal Court at Avignon, and the introduction there of Simone Martini or Memmi, and other painters from Florence and Siena, to decorate the walls of the Pope's Palace[3].

On the whole, however, manuscripts were not produced in such abundance or with such skill in southern France as they were in the north. Paris, Burgundy and the French districts of Flanders were the chief homes of the illuminator's art.

Secular miniaturists. By this time the production of illuminated manuscripts ceased to be almost wholly in the hands of monastic scribes, as it had been in earlier days when manuscripts dealing with profane subjects were scarcely known.

In Paris, Brussels, Antwerp, Bruges, Ghent, Arras and other French and Flemish cities, large classes of secular writers and illuminators of manuscripts grew up, and special guilds of illuminators were formed, exactly like the guilds of other arts and crafts[4].

Before long this great extension of the art of illumination, and the fact that it became a trade, a method of earning a

---

[1] A fine manuscript of Christina's *Romance* is mentioned above, see page 138.
[2] These chivalrous romances were no less popular in England; Dan Lydgate's *Boke of the siege of Troy*, adapted and translated from Guido de' Colonna's romance, was one of the most popular English books in the fifteenth century; see page 123.
[3] See Muntz, *Les Peintres d'Avignon*, 1342—1352, Tours, 1885; and *Les peintures de Simone Martini à Avignon*, Paris, 1885. Many of these paintings still exist in a good state of preservation, especially those on the vault of the small private chapel of the Popes.
[4] This subject is discussed at greater length in Chapter XIII.

CHAP. IX.]   THE DECADENCE OF ILLUMINATION.   141

livelihood, like any other craft, led to a serious decadence in the art. Though wealthy patrons were able to pay large prices for richly illuminated manuscripts, thus keeping up the production of very elaborate and artistically valuable works of miniature art, yet the practical result was a growing decadence of style and workmanship.

No illuminator working mainly for a money reward could possibly rival the marvellous productions of the earlier monastic scribes, who, labouring for the glory of God, and the credit to be won for themselves and for their monasteries, could devote years of patient toil to the illumination of one book, free from all sense of hurry, and finding in their work the chief joy and relaxation of their lives[1]. *Decay of the art.*

In most even of the best productions of the guild-scribes of the fifteenth century one sees occasional signs of weariness and haste; and in the cheap manuscripts, which were turned out by the thousand in France and Flanders during the latter part of the fifteenth century, there is a coarseness of touch and a mechanical monotony of style, which remind one of the artistic results of the triumphant commercialism of the nineteenth century.

It is more especially in the cheap *Books of Hours* of the second half of the fifteenth century that the lowest artistic level is reached in France, Flanders and Holland. Education had gradually been extended among various classes of laymen, and by the middle of the fifteenth century it appears to have been usual not only for all men above the rank of artisans to be able to read, but even women of the wealthy bourgeois class could make use of prayer-books. Hence arose a great demand for pictured *Books of Hours*[2], which appear to have been produced in enormous quantities by the trade-scribes of towns such as Bruges, Paris and many others. These common manuscript *Horae* are monotonous in form and detail; they nearly always have the same set of miniatures, which are *Cheap MSS.*

[1] See page 206 on the favourable conditions under which the monastic illuminators did their work.
[2] *Books of Hours* were the prayer-books of the laity, as the *breviary*, *portiforium*, or "*portoos*" was the prayer-book of the priest.

often coarse in detail and harsh in colour; and the illuminated borders, with which they are lavishly though cheaply decorated, have the same forms of foliage and fruit repeated again and again in dozens of manuscripts, which all look as if they had come out of the same workshop.

It must not however be supposed that all the later French manuscripts, even of the latter half of the fifteenth century, were of this inferior class. Though the best figure painting was far inferior to the glorious miniatures in the *Apocalypses*

Fig. 26. Miniature executed for King René of Anjou about 1475.

of the fourteenth century, yet in their own way, as pictorial rather than decorative illustrations, the French miniatures of this date are often very remarkable for their beauty, their refinement and their interesting and very elaborate details.

Some very fine manuscript illuminations of the highly pictorial type were executed for King René of Anjou, who died in 1480. Fig. 26 shows a good example of this, with a carefully painted landscape background, one of sixteen fine miniatures in a manuscript of the *Roman de la très douce Mercy du Cueur damour épris*, one of the poetical and allegorical romances which were then so popular in France. This miniature represents the meeting of the Knight *Humble Requeste* with the Squire *Vif Désir*. This manuscript is now at Vienna, in the Imperial library, No. 2597.

King René's romance.

The illuminated borders are also not unfrequently of very great merit and high decorative value; they are formed of rich and fanciful combinations of various plants and flowers, treated at first with just the due amount of conventionalism, but tending, towards the end of the fifteenth century, to an excessive and too pictorial realism. As late as the middle of the fifteenth century the "ivy pattern" of the previous century survived with little modification, and very beautiful borders occur with branches of the vine, the oak, the maple and other trees, together with a great variety of flowers, such as the rose, the daisy, the columbine, the clove-pink or carnation, the pansy, the lily, the iris or blue flag, the cornflower, the anemone, the violet, the thistle; and with many kinds of fruit, especially the grape, the strawberry, the pomegranate and the mulberry. Among this wealth of fruit and foliage, variety is given by the introduction of birds, insects, animals, and grotesque monsters half beast and half human, or else living figures growing out of flower blossoms, all designed with much graceful fancy and decorative beauty.

Beauty of fruit and flowers.

Towards the close of the fifteenth century one skilfully treated but less meritorious style of illuminated border became very common in France and Flanders. This consisted of isolated objects, such as sprigs of various kinds of flowers and fruits, especially strawberries, together with butterflies and other insects, shells, reptiles and the like scattered over the margin of the page, very frequently on

Later style.

Imitation of relief. a background of dull fluid gold[1]. A deceptive effect of relief is commonly attempted by the painting of strong shadows, as if each object were lying on the gold ground and casting its shadow on the flat surface. This attempt at relief of course marks a great decadence of taste, and yet it occurs in manuscripts which show much artistic feeling and great technical skill; as, for example, in the magnificent Grimani Breviary, mentioned below at p. 167, see fig. 38.

Use of fluid gold. In French and Flemish miniatures of this period, gold, applied with a brush, is often used to touch in the high lights, not only in the *grisaille* miniatures, but also in paintings with brilliant pigments, much in the same way as in the Umbrian and Florentine pictures of contemporary date.

Many manuscripts of the early part of the sixteenth century have elaborate architectural borders, consisting of tiers of canopied niches containing statuettes, all executed in fluid, *mat* gold.

Harsh colours. The use of a very harsh emerald green is characteristic of this period of decadence in France and in Flanders; and generally there is a want of harmony of colour in the miniatures of this time, in which gaudiness rather than real splendour gradually becomes the main characteristic.

Renaissance style. At the end of the fifteenth century the influence of the classical Renaissance of art in Italy began to affect the French manuscript illuminations, and especially those by Parisian miniaturists. The introduction of architectural forms of Italian classic style into the backgrounds of miniatures was the first sign of this, examples of which occur as early as the year 1475 or 1480. Fig. 27 shows a characteristic example of a French miniature executed under Italian influence. This is a scene of the marriage of the B. V. Mary to the elderly Joseph, who holds in his hand the dry rod which had blossomed. One of the unsuccessful suitors is breaking his rod across his knee, as in Raphael's early *Sposalizio* in the Brera gallery at Milan.

[1] See below, page 230, for an explanation of the difference between "mat" gold applied as a fluid pigment with a brush, and burnished gold leaf laid over a raised "mordant" or enamel-like ground.

Fig. 27. Miniature of the marriage of the B. V. Mary from a French manuscript of about 1480, with details in the style of the Italian Renaissance.

Horae of Jehan Foucquet.

The painting represented in Fig. 27 is from a manuscript *Book of Hours* illuminated by the famous miniaturist Jehan Foucquet of Tours, whose services were secured by Louis XI. from 1470 to 1475. This manuscript *Horae*, which has been horribly mutilated, the miniatures being cut out of the text, was originally executed for Maître Etienne Chevalier. Foucquet and other French illuminators of his time were largely influenced not only by Italian art, but also by the Flemish school of miniaturists who were followers of Memlinc and Rogier van der Weyden; but by the end of the fifteenth century the Italian influence reigned supreme and soon destroyed all remaining traces of the older mediaeval or Gothic style.

Fig. 28 shows part of a border from the same MS. that is illustrated in Fig. 25 on page 134.

Fig. 28. Border illumination from a *Book of Hours* by Jacquemart de Odin; see fig. 25.

CHAPTER X.

PRINTED BOOKS WITH PAINTED ILLUMINATIONS.

DURING the last few years of the fifteenth century and the first twenty or thirty years of the sixteenth century Paris was remarkable for the production of a beautiful class of books which form a link between printed books and illuminated manuscripts.

These are the numerous *Books of Hours* printed on vellum, richly decorated with wood-cut[1] borders and pictures, and frequently illuminated by painting in gold and opaque colours over the engravings. One of the earliest of these vellum-printed *Horae* was produced by Pigouchet for the bookseller Simon Vostre in 1487[2]; the pictures and borders are very simply treated in broad outline, which the illuminator was meant to fill in with colour, aided only in the general design by the wood-cut[3]. In 1498 Pigouchet began to execute for S. Vostre *Books of Hours* of quite a different and still finer style, with engravings of the most exquisite beauty of design and delicacy of detail, perfect masterpieces of the engraver's art. The decorative borders in these lovely books have

Paris Horae on vellum.

[1] In point of technique these beautiful miniatures are exactly like very delicate wood-cuts, though in most cases they appear to have been cut (in relief) on blocks of soft metal, treated just as if it had been wood.
[2] Perhaps the earliest was one issued in 1486 by Antoine Verard.
[3] In these earliest Parisian printed *Horae* the backgrounds of the borders are left plain white; unlike the later ones, in which the borders have dotted or *criblée* backgrounds.

dotted (*criblée*) backgrounds, and the whole effect, though merely in black and white, is rich and decorative in the highest degree. The comparatively coarse touch of the illuminator ruins the beauty of these *Horae*; but luckily a good many copies have escaped this tasteless treatment, which must have appealed only to a very ignorant love of gold and gaudy colour on the part of the purchasers.

Effect of colouring.

In the early part of the sixteenth century immense numbers and varieties of these vellum-printed *Horae*[1] were issued by Pigouchet and Vostre, Antoine Verard[2], Thielman Kerver and his widow, the brothers Hardouyn, and other Paris printers and publishers. The cuts from the earlier, fifteenth century editions[3], were reproduced, and a great number of new ones were cut; but after the year 1500 there was a most rapid deterioration of style. Even between the cuts of 1498 and those of 1503 a very marked change for the worse is apparent, the fine mediaeval French style being replaced by somewhat feeble imitations of the works of the Italian Renaissance.

Decadence of style.

These Parisian prayer-books gradually superseded the coarse manuscript *Horae* which were still produced in the early part of the sixteenth century; and the latest examples of these vellum-printed books, the work of Geoffroi Tory and others as late as 1546, came to be sold without any assistance from the hand, one can hardly say the art, of the illuminator in his extreme decadence.

In a feeble way the art of writing and illuminating manuscripts, as a sort of plaything for the wealthy, lingered on in Paris till the seventeenth century. An illuminated *Book of Hours* (*Office de la Sainte Vierge*), with four miniatures and many floriated head-pieces of very minute

Latest decadence.

---

[1] They include many different *uses*, especially that of Paris, Rome, Rouen and Sarum.

[2] Both Verard and Pigouchet produced *Horae* for the publisher Simon Vostre.

[3] It is incorrect to speak of *editions* of these *Books of Hours*; hardly any two copies appear to have been quite the same; fresh arrangements and combinations of a large stock of engraved blocks were made for the printing of almost every copy, and thus the long list given by Brunet is very incomplete; see the last volume of Brunet's *Manuel du libraire*, Paris, 1865.

CHAP. X.] THE EARLIEST PRINTED BOOKS. 149

workmanship, which was in the Perkins collection[1], is signed *N. Jarry Parisinus Scribebat*, 1660. Other elaborate examples of Nicholas Jarry's work exist in the Paris library, mostly painted in *grisaille*.

A few words on the connection between early printing and the art of manuscript illumination may not here be out of place. The inventors of printing, Gutenberg, Fust and Schoeffer, appear to have had no idea of producing cheap books by their new art, but that for a fixed sum they could produce a more magnificent and beautiful book than a scribe could for the same price. Such a finished masterpiece of art as the *Mazarine Bible*, issued by Gutenberg in the year 1455, was not sold at a lower rate than the price of a manuscript Bible; but it was cheaper than a manuscript of equal splendour. So also very few scribes of the fifteenth century could with the utmost labour have produced such a marvel of beauty as the *Mentz Psalter* of 1559, printed on the finest vellum and illuminated with 280 large initials printed in blue and red—perfect marvels of technical skill in the perfect fit of the two colours, or *registration* as it is now called[2].

Early printing.

The Mentz Psalter.

It is not known at what price this magnificent Psalter was originally sold, but existing records show that copies of the *Vulgate* produced in 1462 at Mentz by the same printers, Fust and Schoeffer, were sold in Paris for no less than sixty gold crowns, equal in modern value to double that number of sovereigns.

For this reason, as beauty rather than cheapness was aimed at by the inventors of printing, they left spaces for the introduction of richly illuminated and historiated initials, which were frequently inserted by the most skilful miniaturists of the time. Thus the art of printing and illumination for more than half a century walked hand in hand. Some of the earliest printers had originally been illuminators of manuscripts, as, for example, Peter Schoeffer de Gernsheim[3], Mentelin of

Illumination and printing.

[1] Sold in June, 1873, for £181, with the rest of the Perkins library.
[2] A copy of this glory of the printer's art in Mr Quaritch's possession is priced in his catalogue of 1891 at £5250; only eight copies are known to exist.
[3] In 1449 Schoeffer was a young illuminator of manuscripts residing in Paris.

150   THE GREAT BEAUTY OF   [CHAP. X.

The various arts of the printer.

Strasburg, Bämler of Augsburg and many others[1]. The workshop of an early printer included not only compositors and printers, but also cutters and founders of type, illuminators of borders and initials, and skilful binders who could cover books with various qualities and kinds of binding[2]. A purchaser in Gutenberg's shop having bought, for example, his magnificent Bible[3] in loose sheets would then have been asked what style of illumination or rubrication he was prepared to pay for, and then what kind of binding and how many brass bosses and clasps he wished to have[4].

Early Italian printing.

In Central and Northern Italy especially, the printed books of the fifteenth and first decade of the sixteenth century were decorated with illuminations of the most beautiful kind. Books printed in Venice about 1470-5 by Nicolas Jenson of Paris and Vendelin of Spires, and Florentine books, even of a few years later date, frequently contain masterpieces of the illuminator's art. The Magnificent Lorenzo de' Medici and others of his family were liberal patrons of this class of work; as were also many of the Venetian Doges and prelates, especially various members of the Grimani family.

There are no grounds whatever for the belief that the early

[1] Mentelin was enrolled as an illuminator in the Painters' Guild at Strasburg in 1447; and Colard Mansion, Caxton's master in the art of typography, belonged, as a scribe and illuminator, to the Guild of St John and St Luke at Bruges. In 1471 he was elected Warden or *Doyen* of his Guild.

[2] In some cases goldsmiths and engravers of coin-dies became printers owing to their knowledge of the technical process necessary for cutting the punches for type. The great French printer Nicolas Jenson, who produced the most magnificent printed books in Venice, was, until the year 1462, Master of the Mint at Tours. And Bernardo Neri, the printer of the Florentine *Editio Princeps* of Homer, was originally a goldsmith, and had assisted Ghiberti in his work on the famous bronze doors of the Florentine Baptistery.

[3] The glorious copy on vellum of the *Mazarine Bible* in the British Museum has illuminated borders and initial miniatures of the finest style and execution. This earliest of printed books is commonly called after the copy in the library of Cardinal Mazarin which contains the illuminator's note that his work was finished in 1456. Sir John Thorold's copy on paper was sold in 1884 for £3900.

[4] Italian books frequently had clasps at the top and bottom as well as two at the side.

CHAP. X.]   THE EARLY PRINTED BOOKS.   151

printed books were passed off as manuscripts, or that Fust was accused of having multiplied books by magical arts. The early printers usually inserted a statement in their *colophon* to the effect that the book was produced "without the aid of a pen (either of reed, quill or bronze), by a new and complicated invention of printing characters." Many different varieties of this statement occur.

Early colophons.

In the Mentz *Psalter* printed by Fust and Schoeffer in 1459 the printer's statement at the end is, *Presens Psalmorum codex venustate capitalium decoratus, rubricationibusque sufficienter distinctus, adinvencione artificiosa imprimendi ac characterizandi; absque ulla calami exaracione sic effigiatus et ad laudem Dei...* In the Mentz *Catholicon* of 1460 the phrase is used, *Non calami, stili aut penne suffragio......*

It was not till about half a century after the invention of printing that the new art grew into an important means for the increase of knowledge through the copious production of cheap books.

No other typographer did so much for the advancement of learning as Aldus Manutius, a Venetian scholar and printer, who, in the year 1501, initiated a new and cheaper form of book by the printing of his Virgil in small 12mo. size, with a new and more compact form of character, now commonly known as the *Italic* type[1]. As Aldus records in three verses at the beginning of the Virgil, the new Italic fount of type was designed and cut by Francesco Francia, the famous Bolognese painter, goldsmith and die-cutter.

Aldine books.

These small *italic* books of Aldus were not all intended for sale at a low rate; many copies exist which are magnificently illuminated, and some are even printed on vellum.

The issue of the cheaper Aldine classics gave the deathblow to the illuminator's art, which the early large and costly printed folios had done little or nothing to supersede.

It should also be noticed that half a century before the invention of printing with moveable types, quite at the

[1] The first or almost the first book printed by Aldus was the *Hero and Leander* of Musaeus of 1494 in small 4to. The Virgil of 1501 was followed rapidly by a Juvenal and a Martial, issued in the same year.

Wood-cuts in MSS.

beginning of the fifteenth or towards the close of the fourteenth century, some few manuscripts of a cheap and inferior sort had their miniature illustrations not drawn by hand, but printed from rudely cut wood-blocks. These prints were afterwards coloured by hand. Manuscripts of this class are very rare, and are now chiefly of value as supplying the earliest known European examples of wood engraving[1].

One of the most notable examples of these manuscripts illustrated with wood-cuts is described by Mr Quaritch in his catalogue No. 291 of 1873[2]. This is a South-German manuscript of about the year 1400, containing certain pious *Weekly Meditations* written on 17 leaves of coarse vellum; throughout the manuscript text are scattered 69 wood-cuts of Saints and Prophets, with Biblical and other sacred scenes, averaging in size three inches by two inches and a quarter. These miniature designs are all richly illuminated with gold and colours; some of them have names and other inscriptions forming part of the engraved block.

Block-books.

This method of combining printing and manuscript very soon led to the next stage, that of *Xylographic* printing or "block-books"; in which not only the illustrations but the text itself was cut on blocks of wood and printed like the wood-cut pictures; each page occupying a separate plank of wood[3].

These block-book illustrations were coloured by hand in a very decorative and effective way, very superior to the coarse gaudy painting in opaque pigments with which the Parisian illuminators so often spoilt the exquisite miniatures and the borders in the vellum-printed *Horae*. The block-books are not painted over with *opaque* pigment, but delicately washed in with *transparent* tints, without obliterating the outlines of the printed pictures, which, though simple and even rude in

---

[1] Chinese wood engravings of considerably earlier date do exist.
[2] See page 1373; this remarkable manuscript was then (in 1873) priced at £650.
[3] Early wood-cuts were not cut on the cross ends of the grain, but on the "plank side" of a wooden board.

treatment, are often full of real beauty and great decorative charm[1].

Thus we see that as early as about the year 1400 the printer's art had begun to supplement that of the manuscript illuminator[2]; and the two arts continued to work, as it were, hand in hand till after the close of the fifteenth century when the illumination of manuscripts ceased to be a real living art and gradually degenerated into a mere appendage to individual pomp and luxury.

Illumination and printing.

[1] The *Cantica Canticorum* of about 1435 has most lovely designs, and the *Apocalypse*, the *Ars Moriendi*, the *Speculum Humanae Salvationis*, and the *Biblia Pauperum* all have wood-cut illustrations of great vigour and spirit, produced between about 1420 and 1450.

[2] Even before 1400 initial letters in manuscripts had been occasionally printed from wooden stamps covered with red or blue pigment.

CHAPTER XI.

ILLUMINATED MANUSCRIPTS OF THE TEUTONIC SCHOOL AFTER THE TENTH CENTURY.

German MSS. of the XIth century.

THOUGH in the main the eleventh century was a period of artistic decadence, mentioned above as having succeeded the brilliant Carolingian period (see page 78), yet we find that in certain places in Germany there was a very distinct beginning of artistic revival, especially in the illumination of manuscripts, about the middle of the eleventh century and even earlier. A school of magnificently decorative art began then to be developed, and though the drawing of the human figure was still weak, yet effects of the noblest decorative character were produced by manuscript illuminators, foreshadowing that marvellous climax of manuscript art which was reached in the thirteenth and fourteenth centuries.

Missal of Henry II.

Fig. 29 shows a sumptuously decorative page from an eleventh century manuscript *Missal* which was executed for the Emperor Henry II. (now in the Munich library). On a brilliant diapered background in gold, red and blue, a standing figure of the Emperor is crowned by Christ, who sits within a *vesica* aureole. The Emperor receives from two angels the great Cross Standard of the Empire and a sword. His arms are supported by a saint on each side, Saints Ulrich and Emmeram. The whole page is a superb piece of decoration, and is specially interesting because illuminations of this type were evidently used by the earliest painters of stained glass windows to supply them with designs.

Fig. 29. A page from the *Missal* of the Emperor Henry II.

Fig. 30 illustrates a stained glass figure of King David, one of five lancet-windows from the Cathedral of Augsburg, executed about 1065, when the Church was consecrated, and

Fig. 30.   Figure of King David from a stained glass window in the Cathedral of Augsburg, dating from 1065.

probably about the oldest existing example of a figure in stained glass. The manuscript-like type of the design is very evident.

Fig. 31 is from a magnificently decorated book of the *Gospels*, executed in the eleventh century for Uota, Abbess of the convent of Niedermünster, at Ratisbon, in the reign of the Emperor Henry II. The whole page is a superbly

Fig. 31. Miniature from an eleventh century manuscript of the *Gospels*, by a German illuminator.

158   GERMAN MSS. OF THE TWELFTH CENTURY.   [CHAP. XI.

Gospels of the XIth century. decorative composition; in the centre is a Crucifixion with figures of Life and Death at the foot of the cross. In the lower angles are minute paintings of the Rent Veil of the Temple, and the opened sepulchres; above, at the sides, are symbolical figures of the Church and the Synagogue, or Grace and Law. At the upper angles are the Sun and Moon veiling their faces before the Passion of Christ. Graceful scroll foliage, of the Oriental textile type, fills in the spandrels.

Revival of art. In the twelfth century the revival of manuscript art in Germany progressed with great rapidity, and an immense number of magnificently illuminated manuscripts were produced, especially in the chief Benedictine Monasteries, which had always been the principal homes of learning and the chief centres of the illuminator's art in Germany as in other European countries[1].

Frederic I. (Barbarossa), b. 1121—d. 1190, imitated the example of Charles the Great in his patronage of art and especially of the art of the illuminator. The manuscripts of *Grotesque forms.* his time are remarkable for the richness and fancy of their twining masses of conventional foliage, mingled with dragons, monkeys, human forms and monsters of all kinds, designed with extreme beauty in their strong sweeping curves and coloured with brilliant and yet harmonious tints in a superbly decorative way. Though the figure drawing of the illuminators had not reached the perfection which was attained a century later, yet in point of decorative ornament nothing could surpass the best German manuscripts of the twelfth century[2]. Figs. 32 and 33 give good examples of the illuminations of this date.

Fig. 32 shows a fine initial S formed out of a winged dragon, and ornamented with conventional foliage of the

[1] Much of the German bronze-work of this period is extremely fine and skilful in execution, such as the fonts and doors of churches at Hildesheim, Augsburg and other places. The bronze font at Liége, cast about 1112 by a sculptor of the German school, is a work of most wonderful grace and beauty.

[2] Till the thirteenth century the art of the Netherlands and Flanders was German in character; after that Flanders was, artistically, as well as politically, partly Teutonic and partly French.

Fig. 32. An initial S, illuminated with foliage of the Northumbrian type, from a German manuscript of the twelfth century.

Fig. 33. Miniature of the Annunciation from a German manuscript of the beginning of the thirteenth century.

Fig. 34. Page of a Kalendar from a German *Psalter* of about 1200 A.D.

162 GERMAN ART OF THE TWELFTH [CHAP. XI.

noblest type. This initial shows the surviving Celtic or rather Northumbrian influence, which in the time of Charles the Great had been so important in the German Empire.

Painting of the Annunciation. Fig. 33 illustrates a miniature of the Annunciation from a fine manuscript *Evangeliarium* or Book of the *Gospels*, which is now in the library at Carlsruhe. The drawing, though stiff in pose, is noble in style; and the whole miniature, with its graceful scroll-work background, is of high decorative value, a prototype of the perfect style of the French and Anglo-Norman illuminations of the second half of the thirteenth century. In this painting, as in many other manuscripts of early date, the B. V. Mary is represented as occupied in spinning with a distaff while the angel Gabriel approaches to announce the birth of the Messiah.

Page of a Kalendar. Fig. 34 shows a very beautifully designed page of the Kalendar at the beginning of a *Psalter* executed about the year 1200 for the Landgrave of Thüringen. On the left is the space in which the scribe inserted the days of the months, and on the right is a noble and gracefully drawn figure of Saint Matthew. The interlaced foliage of the initial K is of characteristic German type.

Fig. 35 shows a very elaborate and graceful initial Y, from another manuscript of the same date, decorated by a vine-plant from which a youth is gathering grapes, while a monkey, sitting in the branches, is eating some of the fruit. The whole design is a masterpiece of decorative beauty, elaborately worked out in gold and colours.

Mural paintings. The fine *mural paintings* of this date are frequently identical in style and design with pages from illuminated manuscripts. This is most remarkably the case with the late twelfth century paintings on the walls and vault of the church of St Michael at Hildesheim; in which the figures, the conventional foliage and the general arrangement of the whole have evidently been copied from manuscript illuminations[1].

Fig. 36 shows a striking example of this, painted about

[1] See above, page 110, for an English example of wall paintings being copied from manuscript miniatures.

1186 on the vault of Saint Michael's. The whole treatment of this grandly decorative painting is precisely like that of the page of an illuminated book.

Vault of St Michael's.

Fig. 35. Initial Y from a German manuscript of the beginning of the thirteenth century, with a most graceful and fanciful combination of figures and foliage.

In the centre is the Fall of Man in a medallion frame with a conventionally treated tree on each side; all round are smaller paintings, including the great Rivers of Paradise and the Jordan, two Evangelists and their Symbols, with a series of medallion busts of Old Testament Saints linked together by scroll-work of foliage exactly like that in illuminations of contemporary date.

The Fall of Man.

11—2

Fig. 36. Paintings on the vault of the church of St Michael at Hildesheim, closely resembling in style an illuminated page in a manuscript.

CHAP. XI.] LATER GERMAN MANUSCRIPTS. 165

The German manuscripts of the thirteenth and fourteenth century are less purely national in style. The finest illuminations of this date show in some cases a marked French influence, and, especially during the fourteenth century, a strong Italian influence was prevalent.

Fig. 37 gives a good example of this from a manuscript *Passionale*, written in 1312 for the Abbess of the Convent of St George at Prague. The figures in this manuscript resemble those in some of the Florentine illuminated manuscripts of Dante's *Divina Commedia*, executed about 1360 to 1390. The subject of the miniatures shown in fig. 37 is a romantic story of a bride who was carried off by brigands and flung into a blazing furnace, from which, by the aid of the B. V. Mary, she was rescued unhurt by the knight, her husband.

MS. of the XIVth century.

In the fifteenth century an important development of Teutonic art took place under the Van Eycks and their pupils. In Flanders, especially in Bruges, Antwerp and Ghent, a very elaborate and beautiful class of illumination was produced, in some respects different in style from the Franco-Flemish school of art.

School of the Van Eycks.

In the latter part of the century magnificent manuscripts were produced by illuminators of the Memlinc and Van der Weyden school, such as the famous Grimani *Breviary* in the Venetian Ducal library, so-called from its having been bought from a Sicilian dealer in 1521 for 500 gold ducats by Cardinal Grimani, a member of the Venetian Grimani family, who were liberal patrons of this class of art; this sum was quite equal to £2000 in modern value. The miniatures in this manuscript were ascribed by the dealer to Hans Memlinc, Gérard of Bruges and Lieven of Antwerp; they were probably by the two latter illuminators, not by Memlinc, who died in 1494 or 1495.

School of Memlinc.

Gérard or Gheeraert of Bruges was a native of Oudewater in Holland; he was born about the middle of the fifteenth century, and settled in Bruges in the year 1483, when he became a member of the Guild of Saint John and Saint Luke, to which all painters and manuscript illuminators were obliged to belong. Gérard took the surname of David, and became a famous painter of triptychs and altar-pieces, as well

Gérard David.

Fig. 37. Miniatures of Italian style from a German manuscript of 1312, showing the influence of Florentine art on the illuminations of southern France.

CHAP. XI.] THE BRANDENBURG AND GRIMANI MSS. 167

as a skilful illuminator of manuscripts. Many fine panel-paintings by him still exist in Bruges and elsewhere[1]. There are also several fine manuscripts with miniatures by his hand in addition to those in the Grimani *Breviary*. Among these are two *Books of Hours* in the collection of the late Baron Anselm Rothschild of Vienna, and another manuscript *Horae*, which was written and illuminated for the Cardinal Prince Albert, Elector of Brandenburg, who was consecrated Archbishop of Magdeburg in the year 1513 at the age of twenty-three. An interesting monograph, with photographic reproductions of the miniatures, was written by Mr W. H. J. Weale for Mr F. S. Ellis, the owner of the manuscript. This lovely manuscript is almost equal in beauty to the Grimani *Breviary*; it is rather later in date, having been illuminated between 1514 and 1523.

The Horae of Prince Albert.

The miniatures in the sumptuous Grimani *Breviary*, which dates from the latter years of the fifteenth century, probably about 1496, are very pictorial in style, with figures which are larger than usual, proportionally to the size of the page. In some of the miniatures the figures are shown only in half length, so that the elaborately finished heads are painted to a large scale. The borders which surround the pages, enclosing both text and miniatures, are of the Franco-Flemish style, with realistic flowers, fruit, insects and the like, scattered over a flat gold ground, as is described above at page 143. The butterflies, dragon-flies, strawberries, irises and lilies are perfect marvels of naturalistic skill and beauty.

The Grimani Breviary.

Fig. 38 illustrates one of the miniatures in the Grimani *Breviary*; it is one of the lovely series representing the characteristic occupations of the twelve months in the Kalendar, which commonly occur as small pictures at the tops of pages in manuscript Kalendars of the fifteenth century, but in this exceptionally magnificent book are full page miniatures. The one copied in fig. 38 represents the month of April, a time for

The month of April.

[1] The National Gallery in London possesses a magnificent panel by Gérard David, a kneeling Canon with three standing figures of Saints, and an exquisitely painted landscape background. This is one wing of an altar triptych which was painted for St Donatian at Bruges. It is numbered 1045 in the Catalogue. Paintings by Gérard David's wife are mentioned below, see page 218.

Fig. 38. Miniature symbolizing the month of April from the Kalendar of the Grimani *Breviary*, executed about 1496.

CHAP. XI.]   LATE FLEMISH SCHOOL.   169

love-making and out-door parties of pleasure; here illustrated by a most beautiful and dignified group of ladies and gentlemen, enlivened by the humour of the scene in the left-hand corner, with a little dog barking jealously at another pet dog which is being petted on a lady's lap.   *The Grimani Breviary.*

The background, with trees and Cathedral spires like those of Antwerp or Malines, is specially beautiful and highly finished.

Though marvels of minute and beautiful workmanship these late Teutonic manuscripts belong to a period of decadence. As has already been remarked, neither in poetic feeling nor in decorative value do they approach the masterpieces of French art during the fourteenth century.

Fig. 39 shows a page from a *Book of Hours* (Paris, *Bibl. Nat. Lat.* 10, 532) which was illuminated for King René II. of Lorraine (1473 to 1508). The figure of the Virgin shows the influence of Italian art, which about this time, 1490, was largely modifying and adding grace to the paintings of Flanders.   *Horae of King René.*

The border, with lupines or vetch-plant realistically painted on a gold ground, is a good typical specimen of the style.

The famous *Prayer-book of Anne of Brittany*, painted about 1500, after her second marriage to Louis XII., is a work of the same magnificent style, with an immense variety of the most exquisitely painted fruits and flowers treated with the most minute realism. It is now in the Paris library[1].   *Horae of Anne of Brittany.*

Fig. 40 gives a page from a magnificent *Book of Hours* in the Imperial Library of Vienna (no. 1857); the miniatures in which are of the finest Teutonic type, in some cases suggesting the school of Van der Weyden, and in others that of Hans Memlinc. The conventional scroll-work of foliage with long serrated leaves in the border is very characteristic of the German and Dutch manuscripts of the fifteenth century.

In some cases this foliage is painted with fluid gold; the

[1] The whole of this gorgeous manuscript was published in fairly good "fac-simile" by Curmer, *Le livre d'Heures de la Reine Anne de Bretagne*, 2 Vols. Imp. 4to., Paris, 1861; see also Laborde, *Ducs de Bourgogne*, Vol. I. p. xxiv.

Fig. 39. A page from the *Book of Hours* of King René, painted about 1480.

Fig. 40. A page from a *Book of Hours* at Vienna, of the finest Flemish style.

Technical methods. high lights being touched in with white, and the shadows with a *grisaille* blue. Another beautiful style of decoration in manuscripts of this class has conventional flower forms painted in transparent lake with white lights over a sheet of burnished gold. The skilful use of gold both in the pigment form, and in leaf on a raised enamel-like ground, is specially characteristic of German and Dutch manuscripts of the fifteenth century. In some manuscripts very beautiful borders are executed in delicate scroll-work with fine lines and dots, all of burnished gold, the effect of which is very magnificent.

The borders and long marginal ornaments, which grow out of the large illuminated initials, are often diversified with figures of a naturalistic or grotesque type, devised with greater fancy and variety than the similar figures of the same sort which occur in so many French manuscripts.

MS. of the Emperor Wenzel. Fig. 41 shows a beautiful example of this, which dates from the last years of the fourteenth century, c. 1390. It is an ornament at the foot of one of the pages in a manuscript which was illuminated for the Emperor Wenzel of Bohemia. Two scenes, a prisoner in the stocks, and a man being bathed by two attendant girls, are placed in the centre of the grand sweeping lines of foliage. The backgrounds with their delicate scroll-work and diaper patterns are imitated from those in the fine French and Anglo-Norman manuscripts of the earlier part of the fourteenth century.

In some marginal illuminations, miniature figures of knights jousting are introduced charging through the scrolls of foliage; and Angels gracefully drawn are very frequently introduced into the elaborate borders, as is shown on fig. 40.

Grotesque figures. Grotesque figures were great favourites with the Teutonic illuminators; devils and monkeys, pigmies fighting cranes, or strange monsters made up (like the Roman *grylli*) of several animals and birds united, are of frequent occurrence in German and Dutch illuminated manuscripts, more especially in *Books of Hours*, where such fancies were probably a relief from the gravity of the text both to the illuminator and to the owner of the book : see below, page 208.

The finest Teutonic manuscripts of the fifteenth century

Fig. 41. Marginal illumination of very beautiful and refined style from a manuscript executed for King Wenzel of Bohemia about the year 1390.

Fig. 42. Miniature of Duke Baldwin, painted about the year 1450 by an illuminator of the school of the Van Eycks of Bruges.

CHAP. XI.]   THE FLEMISH SCHOOL.   175

show in their miniatures the influence of the Van Eycks; as is also the case with many of the manuscripts which fall rather under the head of the Franco-Flemish than the Teutonic school[1].

Fig. 42 gives a fine example of a miniature by an illuminator who must have been an actual pupil of the Van Eycks. It is taken from a fragment of a manuscript of the *Croniques de Jherusalem*, now in the Imperial library of Vienna (no. 2533). It represents Duke Baudouin (or Baldwin), who was crowned King of Jerusalem, in the guise of a fifteenth century German knight, under a graceful Gothic canopy of characteristically German style. The date of this sumptuous manuscript is about 1450.

School of the Van Eycks.

As is remarked below with regard to Italian art, it is interesting to observe the strong influence that miniature painting in manuscripts had upon the larger pictures of Teutonic artists. In many cases the German and Flemish painters of altar-pieces were also illuminators of manuscripts, like Liberale of Verona and Girolamo dai libri, who are mentioned below, see page 197[2].

Influence on painting generally.

And even without this reason for similarity, it was not uncommon for the painter of a retable to borrow his composition and general decorative scheme from an illuminated manuscript by some skilful artist.

Fig. 43 shows a good example of this, the central panel of a retable dated 1473, in the church of St Martin at Colmar, which is almost certainly the work of Martin Schoen or Schöngauer.

In the art of the Cologne School more especially, the relationship between the panel paintings and the miniature illuminations of manuscripts is very close, both in the general

The Cologne School.

---

[1] A very interesting account of the Flemish illuminators of the fifteenth and sixteenth centuries is given by Weale, *Le Beffroi*, Vol. IV. 1873, in which he publishes the accounts of the Guild of St John and St Luke between the years 1454 and 1500.

[2] Gérard David of Bruges was a notable example of skill in both branches of art; see above, page 165. Gérard's wife also practised both these arts, and produced manuscript illuminations and panel paintings of almost equal beauty to those of her husband; see below, page 218.

Fig. 43. Retable painted by Martin Schöngauer, in the style of a manuscript illumination.

Fig. 44. An altar-piece of the Cologne school, showing the influence of manuscript illumination on the painters of panel-pictures, especially retables.

decorative schemes and also in the extreme minuteness and delicacy of the larger paintings.

Retable at Cologne. Fig. 44 shows a beautiful example of this, a small panel, now in the Archiepiscopal Museum at Cologne, representing the Virgin and Child seated on a flowery sward with a trellis covered with roses as a background, and lovely child-angels playing on musical instruments all round. The whole panel is a perfect gem of brilliantly decorative art of the purest and most perfect kind, quite free from the too pictorial realism which at this time, about 1460, was growing rapidly among the miniaturists of France and the Netherlands.

Half a century later, in the early part of the sixteenth century, the same tendency to paint pictures like a magnified manuscript illumination is frequently to be observed.

Triptych by the elder Holbein. Fig. 45 represents one wing of an altar triptych by Hans Holbein the elder, painted about the year 1514. This beautiful figure of Saint Elizabeth of Hungary is interesting as showing the influence of Italian art, which at that time was widely spread throughout Germany and France; it also, in its minutely delicate touch and in the grotesque ornaments at the top and bottom, shows a strong tendency to use the forms and methods of the manuscript illuminator.

Manuscripts of the Teutonic school, which are known to be by the hand of a famous painter, are of rare occurrence; there is therefore special interest in the book of which one *Illuminations by A. Dürer.* of the border-illuminations is illustrated in fig. 46. The text itself (a book of prayers) is *printed* on vellum, but forty-five of the pages are decorated with borders drawn by the masterly hand of Albert Dürer in red, green and violet ink, a method possibly suggested to Dürer by the sight of one of the tenth or eleventh century manuscripts which were illuminated with outline drawings in inks of these three colours. This beautiful prayer-book was decorated by Albert Dürer in 1515 for the Emperor Maximilian; it is now in the Munich Library[1]. There is much that is grotesque and humorous introduced among the finely designed scroll-work of these borders; and

[1] Maximilian's Prayer-book has been described (with copies of the borders) by Stoeger, *Vignettes d'Albert Dürer*, Munich, 1850.

Fig. 45. Wing of a triptych, with a figure of St Elizabeth of Hungary, painted by the elder Hans Holbein; this illustrates the influence on painting of the styles of manuscript illumination at the beginning of the sixteenth century.

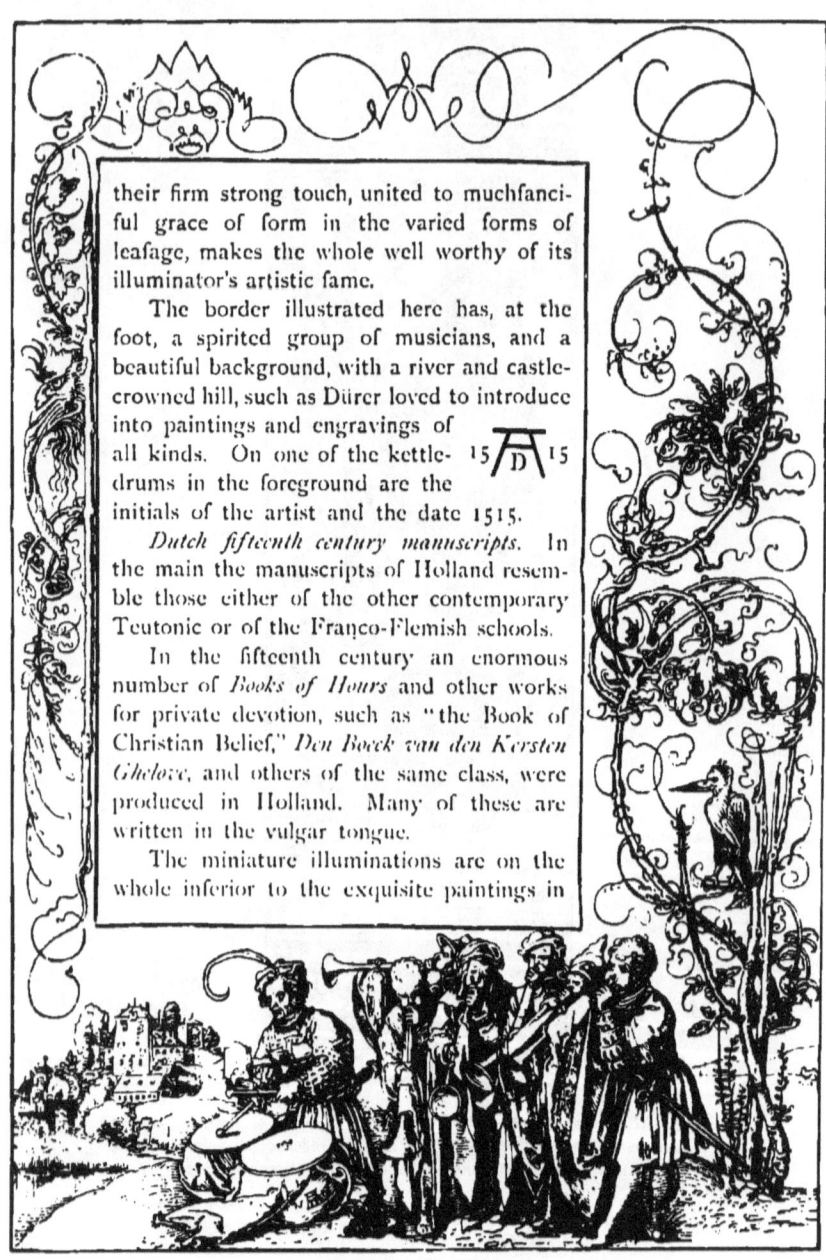

their firm strong touch, united to muchfanciful grace of form in the varied forms of leafage, makes the whole well worthy of its illuminator's artistic fame.

The border illustrated here has, at the foot, a spirited group of musicians, and a beautiful background, with a river and castle-crowned hill, such as Dürer loved to introduce into paintings and engravings of all kinds. On one of the kettle-drums in the foreground are the initials of the artist and the date 1515.

Dutch fifteenth century manuscripts. In the main the manuscripts of Holland resemble those either of the other contemporary Teutonic or of the Franco-Flemish schools.

In the fifteenth century an enormous number of *Books of Hours* and other works for private devotion, such as "the Book of Christian Belief," *Den Boeck van den Kersten Ghelove*, and others of the same class, were produced in Holland. Many of these are written in the vulgar tongue.

The miniature illuminations are on the whole inferior to the exquisite paintings in

Fig. 46. Illuminated border drawn by Albert Dürer in 1515.

CHAP. XI.] DUTCH MANUSCRIPTS. 181

Flemish manuscripts; but they are usually very decorative in treatment, of a simple, homely style, which is not without charm. The decorative initials are often very large and beautiful, in some cases occupying a large proportion of the page; and the borders, which grow gracefully out of these large capitals, are magnificently rich both in design and execution. Gold is used profusely and with remarkable taste and skill in these Dutch illuminations, which frequently have a combination of *mat*, fluid gold applied with the brush over a ground of brilliantly burnished gold leaf. Very beautiful initials are also formed by painting with a transparent lake red over a ground of burnished gold, which shines through the red pigment, thus producing a brilliantly decorative effect. *Dutch methods of ornament.*

The miniatures of the fifteenth century Dutch manuscripts are noticeable for their realistic architectural details, with interiors of rooms full of elaborate furniture, bookshelves, sideboards covered with silver plate, or the humbler jugs and dishes of pewter, with countless other kinds of fittings and furniture. *Realistic details.*

Dutch miniatures with ecclesiastical scenes frequently have elaborately rendered interior views of churches, which are usually very interesting from their illustration of the choir and altar fittings, the retables, the "riddles" or altar-curtains, the tabernacles for the Reserved Host, and many other valuable records of mediaeval church furniture and ritual[1].

One very delicate and beautiful kind of illumination, which occurs in many of the best Dutch manuscripts, is by no means peculiar to Holland, but is also found in many English, French, Flemish and Italian manuscripts.

This consists of capitals, often of large size, decorated with rich ornamentation executed wholly with thin lines of blue and red drawn with a very fine pen. The firmness of touch and spirited quality of this pen illumination is often very remarkable, showing the most perfect training of hand and eye on the part of the illuminator. Though not as *Skilful use of the pen.*

[1] These minutely rendered ecclesiastical scenes occur frequently in other classes of Teutonic illumination.

Pen-work. gorgeous as the usual initials painted with gold and colours, this line ornament is sometimes of the richest and most delicate quality that can be imagined. In some cases a purple or violet ink is used, as well as the brighter blue and red, especially in Italian manuscripts.

The form of the pen ornaments used in this class of illumination is very much the same in all the chief European classes of manuscripts; a somewhat exceptional circumstance, since, as a rule, each country has its own peculiar types of decoration.

Illuminations in printed books. This beautiful pen-work reached its highest point of perfection in the first half of the fifteenth century. It is frequently used for the illuminated initials in the early printed books of Germany. Books printed at Strasburg by Mentelin, about 1460 to 1468, are often decorated with very elaborate and skilfully drawn ornament of this type; in many cases probably by Mentelin's own hand, since he was a skilful manuscript illuminator before he began to practise the art of printing[1].

The printed books of Koburger of Nuremberg are also remarkable for the beauty of their illuminations, both in the blue and red pen-work and also with painted ornaments in gold and colour.

[1] The Fitzwilliam Library possesses a beautiful example of this class of pen illumination in a large folio volume of the *Summa* of Aquinas printed by Mentelin about 1465 or 1466.

Mentelin in his youth was an illuminator of manuscripts in Paris at the same time that he was a student in the University; see page 150.

CHAPTER XII.

THE ILLUMINATED MANUSCRIPTS OF ITALY AND SPAIN.

As has been already mentioned, the old classical forms *Classic* survived in the manuscript miniatures of Italy for many *survival.* centuries with but little alteration.

A slow, but steady degradation in the forms of classic art began to take place about the fifth or sixth century; the fact being that no art can for long remain stationary; there must be either advance or decay, and when the habit of copying older forms has once become the established rule an artistic degradation soon becomes inevitable.

Just as the manuscript art of the Byzantine illuminators *Italian* first lost its vitality and then rapidly deteriorated, so in Italy *decadence.* the late surviving classical style of miniature became weaker and weaker in drawing, feebler in touch, and duller in composition, till in the eleventh and twelfth century a very low stage of degradation was reached, at the very period when the illuminator's art in more northern countries was growing into the most vigorous development of power and decorative beauty.

The great Renaissance of art in Italy, which led to such magnificent results in the fourteenth to the sixteenth centuries, in its first beginnings lagged behind the artistic movement in the north, so that during the thirteenth century, when England, France and Germany had almost reached their climax of artistic growth, Italy had hardly begun to advance[1].

As an example of the degraded state of Italian art during the twelfth century I may mention a manuscript in the Vatican library (*Vat.* 4922)[2] of a poem in honour of the Countess Matilda written by a monk of Canossa named Donizo, which has a number of miniature illustrations. These are of the lowest type, utterly feeble in the drawing of the human form and quite without any feeling for the folds of drapery; the figures are mere shapeless masses without any decorative beauty of colour to make up for the helpless ignorance of the draughtsman; see fig. 47.

MS. of Donizo.

Later on in the twelfth century, and during the first half of the thirteenth century, art in Italy was mainly a feeble reflection of the then degraded art of the Byzantines. This was partly due to the introduction into Italy of mosaic-workers from Constantinople, such as those who decorated the vault of the old Cathedral of Florence (now the Baptistery) with badly drawn but grandly decorative mosaics of the Day of Doom[3].

Oderisi of Gubbio.

Little is known of the two illuminators of manuscripts who are immortalized by Dante (*Purg.* xi. 79—83). Oderisi of Gubbio, whom Dante calls the "Honour of the art that in Paris is called *alluminare*," is said to have been employed by Pope Boniface VIII. to illuminate manuscripts in Rome about the time of the great Jubilee of 1300, when Dante visited Rome as an envoy from Florence.

Franco of Bologna.

Franco (Francesco) of Bologna is the other miniaturist mentioned by Dante as an artist of great merit; nothing is known of him or of his works. During the thirteenth and

---

[1] Such work as the Pisan Baptistery pulpit of Niccola Pisano, executed in about 1260, was an almost isolated phenomenon, and it was not till about half a century later that Giotto and his pupils produced paintings of equal merit to those of France and England during the second half of the thirteenth century.

[2] See *Mon. Germ. Hist.* XII. p. 348 seq.; and Agincourt, *Hist. d'Art*, Pl. 66.

[3] Partly owing to the necessarily decorative beauty of the glass *tesserae*, Byzantine mosaics, even of a degraded period, are usually fine and rich in effect.

Fig. 47. Illumination from an Italian manuscript executed for the Countess Matilda in the twelfth century; this illustrates the extreme decadence of art in Italy before the thirteenth century.

fourteenth centuries Bologna was one of the chief Italian centres for the production of manuscripts, partly on account of its being the seat of one of the oldest and most important Universities of Europe.

MS. of Giotto's school.
One of the finest manuscripts of the Florentine school, executed by an unknown *miniatore* of the school of Giotto, is a *Missal* in the Chapter library of the Canons of Saint Peter's in Rome. The arms of the donor, repeated several times among the floreated borders, show that the manuscript was illuminated for Giotto's patron Cardinal Gaetano Stefaneschi, probably between 1330 and 1340. The same volume contains, by the same illuminator's hand, a richly illuminated *Life of Saint George*, with large historiated capitals of great beauty and finely decorative colouring. Fig. 48 shows one of the initials with Saint George slaying the dragon, and the Princess Saba kneeling at the side.

Italian art in France.
In some cases, especially during the fourteenth century, skilful Italian illuminators appear to have worked in France. Many French and even Flemish manuscripts, such as some of those executed for Philip of Burgundy and the Duc de Berri towards the end of the century, show distinctly two styles of painting, French and Italian, the book evidently being the work of two different artists. Some of these Italian paintings in French manuscripts suggest the hand of a disciple of Simone Martini (Memmi), or some artist of the very decorative Sienese school; this was probably in many cases due to the introduction of Italian painters into Avignon when the Papal court was resident there; see page 140.

Late artistic revival.
It was, however, not till nearly the middle of the fourteenth century that Italy produced many illuminated manuscripts of any remarkable beauty. Those executed under the immediate influence of Giotto, between 1300 and about 1340, were not as a rule to be compared to the illuminations of northern Europe either for decorative value or for minute beauty of detail.

By the middle of the fourteenth century, however, the illuminator's art in Italy, and especially in Florence, had reached a very high degree of excellence.

CHAP. XII.]   THE FOURTEENTH CENTURY.   187

Vasari, in his life of Don Lorenzo Monaco[1], mentions a Camaldolese monk of the Monastery of Santa Maria degli Angeli near Florence, who, about the year 1350, wrote and

Fig. 48. Miniature of St George and the Dragon from a *Missal*, illuminated about 1330 to 1340 by a painter of the school of Giotto.

Monastic painters.

illuminated a number of magnificent choir-books for his monastery, which were very highly valued; so much so that after the death of the monk, whose name was Don Silvestro, his hand was preserved in a shrine as a sacred relic of the

Don Silvestro.

[1] See Vasari, *Vite dei pittori*, Edition of 1568, Parte I. p. 229 seq.; and *ib.* Milanesi's edition, 1878, Vol. II. pp. 17 to 29.

dead monk's piety and skill[1]. Some of Don Silvestro's manuscripts are now preserved in the Laurentian library in Florence, and a number of miniatures cut out of his choir-books were acquired by W. Young Ottley[2].

MSS. of Don Silvestro.

The existing works of Don Silvestro show that the enthusiasm of his fellow monks was not exaggerated. The miniatures are noble in style, finished with the most exquisitely minute touch, splendidly brilliant in colour, and in every way masterpieces of the illuminator's art. These choir-books are of enormous size, being intended to be placed on the central choir lectern so that the whole body of monks standing round could chant the *antiphonalia* from the same book, and the initials are proportionately large to the size of the page. Thus some of the figures of Saints which fill the central spaces of the large initials are as much as from six to seven inches in height, and yet they are painted with the minute detail of an ordinary sized miniature. The grounds of these splendid figures are usually of burnished gold, decorated by incised tooling of diapers or scroll-work; and the floreated borders, which surround the letters and form marginal ornaments to the pages, consist of nobly designed conventional foliage in vermilion, ultramarine and other fine pigments, relieved and lighted up by bosses of burnished gold thickly sprinkled among the sumptuous coloured foliage. Tooled and burnished gold is also used largely for the decoration of the dresses of the figures, their crowns, jewelled ornaments and the apparels and orphreys of their vestments. The whole effect is magnificent in the extreme, and yet, in spite of the dazzling brilliance of the gold and colours, the whole effect is perfectly harmonious and free from the harsh gaudiness which dis-

Methods of decoration.

---

[1] This enshrined hand, and another, said to be that of a later *miniatore* of the same Monastery, Don Lorenzo, still exist in the Sacristy of the church of Santa Maria degli Angeli.

[2] These magnificent miniatures were sold with the rest of the Hailstone Collection in 1891; one of them, in the possession of the present writer, is a magnificent initial O, measuring eight by nine inches, enclosing a very beautiful seated figure of Saint Stephen in a violet dalmatic with richly decorated gold *apparels*.

figures so much of the late fifteenth century work of the French and Flemish manuscript painters.

The special style of ornament used by Don Silvestro survived in Italian illumination for nearly a century and a half. In Italy realistic forms of fruit and flowers, such as were painted with such taste and skill by the northern miniaturists, were scarcely ever used. All through the fifteenth century, alike in the manuscripts of the Florentine, Sienese and Venetian schools, the same purely conventional forms of foliage were used, with great curling leaves, alternately blue and red, lighted up by the jewel-like studs and bosses of burnished gold.

Italian ornament.

According to Vasari, the same Camaldolese Monastery produced another manuscript illuminator whose skill was hardly inferior to that of Don Silvestro. This was Don Lorenzo, who appears to have been born about 1370, and to have died about 1425[1]. Examples of his skill, also in the form of large choir-books, are preserved in the Laurentian library at Florence; they are rich with miniatures of great beauty, and, like Don Silvestro's paintings, show a lavish expenditure of time and patience in the exquisite minuteness with which they are finished. Vasari tells us that his hand also was preserved as a sacred relic in the treasury of Santa Maria degli Angeli.

The monk Don Lorenzo.

In later times Pope Leo X., who, like other members of the Medici family, was an enthusiastic lover of illuminated manuscripts, when on a visit to the Monastery, desired to carry away to the Basilica of Saint Peter in Rome some of these choir-books by the hand of Don.Lorenzo[2].

Visit of Leo X.

The Dominican Convent of San Marco in Florence, where the famous Florentine painter Fra Beato Angelico[3] was a

---

[1] See Vasari, Milanesi Ed. Vol. II. p. 15. Vasari also mentions a monk of the same monastery named Don Jacopo, a contemporary of Don Silvestro, who illuminated twenty large choir-books of extraordinary beauty.

[2] He appears to have abstained from purchasing these choir-books because they were of the special Camaldolese *Use*, and could not therefore be used in the Vatican Basilica.

[3] Fra Angelico's works were executed throughout the first half of the fifteenth

Dominican painters.

Friar, possesses, or till quite recently did possess, a magnificent collection of choir-books richly illuminated with miniatures by various members of the Convent. Some of these are said to have been painted by Fra Angelico himself, others by a brother of his who was a Friar in the same Convent[1].

The records of the Dominican Convent at Fiesole, where Fra Angelico was born, show that he was working there as a painter of illuminated manuscripts in the year 1407 and for some time subsequently.

Fra Angelico's style.

It is noticeable that Fra Angelico's style, even when painting a colossal mural fresco, was essentially that of the manuscript illuminator. He is utterly unrealistic in drawing and still more so in colour; he deals with no possible effects of light and shade, but paints all his figures glowing with the most brilliant effects of gold and colour, in a style far earlier than that of his own date, and with certain technical peculiarities which, as a rule, are to be found only in the illuminations of manuscripts[2].

MSS. of northern Italy.

In the fifteenth century the manuscript art of central and northern Italy, especially Siena, Florence, Venice and Milan, rose to a pitch of beauty and perfection which left it quite without rival in any country in the world. As was the case in writing of the glories of such manuscripts as the French *Apocalypses* of the fourteenth century, words are inadequate to describe the refined beauty of the best Italian manuscripts of this period. As has been already pointed out Italy was late in beginning her artistic Renaissance; and now, just when the rest of Europe was sinking into a more or less

---

century. Vasari mentions some magnificent manuscripts illuminated by him for the Cathedral of Florence, but they are not now known to exist.

[1] This is very doubtful. Fra Angelico's brother Fra Benedetto da Fiesole was a scribe rather than a miniaturist, and probably only wrote the fine large text; the illuminations were probably added by a pupil of Fra Angelico, named Zanobi Strozzi, who died in 1468.

[2] As an example of this I may mention Fra Angelico's system of painting the shadows of drapery in pure colour, using the same colour mixed with white for the rest of the folds. To some extent this method was used by the Sienese school of painting, which in other respects resembles in style the miniatures in illuminated manuscripts; see above, p. 114.

CHAP. XII.] ITALIAN MSS. IN THE FIFTEENTH CENTURY. 191

rapid and complete state of decadence, Italy blossomed out into one of the most magnificent artistic periods that the world has ever seen[1]. The manuscripts of this period are not unworthy of the general artistic glories of the time, and in some cases their technical qualities bear witness to an almost superhuman amount of dexterity and patience.

Renaissance in Italy.

During the first half of the century, by far the greater proportion of the manuscripts written in Italy were for ecclesiastical purposes. Among the most magnificent, but at the same time also the rarest, are folio manuscript *Pontificals*[2], executed for wealthy ecclesiastics of Episcopal rank.

An Italian folio *Pontifical*, dating from early in the fifteenth century, in the library of the Fitzwilliam Museum, is of its kind, one of the most beautiful manuscripts in the world. The delicacy of execution of the figures and especially the faces is little short of miraculous, and the numerous historiated initials, each representing some episcopal act of Consecration or Benediction, scattered thickly all through the volume, are a remarkable proof of the patient, unwearied skill which through years of labour must have been devoted to this one superb volume.

The Fitzwilliam Pontifical.

Among the illuminated manuscripts with secular texts the most important are copies of Dante's *Divine Comedy*, the works of Boccaccio and the Poems of Petrarch. The first page of such works as these is usually richly decorated with a wide border of scroll foliage, studded with the usual gold bosses. Frequently small miniatures in medallion frames are set at intervals among the conventional leafage; and at the bottom is a shield to receive the owner's coat of arms, surrounded with a delicately painted leafy wreath, which is supported on each side by a graceful figure of a flying angel

Italian poems.

---

[1] Taking it all round, in painting, sculpture, the medallist's art and other branches of the fine arts, no country and no period except Athens in the time of Pericles can ever have quite equalled the artistic glories of Florence under Cosimo the Elder and Lorenzo de' Medici.

[2] *Pontificals* contain such Services as only Bishops or Archbishops could celebrate, and therefore comparatively few would be required.

or Cupid[1]. In many cases the shield is still left blank; the book not having been written for any special purchaser and the owner having neglected to insert his arms[2].

The owner's arms.

The painting of the wreath which surrounds the shield is usually very beautiful, and the two flying angels or *amorini* are models of grace. This motive of the wreath held by two flying figures was largely used by the Florentine sculptors of the fifteenth century, such as Ghiberti and Luca della Robbia; it was suggested by the similar design, of very inferior execution, which occurs on so many ancient Roman sarcophagi.

Classical influence.

Some of the most elaborate Italian manuscripts of the second half of the fifteenth century are decorated with very minutely and cleverly painted copies of antique classical gems, cameos, coins and medals, or reliefs in marble and bronze. Wonderful skill is often shown by the way in which the illuminator has given the appearance of relief and the actual texture of the metal or stone[3]. Beautiful as the borders of this class are, they belong to a period of decadence of taste, though not of skill, and they paved the way for the elaborate futilities of Giulio Clovio and other miniaturists of the sixteenth century period of decadence.

Capture of Constantinople.

The influx of Greek exiles into Florence, after the conquest of Constantinople by the Ottoman Turks in 1453, led to the famous revival of classical learning, and for a while made Florence not only the artistic but the intellectual centre of the world. Many of these fugitive Greeks brought with them both Greek and Latin manuscripts of ancient date, and a new development of manuscript art took place in consequence of this.

[1] A beautiful manuscript of about 1460 in the Fitzwilliam Museum has its first page surrounded with a border of this class of design, the interest of which is much increased by the minutely written signature, "Jacopo da Fabriano," introduced among the leavy ornaments of the margin.

[2] This kind of design, with a blank space for the owner's arms, is used for many of the beautiful wood-cut borders in the early printed books of Florence and Venice.

[3] Decorative accessories of this sculpturesque kind are largely used in the paintings of Andrea Mantegna of Padua.

CHAP. XII.] ARCHAISTIC STYLE. 193

Though manuscripts of Service books and other sacred works continued to be written in the mediaeval "Gothic" form of character, for secular manuscripts[1] a very beautiful kind of "Roman" hand was largely used by the scribes of Florence, Venice and other Italian centres of the illuminator's art. This newly developed mode of writing was based on the beautiful clear form of character which had been used by the most skilful northern scribes of the ninth and tenth century; and at the same time a style of illumination for borders and initials was imitated or rather adapted, with the utmost taste and skill from the characteristic interlaced patterns of England, France and Germany during the twelfth century. *Copyism of early writing.*

This beautiful kind of ornament consists of delicately interlaced and plaited bands of white or gold, thrown into relief by filling in the background, or spaces between the laced bands, with alternating colours, blue, red and green. *Celtic style of ornament.*

This style of initial was also largely used for the early printed books of Rome, Florence and Venice[2], many copies of which were illuminated in the most magnificent way, quite equal to the ornaments of the finest vellum manuscripts.

Some of the Italian manuscripts of the second half of the fifteenth century, for delicate beauty and for exquisite refinement of detail, are unrivalled by the illuminated manuscripts of any other country or age.

Among the greatest marvels of human skill that have ever been produced are some of the very small *Books of Hours* which were executed for the merchant princes of Florence and Venice and for other wealthy Italian patrons. The borders in these frequently have minute figures of Cupid-like angels (amorini) playing among decorative foliage, or birds and animals, such as fawns, cheetahs and the like, *Italian Horae.*

[1] And to some extent for manuscripts of religious works as well. This archaic form of letter was also used by Sweynheim and Pannartz and other prototypographers at Subiaco and in Rome; hence it got the name of *Roman* as opposed to *Gothic* letter.

[2] One of the finest examples of this style of illumination is in a volume of the Italian translation of Pliny's *Natural History*, printed on vellum by Nicolas Jenson in Venice in 1476; now in the Bodleian at Oxford.

designed with an amount of grace and modelled with a microscopic refinement of touch that no words can adequately describe.

Beauty of the text. And it is not only the unequalled beauty of the painted decorations and miniatures for which these late Italian manuscripts are so remarkable; the mere writing of the text in the most brilliant black and red ink is of striking beauty in the form of the letters and the perfect regularity of the whole. Last of all the vellum used by the Italian scribes of this period is far more beautiful, from its ivory-like perfection of tint and surface, than that of any other class of manuscripts. Though not, of course, as exquisitely thin as the uterine vellum of the Anglo-Norman thirteenth century scribes, it is more beautiful in texture, and does much to complete the artistic perfection of the manuscripts of fifteenth century Italy, by its exquisitely polished surface and perfect purity of tint.

MSS. of N. Italy. The provinces of Florence, Pisa, Siena, Bologna and Venice, including Verona, were all important centres for the production of fine illuminated manuscripts. On the whole Florence was the most famous in this as in other branches of art, and it was especially to Florence that wealthy foreign Princes sent their commissions when they desired to possess exceptionally beautiful manuscripts.

Corvinus a patron of art. One of the most enthusiastic art patrons of Europe, Matthias Corvinus, King of Hungary from 1458 to 1490, had a large number of most magnificent manuscripts written and illuminated for him by various *miniatori* of Florence; some of these are now in the Imperial library of Vienna.

So also Federigo da Montefeltro, Duke of Urbino about the same time, purchased from a Florentine that most superbly illuminated Bible, in two large folio volumes, dated 1478, which is now in the Vatican library[1].

Among the miniaturists who worked for King Corvinus, the most famous was a Florentine named Attavante di

---

[1] See Wattenbach, *Schriftwesen*, Ed. 2, pp. 411 and 469; and Romer, *Les Manuscrits de la Bibl. Corvinienne*, in *l'Art*, Vol. x. 1877.

CHAP. XII.]   THE FIFTEENTH CENTURY.   195

Gabriello, who was born in 1452. Vasari mentions him as a pupil and friend of Fra Angelico[1], and describes at great length and with much enthusiasm a sumptuous manuscript of Silius Italicus, belonging to the Dominican Monastery of San Giovanni e Paolo in Venice, as being the work of Attavante.

Attavante the miniaturist.

This once magnificent manuscript still exists, but in a much mutilated state, in the Venetian Biblioteca Marciana (Cl. XII. Cod. LXVIII.); all the large miniatures have been cut out, but the borders with winged Cupids, birds and animals among decorative scroll-work are marvels of beauty and minute delicacy of touch. Though quite worthy of Attavante's fame, this manuscript cannot be his work, as it was executed many years too early, in the time of Pope Nicholas V., who reigned from 1447 to 1455.

The same library does, however, possess real examples of Attavante's wonderful illuminations. The borders are specially remarkable for the minute medallion heads which are introduced among the conventional foliage. These minute pictures occur in many of the finest manuscripts of this class; and other *miniatori* painted them with a microscopic refinement of detail, quite equal to the best illuminations of Attavante. Fig. 49 gives a good typical example of this style of border, with two Cupid-like angels and busts of saints in quatrefoil medallions.

MSS. at Venice.

Some of the borders of this class, especially in Venetian and Florentine manuscripts, are decorated with very cleverly painted representations of jewels, such as the emerald and ruby, set at intervals along each margin. These are often wonderful examples of skilful realism, the transparency of the gem, and its bright reflected lights, being rendered with an almost deceptive appearance of reality.

In the fifteenth century Verona was one of the chief Italian centres for the production of magnificent manuscripts. Various members of one family, known from their occupation as "dài Libri," were specially famous as miniaturists. Stefano the eldest was born about 1420; he and his younger brother

The miniaturists called dai Libri.

[1] See Vasari's life of Fra Giovanni da Fiesole, Ed. Milanesi, Vol. II. p. 522 seq.

13—2

Fig. 49. An illuminated border from a manuscript by Attavante of characteristic north Italian style.

CHAP. XII.] DAI LIBRI AND LIBERALE OF VERONA. 197

Francesco were both skilled miniaturists, and Francesco's son Girolamo dai Libri (1474 to 1556) was famous not only as a *miniatore*, but also as a painter of altar-pieces and other sacred pictures on a large scale[1].

Another Veronese painter, Liberale di Giacomo, who was born in 1451, was in his youth a very skilful miniaturist.

Liberale of Verona.

He spent some years in illuminating large choir-books for the Benedictine monastery of Monte Oliveto near Siena, and then after 1469 he was for long occupied in the illumination of similar choir-books for the Cathedral of Siena[2].

The miniatures in these great *Antiphonals* are most exquisitely finished, rich in fancy, brilliant in colour, but wanting decorative breadth of style. With a far greater expenditure of labour and eyesight, these wonderful illuminations are far inferior to the works of the fourteenth century French miniaturists, and show signs of that decadence of taste, which, in the sixteenth century, led to the destruction of the true illuminator's art[3].

In addition to Venice, Padua and Ferrara were both important centres of manuscript illumination of a very high order during the fifteenth century. The Paduan miniatures show strongly the influence of Andrea Mantegna and Gian Bellini, whose styles also appear in the contemporary manuscripts of Venice. The British Museum possesses a magnificent example of the work of one of the ablest *miniatori* of Padua, a *Missal* by Benedetto Bordone, who also illuminated the great choir-books of the Convent of Santa Justina in Padua.

MSS. of N. Italy.

[1] The National Gallery in London possesses (No. 748 in the Catalogue) a good example of Girolamo's work, a Madonna altar-piece, signed *Hieronymus a libris f.* No. 1134 in the same collection is an example of a panel picture by Liberale da Verona. The Bodleian contains an exquisite *Book of Hours* illuminated by Girolamo dai Libri for the Duke of Urbino.

[2] The *Antiphonals* which Liberale illuminated at Monte Oliveto are now preserved in the Chapter library at Chiusi. Those which he painted at Siena are now in the Cathedral library. Records of money paid to Liberale for these choir-books are published by Milanesi, *Documenti per la Storia dell' Arte Sanese*, Vol. II. pp. 384—386; and Milanesi's edition of Vasari, Vol. V. pp. 326—334.

[3] Examples of Attavante's and Liberale's miniatures are illustrated by Eug. Müntz, *La Renaissance en Italie et en France*, Paris, 1885, p. 188 seq.

Fig. 50. A miniature from the Bible of Duke Borso d'Este, painted between 1455 and 1461 by illuminators of the school of Ferrara.

CHAP. XII.] MANUSCRIPTS OF NORTHERN ITALY. 199

Ferrara too produced many very beautiful manuscripts, especially under the patronage of Duke Borso d'Este. It was for this Duke of Ferrara that the magnificent choir-books, now in the Municipal library at Ferrara were executed.

School of Ferrara.

Fig. 50 shows a miniature from a very splendid Bible, which was illuminated for Duke Borso d'Este between 1455 and 1461 by Taddeo di Crivelli and Franco di Messer Giovanni da Russi, two very talented miniaturists of the Ferrarese school, though they were natives of the neighbouring city of Mantua.

Parma, Modena and Cremona also were thriving centres of the illuminator's art; in fact wherever in Italy there was a school of painting a subsidiary school of manuscript miniaturists seems also to have existed. The two classes of painting acted and reacted upon one another; and in some cases, as is indicated below[1], the more important art of painting on a large scale owed more to the manuscript illuminators than has commonly been acknowleged.

Parma and Modena.

Milan, especially under Duke Ludovico and other members of the Sforza family, was an active centre of manuscript illumination. Some very beautiful late manuscripts exist with miniatures which show the influence of Leonardo da Vinci and his pupil Bernardino Luini; a *Book of Hours* in the Fitzwilliam Museum is a good example of this.

School of Milan.

One rather exceptional class of richly illuminated manuscripts was largely produced in Italy during the fifteenth and sixteenth centuries; these were State documents, University diplomas and licences, patents of nobility and legal instruments of various kinds, often very elaborately decorated with illuminations and miniatures in gold and colours.

Illuminated documents.

In Venice especially immense numbers of these were produced; the most elaborate are Appointments of Governors, Commissions of officials of rank, Patriarchal Briefs, together with State records and documents of the most varied kinds. Bologna, Padua, Pisa and others of the chief Universities of Italy issued diplomas for Doctor's degrees, and licences to

[1] See page 200, and compare pages 163 and 175 for examples of similar influence due to the manuscript illuminators of Germany and Italy.

give lectures, which were frequently very magnificently decorated with letters of gold and richly illuminated capitals and borders.

Retables like MSS. Before passing on to the Italian *miniatori* of the last period, it is worth while to notice the strong influence that the art of manuscript illumination had on the painters of large retables and other sacred pictures in Italy and especially in Venice; just as was the case with the contemporary painters of Germany and Flanders[1]. Many of the Venetian altar-pieces, from their minute detail, their use of burnished gold enriched with tooled patterns, their decorative treatment of flowers and their architectural backgrounds and framework, look exactly like a page from an illuminated manuscript.

Retable at Venice. Fig. 51 shows a characteristic example of this, a magnificent retable glowing with brilliant colours and burnished gold, now in the Accademia of Venice, which was painted in 1446 in the little island of Murano by two painters named Johannes and Antonius de Murano[2].

The same strongly marked influence of the decorative style of illuminated manuscripts is to be seen in nearly all the works of Carlo Crivelli, another Venetian painter of the latter part of the fifteenth century, and in the gorgeous retables of Gentile da Fabriano[3], a follower of Fra Angelico's richly decorative and brilliantly coloured method of painting.

The XVIth century. *Italian manuscripts of the sixteenth century.* By about the end of the first decade of the sixteenth century the art of manuscript illumination had ceased in Italy to be a real living art; and, though it continued to be practised with great technical skill for more than half a century later, the art, which once had been one of the most beautiful and dignified of all branches of art, sank into the production of costly toys to please a few Popes and luxurious Princes who were willing to pay very large prices for manuscripts illumi-

[1] For examples of this see above, page 175.

[2] Each of these painters (in some pictures) also signs himself *Alamanus*, meaning not necessarily that they were Germans, but possibly natives of Lombardy, who were often called *Alamani* by their Italian neighbours.

[3] Especially in his magnificently decorative altar-piece of the Adoration of the Magi in the Florentine Academy, dated 1423.

Fig. 51. A Venetian retable by Giovanni and Antonio di Murano, in the style of an illuminated manuscript.

nated by the skilful hands of Giulio Clovio and other miniaturists, whose patience, eyesight and technical skill were superior to their sense of what was fitting and beautiful in an illuminated manuscript.

Giulio Clovio. Of all the illuminators of this class the Dalmatian Giulio Clovio[1] (1498-1578) was the most famous and technically the most skilful. He found many wealthy patrons in Italy and was employed by Charles V. of France.

The Soane Museum in London possesses a characteristic example of his style, a *Commentary on the Epistles of Saint Paul*, executed for Giulio's early patron, Cardinal Marino Grimani of Venice, the brother of the owner of the Grimani *Breviary* mentioned above. Clovio's miniatures are marvels of minute execution, but not truly decorative in style, and in design usually quite unsuited to their purpose. In most cases they resemble large oil paintings reduced to a microscopic scale; the figures are commonly feeble imitations either of large pieces of contemporary tapestry or else of painting in Michel Angelo's grandiose style, both of which of course were utterly unsuited for miniatures in a manuscript[2].

The Vatican MSS. *The Manuscripts in the Vatican Library.* The Archives of the Vatican library contain a number of records of the development of the library during the sixteenth century and later[3].

In mediaeval times manuscripts were rare and costly, so that even Kings, Popes and Universities possessed libraries

---

[1] Clovio is the Italianized form of a harsh Croatian name; the artist adopted the name Giulio as a compliment to his friend and teacher Giulio Romano, Raphael's favourite pupil.

J. W. Bradley, *Life of Giulio Clovio*, London, 1891, gives an interesting account of him and of his times; see also Vasari, Ed. Milanesi, Vol. VII. p. 557.

[2] The ex-king of Naples' library possesses a *Book of Hours*, on the illuminations of which (Vasari tells us) Giulio Clovio spent nine years. It certainly is a marvel of human patience and misdirected skill; the text was written by a famous scribe named Monterchi, who was specially renowned for the beauty of his writing.

[3] An interesting little volume on this subject has been published by Eug. Müntz, *La Bibliothèque du Vatican*, Paris, 1886; it deals chiefly with the growth of the library during the sixteenth century.

which in size were very insignificant compared to those of ancient Alexandria, Rome and Byzantium.

Even in Leo X.'s time (1513-1522) the Vatican library, which was probably the largest in the world, contained only 4,070 manuscripts and printed books. A century earlier, before the invention of printing, two or three hundred volumes would have constituted an enormous library.

The Vatican library.

As a rule even Royal and Public libraries were contained in a few iron-bound chests or *armaria*; and borrowers had to deposit a pledge—a gold ring, a silver cup or some other valuable article, which was retained by the librarian till the manuscript had been restored. In the Vatican this practice survived till the sixteenth century, and books exist among the Archives in which were recorded the date, the title of the book, the borrower's name and a short description of the deposited pledge. When the book was returned the word "restituit" was written in the margin.

The same Archives contain a number of accounts giving the sums paid to various illuminators of manuscripts, especially in the time of Pope Paul III. (Alex. Farnese, 1534 to 1553), who was a great patron of Giulio Clovio and other miniaturists. In 1540 a number of *scriptores et miniatores* employed in the Vatican library received as pay 4 gold ducats each monthly, of 10 Julii to the ducat, equal to about £20 in modern value.

Payments to scribes.

In 1541 Messer Paolo received 30 gold ducats for writing and illuminating four volumes.

It is interesting to note that the famous painter Sebastiano del Piombo[1] ("Fra Bastiano piombator") received payment "pro libris miniatis" in the year 1546 from Pope Paul III.

Del Piombo as an illuminator.

In 1549 Federigo Mario di Perugia received 4½ ducats a month for his labour "in scribendis et ornandis seu pingendis libris." This is the same miniaturist who illuminated some choir-books for the Roman Monastery of Saint' Agostino[2].

[1] Fra Sebastiano was called "del Piombo" from his office as superintendant of the pendant lead seals, *piombi* or *bullae*, which were attached to Papal Briefs and other documents, one class of which were called *Bulls* from their lead *bullae*.

[2] See Montault, *Livres de chœur des églises de Rome*, Arras, 1874, p. 9.

It was especially for the great choir-books that the art of the scribe and illuminator survived, the reason being that no printers' fount of type had characters of sufficient size to be read by a whole circle of singers. Thus we find Italian and Spanish manuscript *Antiphonals*[1] and the like, which have the grand Gothic writing of the fifteenth century executed as late as the year 1620 or even later[2].

Spanish MSS.

The Manuscripts of Spain, Portugal and the East. Little need be said about the manuscript illuminations of the Spanish peninsula since they contain little that is native or original.

In the fifteenth and sixteenth centuries many magnificent illuminations were produced in Spain and Portugal, but they are mainly imitations either of Italian or of Flemish miniatures. In earlier times in Northern Spain the influence of France was paramount, and in Southern Spain the beautiful "Saracenic" art of the Moorish conquerors influenced all branches of the fine arts, including that of manuscript illumination.

Moslem influence.

To some extent the same Moslem influence is apparent in the decorative borders of Sicilian and Venetian manuscripts, especially during the fifteenth century.

The illuminations of Oriental manuscripts do not fall within the limits of this brief treatise, but it should be noted that during the mediaeval period, and down to the present century, Persian and Arabic manuscripts with decorative illuminations of extraordinary beauty and skilful execution have been largely produced in Syria, Persia and India under the Moslem conquerors.

For delicacy of touch, for intricate beauty of ornament,

---

[1] The Fitzwilliam Museum possesses two noble vellum choir-books of this class dated 1604 and 1605. Though the miniatures are poor, the writing of the text and the music might well pass for the work of a fifteenth century scribe.

[2] A valuable but by no means exhaustive list of manuscript illuminators is given by J. W. Bradley, *Dictionary of Miniaturists, Illuminators and Caligraphers*, London, 1887. The names of Italian miniaturists are specially numerous, partly because Italian manuscripts are more frequently signed by their illuminators than the manuscripts of other countries. See also Bernasconi, *Studj sopra la storia della pittura Italiana dei secoli xiv e xv*, Verona, 1864.

CHAP. XII.] ORIENTAL MANUSCRIPTS. 205

and for decorative splendour in the use of gold and colour, these Oriental manuscripts are, in their own way, unsurpassed.

In the orthodox Sunni manuscripts miniatures with figure subjects do not occur, but are lavishly used in the manuscripts of the Persians and other members of the Sufi sect. The drawing of the human form is without the dignity and grace that is to be seen in Western manuscripts, but as pieces of decoration the Oriental miniatures are of high merit. Copies of the *Koran*, and the works of the favourite Persian poets are among the most common kinds of Oriental manuscripts. It is the latter that are so often sumptuously decorated with figure subjects.

Persian MSS.

CHAPTER XIII.

THE WRITERS OF ILLUMINATED MANUSCRIPTS.

The beauty of MSS. *The Monastic Scribes.* It may be interesting to consider what were the causes that made the illuminated manuscripts of the mediaeval period among the most perfect and beautiful works of art that the world has ever produced. No one can examine the manuscripts of any of the chief European countries down to the fourteenth century without a feeling of amazement at their almost unvarying perfection of execution, the immense fertility of fancy in their design, and the utterly unsparing labour that was lavished on their production. Moreover the manuscripts of this earlier period, before their production became a commercial art in the hand of secular scribes, are especially remarkable for their uniform excellence of workmanship, and their complete freedom from any signs of haste or weariness on the part of their scribes and illuminators.

Conditions of life. Now the fact is that the countless illuminated manuscripts which were produced in so many of the Benedictine and other monastic Houses of Europe were executed under very exceptionally favourable circumstances[1]. In the first place the monastic scribe lived in a haven of safety and rest in the middle of a tumultuous and war-harassed world. While at work in the *scriptorium* he was troubled with no thoughts of

[1] J. R. Green, in his *Short History of the English People*, chap. III., gives an interesting sketch of the development of literature and the art of the scribe in the great Monasteries of England, especially from the eleventh to the fourteenth century.

CHAP. XIII.]   MONASTIC ILLUMINATORS.   207

any necessity to complete his task within a limited time in *Absence of hurry.*
order to earn his daily bread. Food and clothing of a simple
though sufficient kind were secured to him, whether he
finished his manuscript in a year or in twenty years. He
worked for no payment, but for the glory of God and the
honour of his monastic foundation, and last, but not least, for
the intense pleasure which the varying processes of his work
gave him.

No one who examines a fine mediaeval manuscript can *Pleasant work.*
help seeing in it the strongest marks of the delight which the
illuminator had in his work ; and this sort of retrospective
sympathy with the pleasure of the workman in his work is an
important element in the beauty of ancient works of art of
many different kinds and dates, from the simple but beautiful
wheel-turned vase of the Greek potter, down to the carved
foliage in a Gothic church, or the complicated ornamentation
of an illuminated initial.

Again, it should be remembered that the life of a medi- *Relief from monotony.*
aeval monk was a very uneventful and monotonous one, and
even the most pious soul must at times have felt a weariness
in the oft-repeated and lengthy *Offices* which made him spend
so large a proportion of each day within the Choir of his
monastic church. Thus it was that his work as an illuminator of manuscripts provided the one great relief from his
otherwise grey and monotonous life, from which he turned to
revel in every variety of fanciful shape and of varied arrangement of gleaming gold and brilliant pigments. Here at
least was no monotony, but the fullest scope for imaginative
fancy and the love of variety which is inborn in the human
mind.

In the illumination of his manuscript the monastic scribe, *Scope for humour.*
even when decorating a sacred book, could lay aside for a
moment the solemn religious thoughts to which his vows had
bound him ; he could sport with every variety of grotesque
monster and of Pagan imagery, and could find vent for his
repressed sense of fun and humour by the introduction of
caricatures and pictorial jokes of all kinds among the foliage
of his borders and initials without any fear of reproof on the

Grotesque figures. part of his superiors[1]. Fig. 52 from a French fourteenth century manuscript shows a characteristic example of an illuminator's humorous fancy, a grotesque Bishop, with a mitre made out of a pair of bellows.

Very frequently the jealousy which existed between the Regular and the Secular Clergy is expressed in the pictorial sarcasms of the monastic illuminators. This feeling, on the Secular side, is vividly set forth in the amusing Latin Poems of Walter Map[2], who, toward the close of the twelfth century, was the Parish Priest of a little church in the Forest of Dean[3]. Walter Map's satire is mainly directed against the Cistercian order of monks, with whom he was specially brought into contact owing to his parish being situated near the Cistercian Abbey of Flaxley.

Fig. 52. Grotesque figure from a French manuscript of the fourteenth century.

Humorous scene. Fig. 53, from a German manuscript of the end of the twelfth century, now in the Chapter library of Prague Cathedral, gives an interesting example of the introduction of a humorous scene into a grave work, Saint Augustine's *De civitate Dei*. The illuminator, who was named Hildebert, has been worried by a mouse, which stole his food; and here on the last leaf of the manuscript he represents himself interrupted in his work and throwing something at the mouse which is nibbling at his food. These explanatory words are written on the open page of his book,

𝔓𝔢𝔰𝔰𝔦𝔪𝔢 𝔪𝔲𝔰, 𝔰𝔢𝔭𝔦𝔲𝔰 𝔪𝔢 𝔭𝔯𝔬𝔟𝔬𝔠𝔞𝔰 𝔞𝔡 𝔦𝔯𝔞𝔪, 𝔲𝔱 𝔱𝔢 𝔡𝔢𝔲𝔰 𝔭𝔢𝔯𝔡𝔞𝔱.

A wicked mouse. "You wicked mouse, too often you provoke me to anger, may God destroy you."

---

[1] The carvings on the *misericords* (or turn-up seats) of choir-stalls were frequently a vent for the pent-up humour and even spite of many a monastic carver.

[2] The Poems of Walter Map were edited by Thos. Wright for the Camden Society, 1841.

[3] Walter Map subsequently obtained various degrees of preferment, and in 1197 became Archdeacon of Oxford.

Fig. 53. Miniature of a comic subject from a German manuscript of the twelfth century, representing a monastic scribe worried by a mouse.

Portrait of the scribe.

At the feet of the scribe a lad named Everwinus, possibly a monastic novice, is seated on a low stool, drawing a piece of ornamental scroll-work. The Monk Hildebert's desk is in the form of a lectern supported by a carved lion; in it are holes to hold the black and red inkhorns, and two pens or brushes. In his left hand the scribe holds the usual penknife, and another pen is stuck behind his ear.

Short hours of labour.

There is yet another of the conditions under which the monastic scribe worked which was not without important effect on the unvarying excellence of his work, and that was that he could never remain long enough at work, at any one time, for his hand or eye to get wearied. Owing to the constantly recurring Choir services, the *Seven Hours*, which he had to attend, the monastic scribe could probably never continue labouring at his illumination for more than about two hours at a time.

No weariness.

The importance of this fact is very clearly seen when we compare one of the earlier monastic manuscripts with one of the fifteenth century French or Flemish *Books of Hours*, executed by a professional secular scribe. Thus in the older manuscripts the firmness of line and delicate, crisp touch never relaxes, and the artist's evident sense of power and the joy in his manual dexterity lasts without diminution from the first to the last page of his book.

Variety of labour.

Additional beauty is given to the mediaeval manuscripts by the fact that each scribe commonly did much important work in the preparation of his inks and pigments; in some cases even to the beating out of the gold leaf he was about to use in his miniatures and borders[1]. No colours bought of a dealer in a commercial age could ever equal in beauty or in durability the pigments that an illuminator made or at least prepared for his own use. And his command over the materials of his art would greatly enhance his pleasure in using them, to say nothing of the relief given by the variety of his labours.

All these influences, combined with others which it might

[1] Theophilus, *Schedula diversarum Artium*, I. 30—33, writes as if every illuminator had to beat out or grind his own gold.

be wearisome to dwell upon, combined to make the manuscripts of the pre-commercial period works of the most unvarying perfection of technique, unspeakably rich in the varied wealth of fancy shown in their decorative schemes, as well as in the minute detail of each part. The illuminated ornament in one place is concentrated into a gem-like miniature within the narrow limit of a small initial letter. At another place it spreads out into the splendour of a full-page picture, which swallows up most of the text, and covers the whole page with one mass of burnished gold and brilliant colour. Or again, springing from its roots in an illuminated capital, it grows over the margin and frames the text with a mass of richly designed and exquisitely graceful foliage.

Varied schemes of ornament.

Every possible scheme of decoration is to be found in these manuscripts; but in all cases the illuminator is careful to make his painted ornament grow out of and form, as it were, an integral part of the written text, which thus becomes not merely a book ornamented with pictures, but is a close combination of writing and illumination, forming one harmonious whole in a united scheme of decorative beauty[1].

The Scriptoria of Monasteries. As I have previously mentioned, it was more especially the Benedictine monasteries[2] that were the centres for the production of mediaeval manuscripts[3]. I will therefore describe the usual arrangements of the *Scriptorium* in a Benedictine House.

Monastic Scriptoria.

In early times, in the eighth and ninth centuries for example, the Scriptorium and library appear usually to have been a separate room, near or over the Sacristy, and adjoining the Choir of the church[4].

[1] In this respect, as is noted above at page 33, the manuscripts of classical date appear to have been inferior to those of the mediaeval period.

[2] Monte Cassino the first and chief of the Benedictine monasteries, founded by Saint Benedict himself, was for many centuries one of the chief centres in Italy for the writing and illumination of manuscripts.

[3] According to the severe Cistercian Rule richly illuminated manuscripts were not allowed to be written or even used in Houses of that Order, which in England from the end of the twelfth century came next in size and importance to the monasteries of the parent Benedictine Order.

[4] See the plan of the Abbey of St Gallen, published by Prof. Willis, *Arch. Jour.*, Vol. V. page 85 seq.

Scriptoria in cloisters. During most of the mediaeval period, however, and in England down to the suppression of the Abbeys by Henry VIII., the system was to devote one whole walk or alley of the cloister, that nearest to the church, to the double purpose of a Scriptorium and library. This was naturally the warmest and dryest portion of the cloister, at least in most cases when the usual arrangement was followed of placing the cloister on the south side of the nave of the Abbey church[1].

This north walk (as it commonly was) of the cloister faced south and so received plenty of sun; at each end of it a screen was placed to shut it off from the rest of the cloister, which formed a sort of common living-room for the monks[2].

Monastic library. Along one side of this alley of the cloister were fixed, against the wall of the church, oak cupboards (*armaria*), with strong locks and hinges, to receive the manuscripts which formed the library of the monastery[3]. At Westminster and in other Benedictine monasteries the marks showing where these *armaria* were fixed are visible on the cloister wall or rather along the wall of the church, which forms one side of this walk of the cloister.

Down the middle of the alley a clear passage was left, and the other side of the passage, that opposite the bookcases, was occupied, at least in the fourteenth century, and probably *Scribes' carrels.* much earlier, by a row of little wooden box-like rooms called *carrels*[4], each of which was devoted to the use of one scribe. As a rule there were either two or three of these carrels to each bay or compartment of the cloister. They were commonly made of wainscot oak, about six by eight feet in

---

[1] The Abbey of Westminster is a well preserved example of the typical Benedictine plan.

[2] One walk of the Benedictine cloister, usually that on the west, was used as the school-room where the novices repeated their "Donats" and other lessons. Hence in many cloisters one sees the stone benches cut with marks for numerous "go-bang" boards—a favourite monastic game.

[3] No monk could borrow a book to read without the express permission of his superiors given in the Chapter House.

[4] The word *carrel* is probably a corruption of the French *carré*, from the *square* form of these little rooms.

CHAP. XIII.] BENEDICTINE CLOISTERS. 213

plan or even less; just big enough to hold the seated scribe and his large desk, on which rested the manuscript he was copying, and the one he was writing, with some extra shelf

Carrels in the cloister.

Fig. 54. View of the scriptorium alley of the cloisters at Gloucester, showing the recesses to hold the wooden *carrels* for the scribes or readers of manuscripts.

space for his black and red inkhorns, his colours and other implements; see fig. 53 on p. 209.

These little rooms were provided with wooden floors and ceilings, so as to be warm and dry; they were set close against the traceried windows, which in most cloisters ran all along the internal sides of the four alleys.

Cloister at Gloucester.

The cloister of Gloucester Abbey[1] has a slightly different arrangement. Here a series of stone recesses, each intended to hold a carrel, extends all along the side of this walk[2] of the cloister. There are two of these recesses to each bay, and the lower part of the outer wall, instead of consisting of open tracery, is of solid masonry, pierced only by a small glazed window to give light to the scribe; above the carrel recess there is the usual large arch filled in with tracery; see fig. 54[3].

When provided with these and other wooden fittings, the cloister of a Benedictine Abbey would not have been either in appearance or fact as cold and comfortless as such places usually look now. With a small portable brazier the monastic scribe in his little wooden cell was safe from damp and probably fairly warm even in cold weather.

The Rites and Monuments of Durham[4] (Cap. XLI.) give the following very interesting description of the *carrels* with which the Durham cloister was fitted up;

Cloister at Durham.

"In the northe syde of the Cloister, from the corner over againste the Church dour to the corner over againste the Dorter (dormitory) dour, was all fynely glased, from the hight to the sole (sill) within a little of the ground into the Cloister garth. And in every windowe iij PEWES or CARRELLS, where every one of the old Monks had his carrell, severall by himselfe, that,

[1] When the great Benedictine Abbey of Gloucester was suppressed, Henry VIII. made the Church into a Cathedral by creating a new See; and so, happily, the very beautiful cloister was saved from destruction.

[2] Gloucester is exceptional in having the cloister on the north side of the Church; and also in having these stone recesses in the *scriptorium* alley.

[3] The Gloucester cloister and the carrel recesses shown in this woodcut date from the latter part of the fourteenth century.

[4] Published by the Surtees Society, London, 1842; see p. 70.

when they had dyned, they did resorte to that place of Cloister and there studyed upon there books, every one in his carrell, all the afternonne, unto evensong tyme. This was there exercise every daie. All there pewes or carrells was all fynely wainscotted (with oak) and verie close, all but the forepart which had carved wourke that gave light in at ther carrell doures of wainscott. And in every carrell was a deske to lye there bookes on. And the carrells was no greater then from one stanchell (mullion) of the windowe to another.

The Durham carrels.

And over againste the carrells against the church wall did stande certaine great almeries (*armaria* or cupboards) of wainscott all full of BOOKES, with great store of ancient manuscripts to help them in their study, wherein did lye as well the old auncyent written Doctors of the Church as other prophane authors, with dyverse other holie men's wourkes, so that every one dyd studye what Doctor pleased them best, havinge the Librarie at all tymes to goe studie in besydes there carrells."

The Durham armaria.

In the sixteenth century, owing to the introduction of printed works, the books in the Benedictine monastery of Durham had become too numerous for the row of *almeries* along the north walk of the cloister to hold them; and so a separate room was provided as a second library. The present library at Durham is the old Dormitory or *Dorter* of the Monks with all its "cubicles" or *sleeping-carrels* removed.

In the Houses of other religious foundations the arrangements for the writing of manuscripts were different from those of the Benedictines. In a Convent of Dominican Friars, for example, each friar worked in his own cell where he slept, and in a Carthusian monastery each monk had a complete little house and garden with a small study and oratory and a larger room, where his labours, literary or mechanical, were carried on.

Other monastic Scriptoria.

The Dominican House of San Marco in Florence, of which Fra Beato Angelico was a member, throughout the fourteenth and fifteenth centuries was famous for the magnificent manuscripts that were illuminated there; see above,

p. 190. And various other Convents of Dominican Friars in Italy were important centres of manuscript illumination. Some of the Regular Canons were also famous as illuminators, especially the Austin Canons.

The Secular Scribes and Illuminators.

Growth of Guilds.
Towards the latter part of the thirteenth and throughout the fourteenth century, secular artisans in all varieties of arts and crafts were gradually throwing off the bonds of the old feudal serfdom under which they had for long been bound. The growth in number and importance of the Trade-Guilds, which in England developed so rapidly under Henry III., was one of the chief signs of the growing importance of the artisans of the chief towns of this and other European countries.

Importance of the Trade-Guilds.
At the end of the thirteenth century, in London, in Florence, and in many other cities no man could possess the rights of a citizen and a share in the municipal government without becoming a member of one of the established Trade-Guilds. Edward I., Edward III. and others of the English Kings set the example of enrolling themselves as members of one of the London Guilds[1]; and in Florence it was necessary for Dante to become a member of a Guild[2] before he could serve the Republic as one of the *Priori*.

At first the scribes and illuminators (*librorum scriptores et illuminatores*[3]) were members of one general Guild including craftsmen in all the decorative arts and their subsidiary processes, such as leather-tanning, vellum-making, and even saddlery[4].

[1] Frequently in the Linen-armourers' Guild, that of makers of defensive armour of linen padded and quilted, a very important protection against assassination, which was used till the seventeenth century.
[2] Dante selected the Apothecaries' and Physicians' Guild.
[3] This phrase was used in the twelfth century by Ordericus Vitalis, *Hist. Eccles.* Lib. III. p. 77, Ed. Le Prevost.
[4] Mediaeval saddlery, with its cut, gilt and stamped leather (*cuir bouillé*), rich and elaborate in design, was a decorative art of no mean character; and in technique was akin to that of the bookbinder, which in most places was included in the same Guild.

CHAP. XIII.]   OF SECULAR ILLUMINATORS.   217

By degrees the Guilds became more numerous and more specialized in character, till their fullest development was reached in the first half or middle of the fifteenth century. Much interesting information about the miniaturists' Guild in Bruges during the second half of the century has been published by Mr Weale[1].

This was the Guild of Saint John and Saint Luke; and every painter, miniaturist, illuminator, rubricator, copyist, maker of vellum, binder or seller of books who lived and worked in Bruges was obliged to belong to this Guild. This rule, which existed in Ghent, Antwerp and most artistic centres, had a double use; on the one hand it protected the individual illuminator from wrong and oppression of any kind; and, on the other hand, it tended to keep up a good standard of excellence in the work which was executed by the Guild-members.

No miniaturist could be admitted till he had laid before the Dean of the Guild a sufficiently good sample of his skill, and all members were liable to be fined if they used inferior materials of any kind, such as impure gold, adulterated ultramarine or vermilion and the like. In this way the officers of the Guild acted as moderators between the artisan and his patrons, securing reasonable pay for the artist, and, in return for that, reasonably good workmanship for his employer or customer. The Guilds also prevented anything like commercial slave-driving by limiting very strictly the number of apprentices or workmen that each master might employ.

Thus it happened that, though fine manuscripts were still written and illuminated in many of the principal monasteries of Europe, a large class of secular illuminators grew up, especially in Paris and the chief towns of Flanders and northern Germany. In this way the production of manuscripts, especially illuminated *Books of Hours*, became a regular commercial process, with the inevitable result that a great deal of work of a very inferior character was turned out to meet the rapidly growing demand for cheap and showy books.

Guilds in the XVth century.

Rules of the Guilds.

Decadence of MS. art.

[1] See *Le Beffroi*, Bruges, Vol. IV. 1873.

An immense number of these cheap manuscript *Horae* were produced after a few fixed patterns, with some mechanical dulness of repetition in every border and miniature with which they were decorated.

Costly Horae.
At the same time manuscripts were still produced, mostly at the special order of some royal patron or wealthy merchant, which, in elaborate beauty and in unsparing labour of execution, are hardly surpassed by the work of the earlier monastic scribes[1]. Examples of this are mentioned above at pages 135 and 169.

The Dukes of Burgundy and the Kings of France, towards the close of the fourteenth and the first half of the fifteenth century, numbered many illuminators among their regular paid adherents. In some cases the artist was permanently engaged, and passed his whole life in the service of one Prince; while in other cases famous illuminators were hired for a few months or years, when the patron wanted a specially magnificent manuscript either for his own use, or as a royal gift on the occasion of a marriage, a coronation or other great event.

Women artists.
In some cases, we find that women learnt to be manuscript illuminators of great skill and artistic taste. For example Cornelia, the wife of Gérard David of Bruges[2], was, like her husband, both an illuminator of manuscripts and a painter of altar retables. A fine triptych painted by Cornelia, in the possession of Mr H. Willett of Brighton, is a work of great beauty and refinement, which it would be difficult to distinguish from a painting by Gérard David himself.

Costly gifts.
In the fifteenth century the commercial value of sumptuously illuminated manuscripts rose to the highest point. No object was thought more suited for a magnificent wedding present to a royal personage than a costly manuscript[3].

---

[1] In poetic beauty, however, they cannot be compared to the glory of the French *Apocalypses* such as that in the library of Trinity College, Cambridge.

[2] Gérard David is mentioned above as one of the illuminators of the famous Grimani *Breviary*; see page 165.

[3] See pages 117 and 122 for examples of this.

CHAP. XIII.]   THE LATER TYPE.   219

And large sums were often advanced by money-lenders or pawnbrokers on the security of a fine illuminated manuscript.

Fig. 55.   Picture by Quentin Matsys of Antwerp, showing a lady selling or pawning an illuminated manuscript.

Fig. 55 shows a lady of the Bourgeois class negociating for the sale or pawn of a *Book of Hours* or some such manuscript, illuminated with a full-page miniature of the Virgin and Child. The money-lender appears to be weighing out to her the money. This beautiful painting which is commonly called the "Money-changer and his wife" is signed and dated 1514 by Quentin Massys or Matsys of Antwerp. It is now in the Louvre.

Painting by Matsys.

In the sixteenth century, especially in Italy, during the last decadence of the illuminator's art, very magnificent and costly manuscripts were produced by professional miniaturists, but these are merely monuments of wasted labour. Some account is given at page 202 of Giulio Clovio, the most skilful though tasteless miniaturist of his age.

Accounts of St George's, Windsor.

Mr J. W. Clark, the Registrary of the University of Cambridge, has procured and kindly allows me to print the following very interesting record of the cost of writing and illuminating certain manuscripts during the fourteenth century. The extract is taken from the manuscript records of the expenses of the Collegiate Church of St George at Windsor. The date is approximately given by the fact that John Prust was a Canon of Windsor from 1379 to 1385.

"Compotus Johannis Prust de diuersis libris per eum factis videlicet j Antiphonarium, j Textus Evangelij, j Martilogium, iij Processionalia.
In primis onerat se de x li. vj s. viij d. receptis de Ricardo
    Shawe per Indenturam.
Item onerat se de xx s. receptis de corpore prebende Edmun-
    di Clouille.
Item onerat se de l s. receptis de dicto Edmundo pro officio
    suo videlicet Precentoris.
            Summa totalis receptorum xiij li. xvj s. viij d.
In xix quaternionibus pergamenti vituli emptis pro libro
    Euangelij precio quaternionis viij d.   xij s. viij d.
Item solutum pro uno botello ad imponendum Incaustum x d.
Item solutum pro incausto   xiiij d.
Item pro vermulione   ix d.
Item pro communibus scriptoris pro xviij°. septimanis solutum
    per septimanam x d.   xv s.
Item pro stipendio dicti scriptoris per idem tempus xiij s. iiij d.
Item solutum Ade Acton ad notandum " Liber generacionis "
    et " Passion[es] " in dicto libro[1]   viij d.
Item pro examinacione et ad faciendum literas capitales
    gloucas [for glaucas]   iij s.
Item pro illuminacione dicti libri   iij s. iiij d.

---

[1] That is, for noting or writing the plain song of certain parts of the service which were sung at Christmas and during Holy Week. This explanation I owe to my friend Mr J. T. Micklethwaite.

Item pro ligacione dicti libri iij s. iiij d.
Item auri fabro pro operacione sua xx s.
Item in uno equo conducto pro Petro Jon per ij vices London
pro dicto libro portando et querendo viij d.
Item pro expensis dicti Petri per ij vices xj d.
Summa lxxv s. viij d.
Item in vij quaternionibus pergamenti vituli emptis pro libro
Martilogij precio quaternionis viij d. iiij s. viij d.
et non plures quia staur[o].
Item pro scriptura xij quaternionum precio quaternionis
xv d. xv s.
Item pro illuminacione dicti libri v s. x d.
Item pro ligacione dicti libri ij s. ij d.
Item ad faciendum literas capitales gloucas viij d.
Summa xxviij s. iiij d.
Item in xxxiiij quaternionibus pergamenti vituli emptis pro
vno Anthiphonario precio quaternionis xv d. xlijs. vj d.
Item xij quaterniones de stauro
Item pro scriptura xl. quaternionum pro nota precio quater-
nionis xv d. l s.
Item pro scriptura vj quaternionum de phalterio[1] precio quater-
nionis ij s. ij d. xiij s.
Item ad notandum antiphonas in phalterio vj d.
Item ad notandum xl. quaterniones pro antiphonis precio
vj d. xx s.
Item ad faciendum literas capitales gloucas xij d.
Item pro illuminacione xv s. xj d.
Item pro ligacione v s.
Summa vij li. vij s. xj d.
Item in xlvj quaternionibus pergamenti multonis emptis pro
iij libris processionalium precio quaternionis ij d. ob.
ix s. vij d.
Item pro scriptura dictarum xlvj quaternionum xv s.
Item ad notandum dictas quaterniones vij s. vj d.
Item pro illuminacione ij s. ix d
Item pro ligacione ij s. vj d.
Summa xxxvij s. iiij d.

[1] Evidently mis-spelt for *psalterio*; and again in the next item.

Summa Totalis Expensarum xiiij li. ix s. iij d. Et sic debentur computanter xij s. vij d. probatur per auditores quos r[ecepit] de Ricardo Shawe tunc precentore. Et sic equatur."

From these accounts we learn that six manuscripts were written, illuminated and bound, one of them with gold or silver clasps or bosses, at a total cost of £14. 9s. 3d., more than £150 in modern value.

The books were a *Textus* or *Evangeliarium*, a *Martyrologium*, an *Antiphonale* and three *Processionals*.

	£	s.	d.
The *Evangeliarium* was written on 19 quaternions (quires)[1] of vellum, costing 8d. each, total......		12	8
Black ink...		1	2
A bottle to hold the ink			10
Vermilion...			9
The scribe's "commons" (food) for eighteen weeks		15	0
Payment to the scribe		13	4
Corrections and adding coloured initials......		3	0
Illumination		3	4
Binding		3	4
Goldsmith's work (on the binding)	1	0	0

Two journeys to London and other smaller items, making a total of £3. 15s. 8d.

The *Martyrologium* was partly written on 7 quaternions of vellum[2], costing 8d. each quaternion

	£	s.	d.
quaternion		4	8
Payment to the scribe		15	0
Illumination		5	10
Binding		2	2
Coloured initials.................................			8
Total	1	8	4

The *Antiphonale* was written on 34 quater-

---

[1] The *quaternion* was a gathering of four sheets of vellum, each folded once; thus forming sixteen pages.

[2] This book was partly written on sheets of vellum which were *in stauro* (in stock), and therefore do not come into the accounts.

CHAP. XIII.]   AT WINDSOR AND BRISTOL.   223

nions of larger and more expensive sheets of
vellum, costing 15*d.* a quaternion[1]............... 2   2   6
   Payments to the scribe 3   3   0
   Adding the musical notation 1   0   6
   Coloured initials..................................   1   0
   Illumination 15 11
   Binding   5   0
                         Total   7   7 11

The three *Processionals* only cost £1. 17s. 4*d.*, being written on 46 quaternions of cheap parchment made of sheep-skin which cost only 2½*d.* the quaternion.

The following extracts from the Parish accounts of the Church of St Ewen, in Bristol[2], give some details as to the cost of writing, illuminating and binding a manuscript *Lectionary* during the years 1469 and 1470. The total expense is £3. 4s. 1*d.*, quite equal to £20 in modern value. *Accounts of St Ewen's, Bristol.*

1468—9.

"Item, for j dossen and v quayers of vellom to perform
   the legend [i.e. to write the lectionary on] ......x[s] vj[d]
Item, for wrytyng of the same .... xxv[s]
Item, for ix skynnys and j quayer of velom to the same
   legend .... v[s] vj[d]
Item, for wrytyng of the forseyd legend .... iiij[s] ij[d]

1470—1471.

Item for a red Skynne to kever the legent ....v[d]
Also for the binding and correcting of the
   seid Boke..v[s]
Also for the lumining of the seid legent ....xiij[s] vj[d]

[1] Twelve quires of vellum which were in stock were also used for this *Antiphonale.*
[2] See *Trans. Bristol and Glouces. Arch. Soc.* Vol. XV. 1891, pp. 257 and 260.

CHAPTER XIV.

THE MATERIALS AND TECHNICAL PROCESSES OF THE ILLUMINATOR.

Finest vellum.
Vellum for scribes[1]. The most remarkable skill is shown by the perfection to which the art of preparing vellum[2] for the scribe was brought. The exquisitely thin uterine vellum, which was specially used for the minutely written Anglo-Norman *Vulgates* of the thirteenth century, has been already described; see page 113. For ivory-like beauty of colour and texture nothing could surpass the best Italian vellum of the fifteenth century.

One occasional use of the very thin uterine vellum should be noted. For example in a German twelfth century copy of the *Vulgate*, now in the Corpus library in Cambridge, some of the miniature pictures have been painted on separate pieces of uterine vellum, and then pasted into their place on the thicker vellum pages of the manuscript. This, however, is an exceptional thing.

High price of vellum.
The vellum used for illuminated manuscripts appears to have been costly, partly on account of the skill and labour that were required for its production, and, in the case of uterine vellum on account of the great number of animals' skins that were required to provide enough material for the writing of a single manuscript such as a copy of the *Vulgate*.

[1] See Peignot, *Essai sur l'histoire du parchemin et du vélin*, Paris, 1812.
[2] Strictly speaking the word *vellum* should denote parchment made from calf-skin, but the word is commonly used for any of the finer qualities of parchment which were used for manuscripts.

CHAP. XIV.] VELLUM FOR MANUSCRIPTS. 225

Even the commoner kind of parchment used for official documents was rather a costly thing. The roll with the Visitation expenses of Bishop Swinfield, Bishop of Hereford from 1282 to 1317, shows that 150 sheets of parchment cost 3s. 4d., about £4 in modern value[1].

Cost of vellum.

The vellum used for manuscripts has a different texture on its two sides. One side, that on which the hair grew, has a *mat*, unglossy surface; the other (interior) side of the skin is perfectly smooth and, in the case of the finest vellum, has a beautifully glossy texture like that of polished ivory.

In writing a manuscript the scribe was careful to arrange his pages so that two glossy and two dull pages came opposite each other[2].

The art of preparing vellum of the finest kind is now lost; the vellum made in England is usually spoilt first by rubbing down the surface to make it unnaturally even, and then by loading it with a sort of priming of plaster and white lead, very much like the paper of a cheap memorandum book.

Bad modern vellum.

The best modern *vellum* is still made in Italy, especially in Rome. Good, stout, undoctored vellum of a fine, pure colour can be procured in Rome, though in limited quantities, and at a high price[3], but nothing is now made which resembles either the finest ivory-textured vellum of fifteenth century Italian manuscripts, or the exquisitely thin uterine vellum of the Anglo-Norman Bibles.

Paper[4]. Though by far the majority of the illuminated manuscripts of the Middle Ages are written on vellum, yet paper was occasionally used, long before the fifteenth century,

Use of paper.

[1] Quoted by Hook, *Lives of Archbishops of Canterbury*, Vol. III. p. 353; the Rev. Canon G. F. Browne kindly called my attention to this passage. Other examples of the cost of vellum are given in the preceding chapter.
[2] The same arrangement is to be seen in books printed on vellum.
[3] For example, the mere vellum required to print a small thick folio, such as Caxton's *Golden Legend*, would now cost about £40.
[4] I owe many of the facts in the following account of early paper to the excellent article on that subject in the *Encyclopædia Britannica*, ninth edition, Vol. XVIII. by Mr E. Maunde Thompson. See also E. Egger, *Le papier dans l'antiquité et dans les temps modernes*, Paris, 1866.

M. C. M. 15

when its manufacture was largely developed to supply the demand created by the invention of printing.

Paper made from the papyrus pith has been already described, see Chap. II. page 22.

Mode of making paper.
A very different process was used for the various kinds of paper which were made in mediaeval and modern times. The essence of the process consists in making a fine pulp of cotton or linen rags by long-continued pounding with water sufficient to give the mixture the consistency of thick cream. A handful of this fluid pulp is then spread evenly and thinly over the bottom of a fine wire sieve, through which the superfluous water drains away, leaving a thin, soft mass which is then turned out of the sieve, pressed, dried and finally soaked with size to make the paper fit to write on. This process leaves the wire-marks of the sieve indelibly printed on to the paper.

These marks are of two kinds, *first*, those of the stouter wires which run longitudinally along the sieve at intervals of about an inch or a little more, and *secondly*, very fine cross wires, placed close together, and woven in at right angles to the first-mentioned stouter wires.

Watermarks.
In the fourteenth century what are called *water-marks* came into use, together with the invention of linen paper. Some simple device indicating the city or province where the paper was made was woven with fine wire into the bottom of the sieve, and this mark was impressed upon the paper, like that of the other (parallel) wires of the sieve. A double-headed eagle, a vase, a letter or a bull's head are among the earliest paper-marks which occur in manuscripts and books of the fifteenth century[1]. In later times, during the sixteenth century, each manufacturer adopted his own mark[2]; and then still more recently the year-date has been added[3].

[1] A good illustrated account of early water-marks is given by Sotheby, *Principia Typographia*, London, 1858.

[2] Some fifteenth century paper has a special maker's mark, but more usually a general town or district mark was used, such as the cross-keys, a Cardinal's hat, an Imperial crown or double-eagle.

[3] What is now called "foolscap paper" originally took its name from a paper-mark in the form of a *fool's cap and bells*, a device which was frequently used in the sixteenth and seventeenth centuries.

CHAP. XIV.]   THE DATES OF ITS USE.   227

These paper-marks in some cases afford useful evidence as to the origin and date of a manuscript or printed book; but too much reliance should not be placed on such evidence, since paper often remained for a long time in stock, and the productions of one manufactory were frequently exported for use by the scribes and printers of more than one distant country[1].

Evidence of date.

Paper of Oriental make has no water-mark, but the earliest linen-paper of the fourteenth century made in Christian Europe always has a water-mark of some kind, very clearly visible.

The dates of paper manufacture. The earliest paper appears to have been made in China at a date even before the Christian Era. Its manufacture was next extended in Syria, and especially to Damascus[2]. This early paper was made of the cotton-plant, the "tree-wool" of Herodotus. Hence it was called *charta bombycina* or *Damascena*, or, from its silky texture, *charta serica*. Paper of this class, almost as beautiful in texture as vellum, is still made in the East and used for the fine illuminated manuscripts of India, Persia and other Moslem countries.

Earliest cotton paper.

Many Arab manuscripts written on cotton-paper of as early a date as the ninth century still exist. The Moslem conquerors of Spain and Sicily introduced the manufacture of this *charta bombycina* into western Europe, and to some small extent it was used for Greek and Latin manuscripts during the tenth and eleventh centuries. It was, however, rarely used in Christian Europe till the thirteenth century.

Arab MSS. on paper.

At first cotton only was used in the manufacture of paper, but gradually a mixture first of wool and then of flax or linen was introduced.

Wool-paper.

Peter, who was Abbot of Cluny from 1122 to 1150, in his treatise *Adversus Judaeos* mentions manuscripts written on wool-paper, made "ex rasuris veterum pannorum."

[1] Some of Caxton's books, printed in Westminster, bear many different paper-marks of Germany and Flanders, even in the same volume.

[2] Paper was also made at an early date in Constantinople, through its intimate relationship with the East. Hence the Monk Theophilus, writing in the eleventh century, calls linen-paper "Greek vellum," *pergamena Graeca*; see I. 24.

Linen paper.   In the fourteenth century linen-paper began to be made; at first mixed with wool, and then of pure linen. This fourteenth century paper is distinguishable by its stoutness, its close texture, and its thick wire-marks; the water-mark being especially clear and transparent. Paper was frequently used for official documents, charters and the like before it came into use for manuscript books[1].

Early MS. on paper.   The British Museum possesses one of the oldest known books on paper (*Arundel Manuscripts*, 268); this is a collection of *Astronomical treatises* written by an Italian scribe early in the thirteenth century.

In the fourteenth century the Spanish manufactories of *cotton*-paper were on the decline, and the first manufactory of *linen*-paper was started at Fabriano in northern Italy. In 1340 another manufactory was set up in Padua, and before the close of the fourteenth century paper was made in nearly all the chief cities of northern Italy, especially in Milan and Venice, and as far south as Florence and Siena.

In Germany paper-making began in Mentz in about 1320; and in 1390 a manufactory was started at Nuremberg with the aid of Italian workmen. South Germany, however, was supplied with paper from northern Italy till the fifteenth century.

In Paris and other places in France paper began to be made soon after the first manufactories in Italy were started.

Paper in England.   In England cotton-paper, especially for legal documents, was largely used in the fourteenth century. In Oxford, in the year 1355, a quire of paper, small folio size, cost five pence, equal in modern value to eight or nine shillings. In the fifteenth century its value had decreased to three pence or four pence the quire.

Paper does not appear to have been made in England till the reign of Henry VII.; before that time it was mainly imported from Germany and the Netherlands.

All Caxton's books are printed on foreign paper, and the first book printed on paper which was made in England was

[1] This old paper is almost as stout, tough and durable as parchment—very unlike modern machine-made paper.

Wynkyn de Worde's Bartholomaeus, *De proprietatibus rerum*, printed about the year 1495, four years after Caxton's death, with the following interesting *colophon*, which alludes to the first paper manufactory in England, set up by John Tate at Hertford.

Earliest English paper.

This *colophon*, which does not do credit to Wynkyn de Worde's literary style, runs thus:

And also of your charyte call to remembraunce
The soule of William Caxton first prynter of this boke
In laten tongue at Coleyn hymself to auance
That every wel disposyd man may theron loke
And John Tate the yonger joye mote he broke
Whiche late hathe in Englond doo make this paper thynne
That now in our englysshe this boke is prynted inne.

During the fifteenth century the making of paper reached its highest degree of perfection, and in the following century its excellence began to decline.

The Venetian paper of about 1470, used, for example, in the printed books of Nicolas Jenson and other printers in Venice, is a substance of very great beauty and durability, inferior only in appearance to the very best sort of vellum. It is very strong, of a fine creamy tint, and sized[1] with great skill, so as to have a beautiful glossy texture. For the illuminator's purpose it appears to have been almost as good as vellum. It even receives the raised mordant for burnished gold of the highest beauty and brilliance.

Beauty of Venetian paper.

The very small quantity of good paper that is now manufactured, mainly for artistic purposes, is made by hand in exactly the same way that was employed in the fourteenth or fifteenth century.

Most paper is now made by machinery, and as a rule contains more esparto grass than pure linen fibre.

[1] The size was made by boiling down shreds of vellum. Blotting-paper is paper that has not been sized. A coarse grey variety was used as early as the fifteenth century, though, as a rule, fine sand was used for this purpose till about the middle of the present century, especially on the Continent.

THE METALS AND PIGMENTS USED IN ILLUMINATED MANUSCRIPTS[1].

Fluid and leaf gold.

Gold and silver or tin. The splendour of illuminated manuscripts of almost all classes, except manuscripts of the Irish school such as the *Book of Kells*, is largely due to the very skilful use of gold and silver. These metals were applied by the illuminator in two ways, *first*, as a fluid pigment, and *secondly* in the form of leaf.

The fluid method appears to have been the older. It is easier to apply, but is not comparable in splendour of effect to the highly burnished leaf gold, which was used with such perfection of skill by the illuminators of the fourteenth century.

Method of grinding.

Fluid gold was made by laboriously grinding the pure metal on a porphyry slab into the finest possible powder. This powdered gold, mixed with water and a little size, was applied with a brush like any other pigment; see Theophilus, I. 30 to 33[2]. When dry, it could be to some extent polished by burnishing, but as it was laid directly on to the comparatively uneven and yielding surface of the vellum it never received a very high polish. As a rule therefore fluid gold was left unburnished, and its surface remained dull or *mat* in appearance.

Dull and burnished gold.

For this reason it was not unfrequently used in conjunction with burnished leaf gold, a fine decorative effect being produced by the contrast of the *mat* and polished surfaces. Thus, for example, in fourteenth and fifteenth century manuscripts a delicate diaper of scroll pattern is sometimes painted with a fine brush over a ground of burnished gold leaf.

[1] Modern "shell gold" is practically the same thing as the fluid gold of the mediaeval illuminators, except that it is not made with the pure, unalloyed metal.

[2] The following are the most useful and easily accessible books on the technical processes of the illuminator; Theophilus, *Schedula diversarum Artium*, Hendrie's edition with a translation, London, 1847; Cennino Cennini, *Trattato della pittura*, 1437, edited, with a translation, by Mrs Merrifield, London, 1844; and a large and valuable collection of early manuscripts on the same subject, edited and translated by Mrs Merrifield under the title of *Original Treatises on the Arts of Painting*, 2 Vols., London, 1849.

In the fifteenth century, during the decadence of the illuminator's art, the use of fluid gold, which had previously greatly diminished, was much revived, especially for the background of the realistic borders in Flemish manuscripts[1], for touching in the high lights of miniatures, and for many other purposes. When used to cover large surfaces, it is always unsatisfactory in effect and has little decorative value.

The preparation of this gold pigment was a very slow and laborious matter. The severe Cistercian rule regarded this process as a waste of precious time; and indeed the use of gold in any form was prohibited in the manuscripts used in Cistercian Abbeys. In the dialogue between a Cistercian and a Cluniac monk, *De diversis utriusque ordinis observantiis* (*Thesaur. Nov. Anecdot.* Vol. v. 1623), the Cistercian asks "what use there can be in grinding gold and painting large capitals with it"; *aurum molere et cum illo molito magnas capitales pingere litteras, quid est nisi inutile et otiosum opus?* St Bernard himself had an even stronger objection, not only to gold in manuscripts, but to any ornaments with grotesque dragons and monsters, on the ground that they did not tend to edification.

Cistercian severity.

Fluid silver was prepared and applied in the same way, but it was much less used than gold pigment. A very beautiful effect is produced in some of the gorgeous Carolingian manuscripts by using in the same ornament both gold and silver, which mutually enhance each other's effect by contrast of colour.

Fluid silver.

Burnished Gold leaf. The extraordinary splendour of effect produced by skilfully applied gold leaf depends mainly on the fact that it was laid, not directly on to the vellum, but on to a thick bed of a hard enamel-like substance, which gradually set (as it got dry) and formed a ground nearly as hard and smooth as glass; this enabled the gold leaf laid upon it to be burnished to the highest possible polish, till in fact the gold gave a reflexion like that of a mirror. This

Leaf gold.

---

[1] See page 144.

Mordant ground.

enamel-like ground, or *mordant* as it was called, was commonly as thick as stout cardboard, and its edges were rounded off, which has the double result of making the gold leaf laid upon it look not like a thin leaf, but like a thick plate of gold[1], and at the same time the rounded edges catch the light and so greatly increase the decorative splendour of the metal.

Convex surface.

Thus, for example, the little bosses and studs of gold, which are strewn so thickly among the foliage in the illuminated borders of Italian manuscripts of the fourteenth and fifteenth centuries, are convex in shape, like an old-fashioned watch-glass, and each boss reflects a brilliant speck of light whatever the direction may be in which the light falls upon the page. Perhaps the most sumptuous use of gold leaf is to be seen in some of the early fourteenth century French manuscripts, in which large miniatures are painted with an unbroken background of solid-looking burnished gold, with a mirror-like power of reflexion.

It was only by slow degrees that the illuminators reached the perfect technical skill of the fourteenth century in their application of gold leaf.

Purity of the gold.

In the first place the purest gold had to be beaten out, not the alloy of gold, silver and copper which now is used for making the gold leaf of what is called "the finest quality." The English illuminators at the close of the thirteenth and in the fourteenth century frequently got their gold in the form of the beautiful florins of Florence, Lucca[2] or Pisa, which were struck of absolutely pure gold[3]. In England there was no gold coinage till the series of *nobles* was begun by Edward

---

[1] That is to say, it looks as if the whole substance, mordant and all, were one solid mass of gold, nearly as thick as a modern half-sovereign; see Theophilus, I. 24 and 25.

[2] So when William Torell was about to gild the bronze effigy of Queen Eleanor in Westminster Abbey he procured a large number of gold florins from Lucca.

[3] Not even the smallest admixture of alloy was permitted in the gold coinages of the Middle Ages. Dante (*Inf.* XXX. 73) mentions the coiner Maestro Adamo who had been burnt at Romena in 1280 for issuing florins which had scarcely more alloy than a modern sovereign.

III.[1], but these were of quite pure gold, like the Italian florins, and so answered the purpose of the illuminator.

Another important point was that the gold leaf was not beaten to one twentieth part of the extreme tenuity of the modern leaf. The leaves were very small, about three by four inches at the most, and not more than from fifty to a hundred of these were made out of the gold ducat of Italy, which weighed nearly as much as a modern sovereign[2].

In many cases, we find, the illuminator prepared his own gold leaf, and it was not uncommon for the crafts of the goldsmith and the illuminator to be practised by the same man. For example the Fitz-Othos, mentioned at page 112 as a distinguished Anglo-Norman family of artists in the thirteenth century, were skilful both as makers of gold shrines and as illuminators of manuscripts. Many interesting notes about the Fitz-Othos and other artists employed at Westminster during the thirteenth and fourteenth centuries are to be found among the royal accounts now preserved in the Record Office: see *Vetusta Monumenta*, Vol. VI., p. 1 seq.

Among the accounts of the expenses of decorating with painting the royal chapel of Saint Stephen at Westminster in Edward III.'s reign, we find that John Lightgrave paid for six hundred leaves of gold at the rate of five shillings the hundred, equal to about £5 or £6 in modern value. And John "Tynbeter" received six shillings for six dozen leaves of tin used instead of silver, not because it was cheap, but because tin was not so liable to tarnish.

These accounts are in Latin, which is not always of

---

[1] The gold penny of Henry III. and the florin and its parts of Edward III. were only struck as patterns. The gold noble was first issued in 1341; its value was 6s. 8d. or half a *mark*. So many nobles were destroyed to make gold leaf for illuminating, and for other purposes, that an Act was passed prohibiting, under severe penalties, the use of the gold coinage for any except monetary purposes.

[2] In the same way the gold leaf used by the Greeks was comparatively thick. The famous Erechtheum inscription of 404 B.C. gives one drachma as the cost of each leaf (πέταλον) used for gilding the marble enrichments; see *Cor. Ins. Att.* I. 324, fragment C, col. ii. lines 35 and 42. Eighteen-pence will now buy 100 leaves of gold.

Ciceronian purity; a classical purist might perhaps carp at such phrases as these,

Item. *Pro reparatione brushorum*, viij^d, under the date 1307; and, in the following year,

Item. *Unum scarletum blanketum*, ij^s vij^d.

The scarlet blanket was not bought to keep the artist warm, but to make a red pigment from, as is described below at page 246.

Goldsmith artists.
This close connection between the arts of the goldsmith and the illuminator had its parallel in other branches of the arts, and with results of very considerable importance. Many of the chief painters and sculptors of Italy, during the period of highest artistic development, were also skilful goldsmiths, as for example Ghiberti, Verrocchio, Ant. Pollaiuolo, Francesco Francia and many others.

This habit of manipulating the precious metals gave neatness and precision of touch to the painter, and in the art of illuminating manuscripts taught the artist to use his gold so as to produce the richest and most decorative effect.

The gold mordant.
The mordant. We now come to the most difficult part of the illuminator's art, that of producing a ground for his gold leaf of the highest hardness and smoothness of surface. It is a subject dealt with at much length by all the chief writers on the technique of the illuminator, from Theophilus in the eleventh century, down to Cennino Cennini at the beginning of the fourteenth[1].

Though differing in details, the general principle of the process is much the same in all; the finest possible sort of *gesso*, plaster, gypsum or whitening, was very finely ground to an impalpable powder, and then worked up with albumen or size to the consistency of cream, so that it could be applied with a brush. After the first coat was dry, a second and a third coat were added to bring up the mordant to the requisite thickness of body, so that it stood out in visible relief upon the surface of the vellum.

[1] The best account of the way to make the mordant was given about 1398 by a Lombard illuminator called Johannes Archerius; see Mrs Merrifield's interesting collection of *Treatises on Painting*, Vol. I. page 259 seq.

In order that the illuminator might see clearly where his brush was going, and keep his mordant accurately within the required outline, it was usual to add some colouring matter, such as bole Armeniac (red ochre), to the white *gesso*, which otherwise would not have shown out very clearly on the cream-white vellum. In many cases, however, this colouring matter is omitted.

When the last coat of the *gesso-mordant* was dry and hard, its surface was carefully polished with the burnisher and it was then ready to receive the gold leaf; several days' waiting would often be required before the whole body of the mordant had set perfectly hard. White of egg was then lightly brushed over the whole of the raised mordant, and while the albumen was still moist and sticky, the illuminator gently slid on to it the piece of gold leaf, which he had previously cut approximately to the required shape. He then softly dabbed the gold leaf with a pad or bunch of wool, till it had completely adhered to the sticky mordant, working it with special care so as completely to cover the rounded edges. After the albumen was quite dry, and the gold leaf firmly fixed in its place, the artist brushed away with a stiff brush all the superfluous gold leaf; all the leaf, that is, under which there was no mordant-ground to hold it fast.

Application of leaf.

The gold was then ready to be polished. For this purpose various forms of burnisher were used, the best being a hard highly polished rounded pencil of crystal or stone, such as haematite, agate, chalcedony and the like; or in lack of those, the highly enamelled tooth of a dog, cat, rat or other carnivorous animal was nearly as good[1]. In fact patience and labour were the chief requisites; one receipt, in Jehan le Begue's manuscript, § 192[2], directs the illuminator to burnish and to go on burnishing till the sweat runs down his forehead. But caution, as well as labour, was required; it was very easy to scratch holes in the gold leaf, so that the mordant showed through, unless great care was used in the rubbing. In that case the illuminator had to apply another

Burnishing process.

---

[1] See Theophilus, I. 25.
[2] See Mrs Merrifield, *op. cit.* Vol. I. p. 154.

piece of leaf to cover up the scratches, and do his burnishing over again. To secure the highest polish, illuminators burnished the hard mordant as described above before laying on the gold leaf. In most cases two layers of gold leaf were applied, and sometimes even more, in order to insure a perfect and unbroken surface.

Application of gold. All writers speak of this burnishing as being a very difficult and uncertain process even to a skilled hand, requiring exactly the right temperature and amount of moisture in the air, or else it was liable to go wrong. If the gold was to be applied in minute or intricate patterns the illuminator did not attempt to cut his leaf to fit the mordant-ground, but laid it in little patches so as to cover a portion of the ornament. The superfluous gold between the lines of the pattern was then brushed away, as the leaf only remained where it was held by the mordant. With all possible care and skill, it was hardly possible always to ensure a sharp clean outline to each patch of gold; and so one commonly finds that the illuminator has added a black outline round the edge of each patch of gold, in order to conceal any little raggedness of the edge.

As examples of mediaeval receipts for making the mordant I may mention the following:—

Receipts for the mordant. "Mix gypsum, white marble, and egg-shells finely powdered and coloured with red ochre or *terra verde;* to be mixed with white of egg and applied in thin coats, and to be burnished before the application of the gold." When dry, this mixture slowly set into a beautiful, hard and yet not brittle substance, capable of receiving a polish like that of marble, and forming the best possible ground to receive the gold leaf. Much of its excellence depended on the patience of the illuminator in applying it in very thin coats; each of which was allowed to dry completely before the next was laid on. When ready to receive the gold leaf, after the burnishing of the mordant was finished, some purified white of egg was brushed over to make the gold leaf adhere firmly so as not to work loose or tear under the friction of the burnisher.

In some cases white lead (*ceruse*) was added to the *gesso*,

CHAP. XIV.]   IN ILLUMINATIONS.   237

as, for example, in a receipt, given by Cennino Cennini (§ 131 to 139, and 157,) for a mordant made of fine gypsum, ceruse and sugar of Candia, that is ordinary pure white sugar[1]. This is to be ground up with white of egg, applied in thin coats and burnished. To colour the mordant Cennino adds *bole Armeniac*, or *terra verde*, or verdigris green.   *Receipts for the mordant.*

Giovanni da Modena, a Bolognese illuminator, gives the following receipt for a different gold-mordant to be used with oil instead of albumen or size[2]. Instead of *gesso* it is to be made of a mixture of white and red lead, red ochre, bole Armeniac and verdigris; the whole is to be ground first with water, then thoroughly dried, and again ground up with a mixture of linseed oil and amber or mastic varnish.

This variety of mordant appears to have been used in a good many fifteenth century Italian manuscripts. It is not such a good mixture as the *gesso* and white of egg, as the oil used to mix with it is liable to stain the vellum through to the other side of the page, and even to print off a mark on the opposite page, especially when the book has been severely pressed by the binder.

Tooled patterns on gold leaf. In many Italian and French manuscripts, especially of the fourteenth and fifteenth centuries, a very rich and brilliant effect is produced with tooled lines impressed into the surface of the flat gold. Diapered and scroll-work backgrounds, the nimbi of Saints, the orphreys and apparels on vestments, and many other kinds of decoration were skilfully executed with a pointed bone or ivory tool, impressed upon the gold leaf after it was burnished, and through the gold into the slightly elastic body of the   *Tooled patterns.*

---

[1] In Cennino's time, the early part of the fourteenth century, in Europe, sugar was sold by the ounce as a costly drug. Apothecaries, not grocers, dealt in it. In Persia, Syria and some other Moslem countries cane sugar was made and used in comparatively large quantities throughout the mediaeval period; but in Europe it did not come into use as an article of food till the 16th century, and even then it was very expensive.

[2] The date of this receipt is about 1410; it is quoted in Jehan de Begue's manuscript published by Mrs Merrifield, Vol. I. pp. 9, 95, and 154; see also Theophilus, I. 31, who speaks of burnishing fluid gold laid on a mordant of red lead and cinnabar.

Stamped patterns. gesso-mordant. Patterns were also produced by the help of minute punches, which stamped dots or circles; these, when grouped together, formed little rosettes or powderings, like those used in the panel paintings of the same time. Gold treated in this way had to be of considerable thickness, and in some cases, when a large flat surface of mordant was to be gilt, as many as three layers of stout gold leaf were employed to give the requisite body of metal.

Silver leaf. Burnished silver leaf was occasionally used by the mediaeval illuminators, though not very often, as it was very liable to tarnish and blacken. For this reason *leaf tin* was not unfrequently used instead of silver, as tin does not oxydize in such a conspicuous way; see above, p. 233.

The use of all three metals, gold, silver and tin, is described by Theophilus, *Schedula diversarum Artium*, I. 24, 25 and 26. Theophilus speaks of laying the gold leaf directly on to the vellum with the help only of white of egg. This method was not uncommon in early times, and it was not till the end of the thirteenth century that the full splendour of effect was reached by the help of the thick, hard mordant-ground.

Cheap methods. Inferior processes were sometimes used for the cheap manuscripts of later times. Thus tin leaf burnished and then covered with a transparent yellow lacquer or varnish made from saffron was used instead of gold.

Cennino and other writers describe a curious method of applying gold easily and cheaply. The illuminator was first to paint his design with a mixture of size and pounded glass or crystal; this, when dry, left a surface like modern sand-paper or glass-paper, the artist was then to rub a bit of pure gold over the rough surface, which ground off and held a sufficient amount of gold to produce the effect of gilding. Only a very coarse effect, worthy of the nineteenth century, could have been produced by this process.

CHAPTER XV.

THE MATERIALS AND TECHNICAL PROCESSES OF THE ILLUMINATOR (continued).

THE coloured pigments of the illuminators. Though mediaeval manuscripts are splendid and varied in colour to the highest possible degree, yet all this wealth of decorative effect was produced by a very few pigments, and with the simplest of *media*, such as *size* made by boiling down shreds of vellum or fish-bones[1], or else gum-arabic, or occasionally white of egg or a mixture both of the yoke and the white[2]. In the main the technique of manuscript illumination is the same as that of panel pictures executed in distemper (*tempera*). An oil medium was unsuited to manuscript work because the oil spoilt the beautiful opaque whiteness of the vellum and made the painting show through to the other side[3].

Vehicles used.

[1] See Theophilus, I. 33 and 34; he recommends white of egg as a medium for ceruse, minium and carmine, and for most other pigments, ordinary vellum *size*.
    Jehan le Begue's manuscript gives the same advice as to the use of white of egg, but advises the use of gum Arabic with other pigments; see § 197.

[2] The British Museum possesses an interesting manuscript on pigments, entitled *De coloribus Illuminatorum* (Sloane manuscripts, 1754); see also Eraclius, *De artibus Romanorum*, published by Raspe, London, 1783 and 1801; and the twelfth century *Mappae Clavicula* printed in *Archaeologia*, Vol. XXXII. pp. 183 to 244. The first book of Theophilus, *Diversarum artium schedula*, written in the eleventh century, contains much interesting matter on this subject; see also the works mentioned above at page 230.

[3] *The Journal of the Society of Arts*, Dec. 25, 1891, and Jan. 8 and 15, 1892, has a valuable series of papers on "The pigments and vehicles of the Old Masters" by Mr A. P. Laurie, who throws new light on the treatises edited by Mrs Merrifield with the help of his own chemical investigations.

240 ULTRAMARINE BLUE. [CHAP. XV.

Blue pigments. The most important blue pigment, both during classical and mediaeval times, was the costly and very beautiful *ultramarine* (*azzurrum*[1] *transmarinum*), which was made from *lapis lazuli*, a mineral chiefly imported from Persia. This *ultramarine* blue was the *cyanus* or *coeruleum* of Theophrastus and Pliny. It is not only the most magnificent of all blue pigments, but is also the most durable, even when exposed to light for a very long period.

Ultramarine blue.

The general principle of the manufacture of ultramarine is very simple; consisting merely in grinding the *lapis lazuli* to powder, and then separating, by repeated washing, the deep blue particles from the rest of the stone[2]. The process of extracting the blue was made easier if the *lapis lazuli* was first calcined by heat. This is the modern method, and was occasionally done in mediaeval times, but it injures the depth and brilliance of the pigment, and in the finest manuscripts ultramarine was used which had been prepared by the better though more laborious process without the aid of heat.

Its manufacture.

The proportion of pure blue in a lump of *lapis lazuli* is much smaller than it looks; the stone was and is rare and costly, and thus the finest ultramarine of the mediaeval painters was often worth considerably more than double its weight in gold[3].

Its great value.

Both in classical and mediaeval times it was usual for the patron who had ordered a picture to supply the necessary *ultramarine* to the artist, who was only expected to provide the less costly pigments in return for the sum for which he had contracted to execute the work.

Pliny (*Hist. Nat.* XXXIII. 120) tells a story of a trick played by a painter on his employer, who suspiciously

---

[1] This word is spelt in many different ways.

[2] In mediaeval times this was done by first embedding the powdered stone in a lump of wax and resin, from which the blue particles were laboriously extracted by long-continued kneading and washing. The theory of this apparently was that the wax held the colourless particles and allowed the blue to be washed out; see Mrs Merrifield, *Treatises on Painting*, Vol. I. pp. 49, and 97 to 111.

[3] The modern value of ultramarine is about equal to its weight in gold. Sir Peter Lely, in the time of Charles II., paid £4. 10s. an ounce for it.

CHAP. XV.] THEFT OF ULTRAMARINE. 241

watched the artist to see that he did not abstract any of the precious *ultramarine* which had been doled out to him. At frequent intervals the painter washed his brush, dipped in the ultramarine, in a vessel of water; the heavy pigment sank to the bottom, and at the end of the day the artist poured off the water and secured the mass of powdered ultramarine at the bottom. *Method of theft.*

It is interesting to note that Vasari, in his *life of Perugino*, tells precisely this story about Pietro, who was annoyed at the suspicions expressed by a certain Prior for whom he was painting a fresco[1]. The Prior was in despair at the enormous amount of pigment that the thirsty wall sucked in, and he was agreeably surprised when, at the conclusion of the work, Perugino returned to him a large quantity of *ultramarine*, as a lesson that he should not suspect a gentleman of being a thief.

The library of Corpus Christi College, Cambridge, possesses a manuscript which affords a curious proof of the great value of ultramarine to the mediaeval illuminator. This is a magnificent copy of the *Vulgate* by a German scribe of the twelfth century, copiously illustrated with miniature pictures, many of which had backgrounds, either partially or wholly, covered with ultramarine. 'All through the book the ultramarine has in mediaeval times been very carefully and completely scraped off, no doubt for use in another manuscript. This theft has been accomplished with such skill that wonderfully little injury has been done to the beautiful illuminations, except, of course, the loss of splendour caused by the abstraction of the ultramarine. *Ultramarine scraped off.*

In illuminated manuscripts *ultramarine* is very freely used. It is specially noticeable for the thick body (*impasto*) in which it is applied, so as very often to stand out in visible relief. The reason of this is that this, and some other blue pigments, lose much of their depth of colour if they are ground into very fine powder. Hence both the ultramarine *Impasto.*

---

[1] The Prior in question was the Superior of the Convent of the Frati Gesuati in Florence.

242   SMALTO BLUES.   [CHAP. XV.

and *smalto* blues are always applied in comparatively coarse grained powder; and this of course necessitates the application of a thick body of colour.

Ancient cyanus. Smalto blues. Next in importance to the real ultramarine come the artificial *smalto* or "*enamel*" blues, which were used largely in Egypt at a very early date under the name of artificial *cyanus*; see Pliny, *Hist. Nat.* XXXVII. 119. Among the Greeks and Romans too this was a pigment of great importance, and when skilfully made is but little inferior in beauty to the natural ultramarine.

Vitreous pigment. Smalto blue is simply a powdered blue glass or vitreous enamel, coloured with an oxide or carbonate of copper. Vitruvius (VII. xi. 1) describes the method of making it by fusing in a crucible the materials for ordinary bottle-glass, mixed with a quantity of copper filings. The alcaline silicate of the glass frit acts upon the copper, which slowly combines with the glass, giving it a deep blue colour. The addition of a little oxide of tin turns it into an opaque blue enamel, which when cold was broken up with a hammer, and then powdered, but not too finely, in a mortar.

Smalto blue is largely used for the simple blue initials which alternate with red ones in an immense number of manuscripts. The glittering particles of the powdered glass can easily be distinguished by a minute examination. Like the ultramarine, the smalto blue is always applied in a thick layer.

The monk Theophilus (II. 12), who wrote during a period of some artistic and technical decadence, the eleventh century, advises the glass-painter who wants a good blue to search among some ancient Roman ruins for the fine coloured *tesserae* of glass mosaics, which were so largely used by the Romans to decorate their walls and vaults, and then to pound them for use.

German blue. Azzurro Tedesco or Azzurro della Magna, German blue, was much used by the illuminators as a cheap substitute for ultramarine. This appears to have been a native compound of carbonate of copper of a brilliant blue colour. It was occasionally used to adulterate the costly ultramarine, but

CHAP. XV.]   DYES USED AS PIGMENTS.   243

this fraud was easily discovered by heating a small quantity of the pigment on the blade of a knife; it underwent no change if it was pure; but if adulterated with *Azzurro della Magna* it showed signs of blackening[1].

Indigo blue. The above-mentioned blues are all of a mineral character, and are durable under almost any circumstances. To some extent however the vegetable *indigo* blue was also used for manuscript illuminations, both alone and also to make a compound purple colour.

Indigo.

Colours of all kinds prepared from vegetable or animal substances required a special treatment to fit them for use as pigments in solid or *tempera* painting. Though indigo and other colours of a similar class are the best and simplest of dyes for woven stuffs, yet they are too thin in body to use alone as pigments. Thus both in classical and mediaeval times these dye-pigments were prepared by making a small quantity of white earth, powdered chalk or the like absorb a large quantity of the thin dye, which thus was brought into a concentrated and solid, opaque form, not a mere stain as it would otherwise have been.

Method of using dyes.

These kinds of pigments are described by Pliny, *Hist. Nat.* XXXV. 44 and 46; and by Vitruvius, VII. xiv. Eraclius in his work on technique, *De artibus Romanorum*, calls them *colores infectivi,* "dyed colours," an accurately expressive phrase.

One method, occasionally used for the cheaper class of manuscripts, was to paint on to the vellum with white lead, and then to colour it by repeated application of a brush dipped in the thin dye-pigment. Many of the colours mentioned below belong to this class.

Green pigments. A fine soft green much used in early manuscripts is a natural earthy pigment called *terra verde* or green *Verona earth.* This needs little preparation, except

Terra verde.

---

[1] The German blue was also liable to turn to a bright emerald green if exposed to damp air. This change has taken place in a great part of the painted ceilings of the Villa Madama, which Raphael designed for Cardinal de' Medici (afterwards Clement VII.) on the slopes of Monte Mario, a little distance outside the walls of Rome.

16—2

244 GREEN PIGMENTS. [CHAP. XV.

washing, and is of the most durable kind; it is a kind of ochre, coloured, not with iron, but by the natural presence of copper.

Verdigris green. A much more brilliant green pigment was made of verdigris (*verderame*) or carbonate of copper, produced very easily by moistening metallic copper with vinegar or by exposing it to the fumes of acetic acid in a closed earthen vessel; see Theophilus, I. 37.

Verdigris green was much used by manuscript illuminators, especially during the fifteenth century, when a very unpleasant harsh and gaudy green appears to have been popular. When softened by an admixture of white pigment, verdigris gives a pleasanter and softer colour.

Chryso-colla. A native carbonate of copper, which was called by the Romans *chrysocolla*[1], was also used for mediaeval manuscripts. It is, however, harsh in tint if not tempered with white. Both the last-named pigments were specially used with yoke of egg as a medium.

Prasinum, a vegetable green made by staining powdered chalk with the green of the leek, was sometimes used.

Cennino Cennini also recommends a grass green made by mixing orpiment (sulphuret of arsenic) and indigo.

One of the best and most commonly used greens was made by a mixture of smalto blue and yellow ochre; other mixtures were also used.

Red pigments. Red and blue are by far the most important of the colours used in illuminated manuscripts, and it is wonderful to see what variety of effect is often produced by the use of these two colours only.

Vermilion and minium. The chief red pigments used by illuminators are vermilion (*cinnabar* or sulphuret of mercury) and red lead (*minium*), from which the words *miniator* and *miniature* were derived, as is explained above at page 31[2].

Both these pigments are very brilliant and durable reds,

---

[1] Because it was used by goldsmiths in *soldering gold*.

[2] *Minium* was largely used in the manuscripts of classical times; this is mentioned by Pliny (*Hist. Nat.* XXXIII. 122) who says *minium in voluminum quoque scriptura usurpatur*.

the more costly vermilion is the more beautiful of the two; it has a slightly orange tint.

Illuminators commonly used the two colours mixed. One receipt recommends one-third of red lead combined with two-thirds of vermilion; Jehan le Begue's manuscript, § 177 (Mrs Merrifield's edition, Vol. I. page 141). Vermilion was prepared by slowly heating together metallic mercury with sulphur. Red lead (a protoxide of lead) was made by roasting white lead or else *litharge* (ordinary lead oxide) till it absorbed a larger proportion of oxygen. *Mixed reds.*

Rubrica or *Indian red* was a less brilliant pigment, which also was largely used in illuminated manuscripts, especially for headings, notes and the like, which were hence called *rubrics*. *Rubrica* is a fine variety of *red ochre*, an earth naturally coloured by oxide of iron[1]; another variety was called bole Armeniac. In classical times the *rubrica of Sinope* was specially valued for its fine colour. *Ochre reds.*

In addition to these mineral and very permanent reds there were some more fugitive vegetable and animal scarlets and reds which were used in illuminated manuscripts.

Murex. One of these, the *murex* shell-fish, has already been mentioned for its use as a dye for the vellum of the magnificent Byzantine and Carolingian gold-written manuscripts. The *murex* was also used as a *color infectivus* by concentrating it on powdered chalk[2]. *Murex.*

Kermes. Another very beautiful and important carmine-red pigment was made from the little *kermes*[3] beetle (*coccus*) which lives on the ilex oaks of Syria and the Peloponnese. It is rather like the *cochineal* beetle of Mexico, but produces a finer and more durable colour, especially when used as a dye. *Kermes.*

---

[1] All natural earthy pigments owe their colours to the various metals, which in combinations with different substances give a great variety of tints. Thus, *iron* gives red, brown, yellow and black; *copper* gives many shades of brilliant blues and greens; and *manganese* gives a quiet purple, especially in combination with an alcaline silicate.

[2] Plutarch (*De defec. Or.* § 41) mentions flour made from beans as being used with *murex* purple and *kermes* crimson to give them sufficient body for the painter's purpose.

[3] Kermes is the Arabic name for this insect.

Kermes red. For the woven stuffs of classical and mediaeval times, and in the East even at the present day, the kermes is one of the most beautiful and important of all the colours used for dyeing. The mediaeval name for the kermes red was *rubeum de grana;* when required for use as a pigment it appears to have been usual, not to extract the colour directly from the beetle, but to get it out of clippings of red cloth which had been dyed with the kermes, by boiling the cloth in a weak solution of alkali and precipitating the red pigment from the water with the help of alum.

The reason for this method is not apparent. Possibly it was first done as a means of utilizing waste clippings of the costly red cloth, and then, when the habit was established, no other method was known to the colour-makers, who in some cases bought pieces of cloth on purpose to cut them up and use in this way[1]. The *scarletum blanketum* mentioned at page 234 was bought for this purpose.

Madder. *Madder-red* was also used as a pigment by boiling the root of the madder-plant (*rubia-tinctorium*), and then using the concentrated extract to dye powdered chalk. Various red and purple flowers, such as the violet, were used in the same way as *colores infectivi.*

Lac. *Lake-red* (*lacca* or *lac*) was made and called after a natural gum or resin, the *lach* of India ; see Cennino Cennini, § 44.

This is a beautiful transparent colour, which, in some fine manuscripts of the fifteenth century, is used as a transparent glaze over burnished gold, the effect of which is very magnificent, as the metallic gleam of the gold shines through the deep transparent red of the over-painting. Lake was also used as an opaque, solid pigment by mixing it with white, which at once gave it "body," and destroyed its transparency.

Purple of a very magnificent tint was occasionally made by a mixture of *ultramarine* with the carmine-red of the

---

[1] It should be remembered that a large number of the mediaeval receipts and processes were not based on any reasonable principle, and endless complications were often introduced quite needlessly; this is well shown in a very interesting paper by Prof. John Ferguson of Glasgow on *Some Early Treatises on Technological Chemistry*, read before the Philos. Soc. Glasgow, Jan. 6, 1886.

CHAP. XV.] YELLOWS AND WHITES. 247

kermes beetle; this was specially used by the illuminators of the fourteenth and fifteenth centuries.

Yellow ochre, a fine earth pigment coloured by iron, was the principal yellow of the illuminators. *Yellows.*

In late manuscripts *orpiment* (sulphuret of arsenic), which is a more brilliant lemon-yellow, was occasionally used; see Cennino Cennini, § 47.

Litharge yellow, an oxide of lead, was another important colour, but more especially for the painter in oil, who used it very largely as a drier[1].

Another fine ochreous earth of a rich brown colour was the *terra di Siena* or "raw Siena"; the colour of this was made warmer in tint by roasting, thus producing "burnt Siena."

White pigments were perhaps the most important of all to the illuminator, who usually only used pure colours for his deepest shadows; all lights and half tints, both in miniature pictures and in decorative foliage, being painted with a large admixture of white. The use of this system of colouring by Fra Angelico and many painters of the Sienese school has been already referred to; see page 190. *Use of white.*

For this reason it was very important to use a pure and durable white pigment which would combine well with other colours.

Bianco di San Giovanni was in all respects one of the best of the whites used by illuminators. *Lime white.*

This was simply pure *lime-white*, made by burning the finest white marble; the lime was then washed in abundance of pure water, then very fine ground and finally dried in cakes of a convenient size; see Cennino Cennini, § 58; and

---

[1] The use of litharge as a drier was one of the most important improvements made in the technique of oil painting by the Van Eycks of Bruges in the first half of the fifteenth century. Before then, oil paintings on walls had often been laboriously dried by holding charcoal braziers close to the surface of the picture. Among the accounts of the expenses of painting the Royal Palace of Westminster in the thirteenth century (see above, page 110) charcoal for this purpose is an important item in the cost. Paintings on panel, being moveable, were usually dried by being placed in the sun; but, in every way, a good drier like litharge answers better than heat, either of the fire or of sunshine.

Theophilus, I. 19. The medium used with it was the purest size or gum Arabic of the most colourless kind.

Another white pigment was made of powdered chalk and finely ground egg-shells; this was a less cold white than the bianco di San Giovanni.

White lead.
 White lead (*cerusa* or *biacca*) was also used[1], especially by the later illuminators, but with very unfortunate results, since white lead is liable to turn to a metallic grey or even black if exposed to any impure sulphurous atmosphere.

Many beautiful manuscripts have suffered much owing to the blackening of their high lights which had been touched in with white lead; especially manuscripts exposed to the gas- and smoke-poisoned air of London or other large cities.

Process of manu- facture.
 The *biacca* of the mediaeval illuminator was made in exactly the same way that Vitruvius and Pliny describe; see Vitr. VII. xii.; and Pliny, *Hist. Nat.* XXXIV. 175.

A roll of lead was placed in a clay *dolium* or big vase, which had a little vinegar at the bottom. The top was then luted down, and the jar was left in a warm place for a week or so, till the fumes of the acetic acid had converted the surface of the lead into a crust of carbonate. This carbonate of lead was then flaked off and purified by repeated grinding and washing.

In order to keep the white pigments perfectly pure, some illuminators used to keep them under water, so that no dust could reach them.

Black inks. Two inks of quite different kinds were used for the ordinary text of mediaeval manuscripts.

Carbon ink.
 One of these was a pure carbon-black (modern Indian or Chinese ink); this has been described under the classical name *atramentum librarium*[2]; see above, page 27. The great advantage of this carbon ink is that it never fades; it is not a *dye* or *stain*, but it consists of very minute particles of carbon which rest on the surface of the vellum.

The other variety was like modern black writing ink, only

---

[1] See Theophilus, I. 39.
[2] See Vitruvius, VII. 10; and Pliny, *Hist. Nat.* XXXV. 41; and Dioscorides, V. 183.

CHAP. XV.] BLACK INKS. 249

of very superior quality. This acts as a dye, staining the *Iron ink.*
vellum a little below the surface. Unfortunately it is liable to
fade, though when kept from the light (as in most manuscripts) it has stood the test of time very well.

Sometimes the mediaeval illuminators distinguished these
two kinds of black ink, calling the first *atramentum* and the
second *encaustum;* but frequently the names are used indif-
ferently for either: see Theophilus, I. 40. The *encaustum* was
made by boiling oak-bark or gall-nuts, which are rich in
tannin, in acid wine with some iron filings or vitriol (sulphate
of iron). The combination of the iron and the tannin gives
the inky black[1]. Both these black inks were used with gum
Arabic.

A great part of the beauty of mediaeval manuscripts is *Beauty of*
quite unconnected with their illumination. The plain portion *text.*
of the text, from the exquisite forms of its letters and the
beautiful glossy black of the ink on the creamy ivory-like
vellum page, lighted up here and there by the crisp touch of
the rubricator's red, is a thing of extraordinary beauty and
charm. This perfection of technique in the writing and
beauty of the letters lasted considerably longer than did the
illuminator's art. Hence in some of the manuscripts of the
period of decadence, executed during the fifteenth century,
the plain black and red text is very superior in style to
the painted ornament; and one cannot, in some cases, help
regretting that the manuscript has not escaped the disfigurement of a coarse or gaudy scheme of illumination.

Red inks were of three chief kinds, namely the *vermilion,
red lead,* and *rubrica* or red ochre, which have been already
mentioned.

Purple ink was used largely, not often for writing, but for *Purple*
the delicate pen ornaments of the initials in certain classes of *ink.*
late Italian and German manuscripts. A vegetable pigment
seems to have been used for this; the lines appear to be
stained, and do not consist of a body-colour resting on the
surface of the vellum.

[1] Sometimes accidentally produced in domestic life by some overdrawn tea
remaining on a steel knife.

Gold writing is usually executed with the fluid gold pigment, but in later manuscripts very gorgeous titles and headings are sometimes done with burnished leaf gold applied on the raised mordant, the writing being first done with a pen dipped in the fluid mordant.

The pencils and pens of the Illuminator. Two quite different classes of pencils were used for lightly sketching in the outline of the future floral design or miniature.

Lead point. One of these was the silver-point or lead-point[1], very much like the metallic pencil of a modern pocket-book. The use of the silver-point was known in classical times; Pliny (*Hist. Nat.* XXXIII. 98) remarks as a strange thing that a white metal like silver should make a black line when used to draw with. It is, however, rather a faint grey than a black line that a point of pure silver makes, especially on vellum, and so it was more usual for illuminators to use a softer pencil of mixed lead and tin; Cennino recommends two parts of lead to one of tin[2] for making the lead point, *piombino*.

Red pencil. Another kind of pencil was made of a soft red stone, which owed its colour to oxide of iron. From its fine blood-red tint the illuminators called it *haematita, lapis amatista* or *amatito*, hence an ordinary lead pencil is now called either *lapis* or *matita* in Italy. This stone is quite different from the hard *haematite* which was used in classical times for the early cylinder-signets of Assyria.

Burnisher. The harder varieties of the *amatista* or *haematite* were used to burnish the gold leaf in manuscripts, small pieces being polished and fixed in a convenient handle. They were also used as a red pigment, the stone being calcined, quenched in water and finely ground; see Cennino Cennini, § 42.

[1] The modern "lead-pencil" is wrongly named, being made of *graphite*, which is pure carbon. This does not appear to have been used in mediaeval times.

[2] The vellum was not prepared in any way to receive the silver-point drawing; but when an artist wanted to make a finished study in silver-point he covered his vellum or paper with a priming of fine *gesso*, powdered marble, or wood-ashes; this gave a more biting surface to the paper, and made the silver rub off more easily and mark much more strongly. In the case of manuscript illuminations a strongly marked line was not needed, as the outline was only intended as a guide to the painter.

Besides the hard red chalky stone (*amatita rossa*) used for outlines by the illuminators, a somewhat similar black stone (*amatita nera*) was also used, but not so commonly as the red.

The pens of illuminators. In early times, throughout, that is, the whole classical period and probably till about the time of Justinian, the sixth century A.D., scribes' pens were mostly made of reeds (*calamus* or *canna*); and occasionally silver or bronze pens were used; see above, page 29. *Reed pens.*

But certainly as early as the eighth century A.D. and probably before that, quill-pens came into use and superseded the blunter and softer reed-pen.

Such exquisitely fine lines as those in many classes of mediaeval manuscripts could only have been made with some very fine and delicate instrument like a skilfully cut crow's quill or other moderately small feather. *Fine quills.*

The pen was a very important instrument for the illuminator, not only when his pictures were mainly executed in pen outline, like many of those in the later Anglo-Saxon manuscripts, but also in such microscopically delicate miniature work as that in the Anglo-Norman *historiated Bibles* of the thirteenth century; in these much of the most important drawing, such as the features and the hair of the figures, was executed, not with a brush, but with a quill-pen, which in the illuminator's skilful hand could produce a quality of line which for delicacy and crisp precision of touch has never been surpassed by the artists of any other class or age.

Brushes were, as a rule, made by the illuminators themselves, so as to suit their special needs and system of working. Cennino (§§ 63 to 66) and other writers give directions for the selection of the best hair and the mode of fixing it so as to give a finely pointed brush. Ermine, minever and other animals of that tribe supplied the best hair for the brushes required for very minute work. But a great number of other animals provided useful material to the craftsman who knew the right places to select the hair from, and, a still more important thing, understood how to arrange and fix it in a bundle of the best form. *Brushes.*

List of tools.   *The implements of scribes and illuminators.* The following is a list of the principal tools and materials required by the illuminator of manuscripts, including those which have been already described[1].

    Pens, pencils and chalk of various sorts, as described above.
    Brushes made of minever, badger and other kinds of hair.
    Grinding-slabs and rubbers of porphyry or other hard stone, and a bronze mortar.
    Sharp penknife and palette knife.
    Rulers, and a metal ruling-pen.
    Dividers to prick out the guiding-lines of the text.
    Scissors for shaping the gold leaf.
    Burnishers, stamps, and *stili* for ornamenting the gold.
    Small horns to hold black and red ink; see fig. 53 on page 209.
    Colour-box, palette, pigments, gold leaf and *media* of various kinds.
    Sponge and pumice-stone for erasures.

Paintings of scribes.   Miniatures representing a scribe writing a manuscript are the commonest of all subjects in several classes of illuminated manuscripts. For example the first capital of Saint Jerome's *Prologue* in the historiated Anglo-Norman *Vulgates* almost always has a very minute painting of a monastic scribe[2], seated, writing on a sloping desk, with his pen in one hand and his penknife in the other[3].

In one respect such scenes are always treated in a conventional way; that is, the scribe is represented writing in a

---

[1] See above, pages 29 and 30, on the pens and inkstands of the classical scribes.
[2] Usually meant for Saint Jerome translating or revising the Latin edition of the Bible.
[3] Again, the first miniature in the French and Flemish *Horae* usually represents *Saint John in Patmos* writing his Gospel. The eagle stands by patiently holding the Evangelist's inkhorn. In some manuscripts the Devil, evidently in much awe of the eagle's beak, makes a feeble attempt to upset the ink. In the latest manuscript *Horae* this scene is replaced by the one of *Saint John at the Latin Gate.*

complete and bound book, whereas both the writing of the text and the illuminations were done on loose sheets of vellum, which could be conveniently pinned down flat on the desk or drawing-board.

The scribes' processes.

The processes employed in the execution of an illuminated manuscript of the fourteenth or fifteenth century were the following;

First, if the text were to be in one column, four lines were ruled marking the boundaries of the patch of text and the margin. These four lines usually cross at the angles and are carried to the extreme edge of the vellum[1].

Next, the scribe, with a pair of dividers or compasses, pricked out at even distances the number of lines which were to be ruled to serve as a guide in writing the text. These pricked holes were, as a rule, set at the extreme edge of the vellum, and were intended to be cut off by the binder, but in many manuscripts they still remain. The scribe then filled the space within the first four marginal lines with parallel ruled lines at the intervals indicated by the pricks at the edge.

Ruled lines.

In early manuscripts the guiding lines to keep the text even are usually ruled, not with colour or ink, but simply traced with a pointed *stilus*, which made a sufficiently clear impressed line on the vellum, showing through from one side to the other.

Stilus lines.

In the twelfth and thirteenth centuries the practice began of ruling the lines with a *lead point;* and then, from the fourteenth century onwards, they were usually ruled with bright red pigment[2]; this has a very decorative effect in lighting up the mass of black text, and thus we find in many early printed books[3] these red guiding lines have been ruled in merely for the sake of their ornamental appearance.

Lead lines.

Red lines.

---

[1] A two-columned page of text had, of course, two sets of framing lines, one for each patch of writing.

[2] In some manuscripts lines are ruled in blue or purple, but much less frequently than in the more decorative vermilion.

[3] In certain classes of books, such as large Bibles and Prayer-books, the custom of ruling red lines lasted till the present century.

This ruling was nearly always done with special metal ruling-pens, very like those now used for architectural drawing; and thus the lines are perfectly even in thickness throughout.

The plain text.
The next stage in the work was the writing of the plain black text. In early times it appears to have been usual, or at least not uncommon, for the same hand to write the text and add the painted illuminations, but when the production of illuminated manuscripts came mostly into secular hands, the trades of the scribe and the illuminator were usually practised by different people; and in late times a further division still took place, and the miniaturist frequently became separated from the decorative illuminator.

Guiding letters.
Thus we find that in many manuscripts the scribe has introduced in the blank spaces minute guiding letters[1] to tell the illuminator what each initial was to be, and, especially in fifteenth century Italian manuscripts, instructions are added for the miniaturist, telling him what the subject of each picture was to be. These instructions were commonly written on the edge of the page so that they were cut off by the binder, but in many cases they still exist, not obliterated by the subsequent painting.

But to return to the progress of the page, when the scribe had finished the plain text, leaving the necessary blank spaces for the illuminated capitals and miniatures, the work of decoration then began.

Decoration.
As a rule the decorative foliage and the like was finished before the separate miniatures, if there were any, were begun. First the illuminator lightly sketched in outline the design of the ornament, using a lead point. Next, wherever burnished gold was to be introduced, the thick mordant-ground was laid on; the gold leaf was then applied and finished with tooling and burnishing.

The reason why the gold was applied before any of the painting was begun was this; the long rubbing with the

---

[1] These guiding letters were used in all the early printed books which had initials painted in by an illuminator.

burnisher acted not only on the gold leaf, but also naturally rubbed the vellum a little way all round it. This would have smudged the painting round the gold if it had been applied first. Moreover, the burnisher was liable to carry small particles of gold on to the surrounding vellum, which would have given a ragged look to the design, if the adjacent surfaces had not been subsequently covered with pigment. In cases where there is an isolated gold boss there is usually a slight disfigurement from the burnisher rubbing the vellum all round the gold. In these cases the outline of the gold was made clean and definite by the addition of a strong black outline, as is mentioned above.

Gold leaf.

When the whole of the burnished gold was finished, the painting was then executed. If any fluid gold pigment were used, that was usually added last of all.

The painting.

In some cases, in the later and cheaper French and Flemish manuscripts, the ornaments in the borders were not specially designed and sketched in for the manuscripts but previously used outline patterns were transferred on to the vellum by a bone *stilus* and ordinary transfer paper, made by rubbing red chalk all over its surface.

Transferred patterns.

In some of the better class of manuscripts with the "ivy-leaf" border, the illuminator has made the general design of one page serve for the next one in this way; when he had drawn in the main lines of the scroll-pattern on the borders of one page, he held the vellum up to the light and so was able to trace the pattern through from the other side of the leaf. To prevent monotony he varied the design by introducing different little blossoms among the repeated scroll-work which formed the main pattern.

When the *scribe*, the *rubricator*, the *illuminator* and the *miniaturist* (either as one or as several different people) had completed the manuscript it was ready for the *binder*. As an indication of the order in which the leaves of the manuscript were to be bound, the scribe usually placed on the lower margin of the last page of each "gathering" of leaves a letter or number.

Preparation for binding.

In the earliest printed books these guiding letters, or *signatures* as they are called, were added by hand in the same way[1]; but in a few years the regular and more developed system of printed *signatures* was introduced[2].

Scribes' signatures. Scribes' signatures at the end of manuscripts are comparatively rare, but they do occasionally occur in various interesting forms. My friend Mr W. J. Loftie kindly sends me the following:

In a Sarum *Missal* of the fifteenth century at Alnwick Castle,

"Librum scribendo Jon Whas[3] monachus laborabat,
Et mane surgendo multum corpus macerabat."

More commonly manuscripts terminate with a vague phrase invoking a blessing on the scribe, such as this, from a Bible in the Bodleian (No. 50),

"Qui scripsit hunc librum
Fiat collectum in paradisum."

Or this, which occurs in several manuscripts,

"Qui scripsit scribat,
Semper cum Deo vivat."

Owner's name. In another manuscript *Vulgate* in the Bodleian (No. 75), the owner of the book, who was named *Gerardus*, has recorded the fact in this fanciful way,—

"Ge ponatur et rar simul associatur
Et dus reddatur cui pertinet ita vocatur."

[1] As a rule these manuscript signatures in printed books were written close to the edge of the page, and so have been cut off by the binder; in some tall copies, however, they still exist.

[2] The next stage was the numbering of each *folio* or leaf, and the last system was to number each page. Folios appear to have been first numbered in books printed at Cologne about the year 1470. A further modification has recently been introduced, namely, in two column pages, to number each column separately.

[3] The *Lectionary* mentioned on p. 120 was written and signed by a monastic scribe called Sifer Was.

CHAPTER XVI.

THE BINDINGS OF MANUSCRIPTS.

FOR the more magnificent classes of manuscripts, such as the *Textus* (*Gospels*) used as altar ornaments, every costly and elaborate artistic process was employed. In addition to the sumptuous gold and jewelled covers mentioned above at page 55, manuscripts were bound in plates of carved ivory set in gold frames, in plaques of Limoges enamel, especially the *chamlevé* enamels with the heads of the figures attached in relief, such as were produced with great skill at Limoges during the eleventh to the thirteenth century. Some *Evangeliaria* were bound in covers made of the ancient Roman or Byzantine ivory diptychs, a custom to which we owe the preservation of the most important existing examples of these[1]. Such costly methods of binding were of course exceptional, and most manuscripts were covered in a much simpler manner.

Costly bindings.

The commonest form of binding was to make the covers of stout oak boards, which were covered with parchment, calf-skin, pig-skin or some other leather. Five brass or bronze bosses were fixed on each cover, arranged thus :·:, and two or four stout clasps made of leather straps with brass catches were firmly nailed on to the oak. The angles of the covers were often strengthened by brass or *latten* corner-pieces, and in some cases metal edgings were nailed all along

Common bindings.

[1] Some fine examples of magnificently bound manuscripts are illustrated by Libri, *Monumens inédits; Hist. Ornam.* Paris, 1862—1864.

M. C. M. 17

the edges of the oak, making a very strong, massive and heavy volume. Large pieces of rock crystal, amethyst or other common gem were frequently set in the five bosses of the covers. These were always cut in rounded form *en cabochon*, not faceted as is the modern custom.

The small amount of decoration, which was usually employed on early bindings, was often limited to tooled lines joining the five bosses on the covers[1].

Titles of MSS. If the title of the manuscript was placed on the binding, a not very common practice, it was usually written on the upper part of one of the covers. In some cases the title was written on a separate slip of vellum and was protected by a transparent slice of horn, fixed with little brass nails.

This appears to have been the usual system as long as books were kept in coffers or *armaria*; but when open bookshelves with chained books came into use, about the time when printing was invented, the title of a book was usually written on the front edges of the leaves.

At that time books were set on the shelves in the opposite way to that now used, so that, not the back, but the edge of the volume was visible.

Painted edges. Towards the close of the fifteenth and throughout the sixteenth century, the front edges of printed books and manuscripts were sometimes decorated with painted illumination, usually a portrait figure of the author of the work or some object illustrating its subject[2].

The parchment which was used to cover the oak bindings of manuscripts was often coloured by staining or painting; red and purple being the favourite colours. Chaucer, in the

[1] In Geyler's *Fatuorum Navicula*, of which many editions, copiously illustrated with woodcuts, were published shortly before and after the year 1500, the cut showing the first fool of the series, the Bibliomaniac, represents him surrounded with books, all of which are bound after this design.

[2] A complete sixteenth century Venetian library, consisting of a hundred and seventy volumes, all with painted illuminations on their edges, is now in the library of Mr Thos. Brooke, at Armitage Bridge, near Huddersfield. The whole collection forms a beautiful array of delicately painted miniatures, mostly the work of Cesare Vecellio, a Venetian illuminator of the latter part of the sixteenth century; see *Catalogue of Mr Brooke's library*, London, 1891, Vol. II., pp. 663 to 681.

Prologue to the *Canterbury Tales*, describing the Clerke of Oxenford says,

> For him was lever habe at his beddes heed,
> Twenty bookes, clothed in blak and red
> Of Aristotil and of his philosophie
> Then robes riche or fithul or sawtrie.

In some cases the oak covers of manuscripts were not hidden by leather, but were decorated by elaborate paintings. A very interesting series of folio account-books of the Cathedral of Siena, now preserved in the *Opera del Duomo*, are specially remarkable for their pictured bindings. These manuscripts date from about 1380 to 1410, one volume being devoted to the expenses and records of each year. On one of the covers of each is a large painting on the oak, frequently of a view of some part of Siena or of the interior of the Cathedral. Very interesting evidence with regard to the old fittings of the high altar, with Duccio di Buoninsegna's great retable, and the original position of the magnificent pulpit are given by some of these pictured covers. One volume of this Sienese series is now in the South Kensington Museum.

Painted bindings.

In the fourteenth century bindings of books began to be decorated by stamping patterns with dies or punches on the vellum or pigskin covering of the oak board; a method of decoration which was greatly elaborated and developed in the sixteenth century, especially by the German and Dutch bookbinders.

Stamped leather.

The earlier stamped designs were of a much simpler character, usually consisting of powderings all over the surface of the cover, with small flowers or animals, such as lions, eagles, swans and dragons of heraldic character. In many cases these punches, or at least their designs, continued in use for a long time, and so one occasionally meets with a fifteenth century book, the binding of which is decorated with stamps of fourteenth or even thirteenth century style.

The later class of stamped bindings, belonging rather to printed books than to manuscripts, is often very beautiful and

260   STAMPED BINDINGS.   [CHAP. XVI.

Stamped bindings. decorative in character, the whole surface of the cover being completely embossed in relief by the skilful application of a great number of punches used in various combinations, so as to form one large and perfectly united design. In these later times, from about the middle of the sixteenth century the tendency was to cut larger designs on one punch or die; and the leather or parchment was softened by boiling so that a large surface could be embossed at one operation. This process was much aided by the invention of the screw-press, which enabled the workman to apply a steady and long-continued pressure. But in the older stamped bindings, as a rule, small punches were used, and the force was simply applied by the blow of a hammer[1].

English bindings. In England very fine stamped bindings of this class were made even in the first half of the fifteenth century. And, just as in earlier times the operations of the binder and the manuscript illuminator had been carried on by the same man, or at least in the same workshop, so we find that some of the earliest English printers, such as Julian Notary, were also skilful binders of their own printed books. The very fine stamped bindings of Julian Notary and other English craftsmen are commonly decorated on one side with the Tudor arms and badges supported by angels, and on the other side with a pictorial scene of the Annunciation of the B. V. Mary with I. N. or other maker's initials.

Walled bindings. Returning now to the earlier bindings of manuscripts, we should mention one system which was frequently applied to *Books of Hours, Breviaries (portiforia)*, and other *portable* books. This system was to extend the leather covering far beyond the edges of the wooden boards, which formed the main covers of the manuscripts, so that the book, edges and all were protected, very much as if it were kept in a bag. In fact this sort of binding really was a leather bag to the inside of which the book was attached.

The mouth of the bag was closed by a running thong,

[1] An analogous change took place in the reign of Elizabeth in England when coins, which up to that time had always been made by hammering, were first struck by the "mill and screw."

a loop or some other fastening, and the book was thus carried about, hung from its owner's girdle[1].

In bindings of this class the leather covering was frequently dressed with the hair on. Corpus Christi College at Oxford possesses a very well-preserved example of this, a manuscript of the thirteenth century in a contemporary bag-covering made of deer's skin, with its soft brown fur in a perfect state of preservation.

Bindings of red or violet velvet were also frequently used for manuscripts. Plain red velvet, with elaborate clasps and corner-pieces of chased gold or silver, was perhaps the most usual form of binding for costly manuscripts of the fourteenth and fifteenth centuries. Fine gems, especially the carbuncle and turquoise, were set in the gold mounts of some of these princely books. *Velvet.*

Vellum dyed with the *murex* was used to cover the oak boards of manuscripts at a time when purple-stained vellum was no longer used for the pages of manuscripts. A fine green dye and other colours were also used for vellum bindings. The Vatican records of books borrowed (and returned) usually mention how each volume was bound. Among the earliest of these records, dating from the Pontificate of Leo X. (1513 to 1522) the commonest descriptions of bindings are *in tabulis, in rubio, in albo, in nigro,* and *in gilbo,* indicating the colour of the skin or velvet in which the manuscript was bound. *Dyed vellum.*

In the sixteenth century, when private luxury and pomp were taking the place of the earlier religious feelings and beliefs which had so greatly fostered the decorative arts, bindings as costly as those of the *Altar-textus* of the great Cathedral and Abbey churches were again made at the command of wealthy patrons. Thus, for example, Cardinal Grimani had his famous *Breviary*[2] bound in crimson velvet, the greater part of which is concealed by the most elaborate *Later bindings.*

---

[1] In the miniature pictures in manuscripts of the fourteenth and fifteenth centuries one often sees ladies represented with their *Horae* suspended in this way from their girdle.

[2] See page 167.

Gold mounts.

mounts, clasps, corner-pieces and borders of solid gold, of the most exquisite workmanship, decorated with a medallion portrait head of the Cardinal himself.

So also the very similar *Horae* of Albert of Brandenburg[1] is decorated with clasps and other mounts of pure gold; and an immense number of other sumptuous bindings, rich with embossed and chased gold, studded with precious gems, were made to enshrine the costly manuscripts of Giulio Clovio and other famous miniaturists of the sixteenth century period of decadence.

Bindings of needle-work.

At the close of the fifteenth century or rather earlier, the custom became popular of having *Horae* and other manuscripts owned by wealthy secular personages bound in velvet, richly decorated with embroidery in gold and silver thread and silk mixed with a great number of seed pearls. The arms, badges and initials of the owner are the commonest designs for these embroideries.

Some of the German examples of this class of binding are especially elaborate and magnificent; but on the whole this method of decoration is not at all suited for covering books.

Works on bindings.

With regard to books on the subject of early bindings; it is much to be regretted that existing works, of which there are a great many, especially in French, all begin just about the period when bindings of the greatest interest and the truest artistic value were no longer made. Plenty has been written about the costly bindings in which Grolier, Maioli, and other wealthy book-buyers had their purchases encased, but no work exists on the bindings of the mediaeval period, when, frequently, the covers of a manuscript were as much a labour of love as the illuminated pages within. The sixteenth century binders, who worked for Grolier and other rich patrons of art, lived at the verge of a commercial epoch, and though their works are often very pretty and technically of high merit, yet they cannot be compared, as true works of art, with the bindings of the period before printing was invented.

---

[1] See page 167.

CHAP. XVI.] VALUE OF MANUSCRIPTS. 263

The present value of illuminated manuscripts. On the whole a fine manuscript may be regarded as about the cheapest work of art of bygone days that can now be purchased by an appreciative collector. Many of the finest and most perfectly preserved manuscripts which now come into the market are actually sold for smaller sums than they would have cost when they were new, in spite of the great additional value and interest which they have gained from their antiquity and comparative rarity. *Small cost of MSS.*

For example, a beautiful and perfectly preserved historiated Anglo-Norman *Vulgate* of the thirteenth century, with its full number of eighty-two pictured initials, written on between six and seven hundred leaves of the finest uterine vellum, can now commonly be purchased for from £30 to £40. This hardly represents the original value of the vellum on which the manuscript is written.

Manuscripts of a simpler character, however beautifully written, if they are merely decorated with blue and red initials, commonly sell for considerably less than the original cost of their vellum[1].

Again, the more costly manuscripts of fine style, which now fetch several hundred pounds, usually contain a wealth of pictorial decoration and laborious execution far in excess of that which could be purchased for a similar sum in any other branch of art.

Another noticeable point is that the modern pecuniary values of manuscripts, even those which are bought only as works of art, are by no means in proportion to their real artistic merits. Manuscripts of the finest period of the illuminator's art, the thirteenth and fourteenth centuries, are now sold for very much smaller sums than the immeasurably inferior but more showy and over-elaborated manuscripts of the period of decadence in the fifteenth and sixteenth centuries. *Want of taste.*

---

[1] The same want of appreciation extends to bindings. As a rule a book in a fine mediaeval binding sells for no more than if it were in a modern binding by Bedford. It is only the sixteenth century bindings of so-called "Grolier style" and the like which add largely to the value of a book.

Modern want of taste.

A melancholy example of the existing want of taste and lack of appreciation of what is beautiful in art is afforded by the fact that such a thing as a manuscript signed and illuminated by Giulio Clovio would fetch a far larger sum than so perfect a masterpiece of poetic art as a fine example of a fourteenth century Anglo-Norman *Apocalypse*.

So also the late and inferior *Horae* of about 1480 to 1510 often sell for much higher prices than simpler but far more beautiful manuscripts of earlier date. Of course I am here speaking of the values of manuscripts regarded simply as works of art, not of those which are mainly of importance from the interest of their text.

The result of this is that a collector with some real knowledge and appreciation of what is artistically fine can perhaps lay out his money to greater advantage in the purchase of manuscripts than by buying works of art of any other class, either mediaeval or modern.

APPENDIX.

Mr Jenkinson, the Librarian of the University of Cambridge, has kindly supplied me with the following interesting extracts, from a manuscript of the thirteenth century in the Parish Library of St James' at Bury St Edmunds (M 27 + B 357)[1], which gives instructions to scribes and illuminators of manuscripts as to the various tools they are to use.

"Scriptor habeat rasorium siue nouaculam ad radendum sordes pergameni vel membrane. Habeat etiam pumicem mordacem et planulam ad pactandum (?) et equandum superficiem pergameni. Plumbum habeat et linulam quibus liniet pergamenum, margine circumquaque tam ex parte tergi quam ex parte carnis existente libera......

Scriptor autem in cathedra resideat ansis utrimque eleuatis pluteum siue ait'em (?) sustinentibus, scabello apte pedibus posito.

.i.asserem

Scriptor habeat epicaustorium centone copertum. Arcanum habeat quo pennam formet ut habilis sit et ydonea ad scribendum...... Habeat dentem canis (?) sive apri ad polliandum pergamenum...... Et spectaculum habeat ne ob errorem moram disspendiosam (?). Habeat prunas in epicausterio ut cicius in tempore nebuloso vel aquoso desicari possit...... Et habeat etiam mineum ad formandas literas puniceas, vel rubeas, vel feniceas et capitales. Habeat etiam fuscum pulverem; et azuram a Salamone repertam[2]."

[1] This library is now deposited in the Guildhall; the press-mark is probably that of an old monastic library.
[2] Probably a blundered version of Pliny's statement (*Hist. Nat.* xxxvii. 119) that azure blue (*cyanus*) was invented by a king of Egypt.

Translation.

"The scribe should have a sharp scraper or knife to rub down the roughnesses of his parchment or vellum. He should also have a piece of 'biting' pumice-stone and a flat tool to smooth down and make even the surface of his parchment.

He should have a lead pencil and a ruler with which to rule lines on the parchment, leaving a margin free (from lines) on both sides of the parchment, on the back of the leaf as well as on the flesh side......

The scribe should sit in an arm chair, with arms raised on each side to support a desk or ?; a footstool should be conveniently placed under his feet. The scribe should have an *epicaustorium*[1] covered with leather; he should have an *arcanum* (pen-knife?) with which to shape his pen, so that it may be well formed and suitable for writing......

He should have the tooth of a dog (?) or of a wild boar for the polishing of his parchment...... And he should have spectacles. lest troublesome delay be caused through blunders. He should have hot coals in a brazier so that [his ink] may dry quickly [even] in cloudy or rainy weather...... He should also have mineum (*minium*) for the painting of red, crimson or purple letters and initials. He should also have a dark powder (pigment), and the azure which was invented by Solomon."

The following excellent description of the chief kinds of Service-books which were used during the later mediæval period was originally written in 1881 by Henry Bradshaw, the Cambridge University Librarian, for *The Chronicles of All Saints' Church, Derby*, by the Rev. J. C. Cox and Mr W. H. St John Hope. It is by the kind permission of Mr Cox and Mr Hope that I am able to reprint Mr Bradshaw's valuable note, which, with admirable clearness and conciseness, explains the character of each of the principal classes of Service-books used in English Churches and the manner in which these books became differentiated and multiplied down to the time of the Reformation.

---

[1] This is evidently a different thing from the *epicausterium* or brazier for hot coals mentioned below. My friend Mr J. T. Micklethwaite suggests that it was a board covered with leather on which to stretch and dry vellum before writing on it.

Note by Henry Bradshaw.

In the old Church of England, the Services were either—
1. For the different hours (Mattins, Lauds, Prime, Terce, Sext, None, Vespers, and Compline), said in the Choir, *The Hours.*
2. For Processions, in the Church or Churchyard,
3. For the Mass, said at the Altar, or
4. For occasions, such as Marriage, Visitation of the Sick, Burial, &c., said as occasion required.

Of these four all have their counterparts, more or less, in the English Service of modern times, as follows:

1. The Hour-Services, of which the principal were Mattins and Vespers, correspond to our Morning and Evening Prayer.
2. The Procession Services correspond to our Hymns or Anthems sung before the Litany which precedes the Communion Service in the morning, and after the third Collect in the evening, only no longer sung in the course of procession to the Churchyard Cross or a subordinate Altar in the Church; the only relic (in common use) of the actual Procession being that used on such occasions as the Consecration of a Church, &c. *Processions.*
3. The Mass answers to our Communion Service.
4. The Occasional Services are either those used by a Priest, such as Baptism, Marriage, Visitation and Communion of the Sick, Burial of the Dead, &c., or those reserved for a Bishop, as Confirmation, Ordination, Consecration of Churches, &c. *Occasional Services.*

All these Services but the last mentioned are contained in our "Prayer-book" with all their details, except the lessons at Mattins and Evensong, which are read from the Bible, and the Hymns and Anthems, which are, since the sixteenth century, at the discretion of the authorities. This concentration or compression of the Services into one book is the natural result of time, and the further we go back the more numerous are the books which our old inventories show. To take the four classes of Services and Service-books mentioned above:

1. The Hour-Services were latterly contained, so far as the text was concerned, in the *Breviarium*, or *Portiforium*, as it was called by preference in England[1]. The musical portions of this book were *The Breviary.*

---

[1] An explanation of the nature and constitution of the Breviary will be found in the preface to the Psalter-volume of the Cambridge University Press edition of the Sarum Breviary, lately published.

contained in the *Antiphonarium*. But the Breviary itself was the result of a gradual amalgamation of many different books:

The Breviary.

(*a*) The *Antiphonarium*, properly so called, containing the Anthems (*Antiphonae*) to the Psalms, the Responds (*Responsoria*) to the Lessons (*Lectiones*), and the other odds and ends of Verses and Responds (*Versiculi et Responsoria*) throughout the Service;

(*b*) The *Psalterium*, containing the Psalms arranged as used at the different Hours, together with the Litany as used on occasions;

(*c*) The *Hymnarium*, or collection of Hymns used in the different Hour-Services;

(*d*) The *legenda*, containing the long Lessons used at Mattins, as well from the Bible, from the *Sermologus*, and from the *Homiliarius*, used respectively at the first, second, and third Nocturns at Mattins on Sundays and some other days, as also from the *Passionale*, containing the acts of Saints read on their festivals; and

(*e*) The *Collectarium*, containing the *Capitula*, or short Lessons used at all the Hour-services except Mattins, and the *Collectæ* or *Orationes* used at the same.

Procession Services.

2. The Procession Services were contained in the *Processionale* or *Processionarium*. It will be remembered that the Rubric in our "Prayer-Book" concerning the Anthem ("In Quires and places where they sing, here followeth the Anthem") is *indicative* rather than *imperative*, and that it was first added in 1662. It states a fact; and, no doubt, when processions were abolished, with the altars to which they were made, Cathedral Choirs would have found themselves in considerable danger of being swept away also, had they not made a stand, and been content to sing the Processional Anthem without moving from their position in the Choir. This alone sufficed to carry on the tradition; and looked upon in this way the modern Anthem Book of our Cathedral and Collegiate Churches, and the Hymn Book of our parish Churches, are the only legitimate successors of the old *Processionale*. It must be borne in mind, also, that the Morning and Evening Anthems in our "Prayer-Book" do not correspond to one another so closely as might at first sight appear to be the case. The Morning Anthem comes immediately before the Litany which precedes the Communion Service, and corresponds to the Processional Anthem or Respond sung at the

churchyard procession before Mass. The Evening Anthem, on the other hand, follows the third Collect, and corresponds to the Processional Anthem or Respond sung "*eundo et redeundo*," in going to, and returning from, some subordinate altar in the church at the close of Vespers.

3. The Mass, which we call the Communion Service, was contained in the *Missale*, so far as the text was concerned. The Epistles and Gospels, being read at separate lecterns, would often be written in separate books, called *Epistolaria* and *Evangeliaria*. The musical portions of the Altar Service were latterly all contained in the *Graduale* or Grayle, so called from one of the principal elements being the *Responsorium Graduale* or Respond to the *Lectio Epistolae*. In earlier times, these musical portions of the Missal Service were commonly contained in two separate books, the *Graduale* and the *Troparium*. The *Graduale*, being in fact the *Antiphonarium* of the Altar Service (as indeed it was called in the earliest times), contained all the passages of Scripture, varying according to the season and day, which served as Introits (*Antiphonae et Psalmi ad Introitum*) before the Collects, as Gradual Responds or Graduals to the Epistle, as *Alleluia* versicles before the Gospel, as *Offertoria* at the time of the first oblation, and as *Communiones* at the time of the reception of the consecrated elements. The *Troparium* contained the *Tropi*, or preliminary tags to the Introits; the Kyries; the *Gloria in excelsis*; the Sequences or *Prosae ad Sequentiam* before the Gospel; the *Credo in unum*; the *Sanctus* and *Benedictus*; and the *Agnus Dei*; all, in early times, liable to have insertions or *farsurae* of their own, according to the season or day, which, however, were almost wholly swept away (except those of the *Kyrie*) by the beginning of the thirteenth century. Even in Lyndewode's time (A.D. 1433), the *Troparium* was explained to be a book containing merely the Sequences before the Gospel at Mass, so completely had the other elements then disappeared or become incorporated in the *Graduale*. This definition of the *Troparium* is the more necessary, because so many *old* church inventories yet remain, which contain books, even at the time of writing the inventory long since disused, so that the lists would be unintelligible without some such explanation.

The Mass.

4. The Occasional Services, so far as they concerned a priest, were of course more numerous in old days than now, and included the ceremonies for *Candle*mas, *Ash* Wednesday, *Palm* Sunday, &c.,

Occasional Services.

besides what were formerly known as the Sacramental Services. The book which contained these was in England called the *Manuale*, while on the Continent the name *Rituale* is more common. No church could well be without one of these. The purely episcopal offices were contained in the *Liber pontificalis* or Pontifical, for which an ordinary church would have no need.

The Ordinale.

5. Besides these books of actual Services there was another, absolutely necessary for the right understanding and definite use of those already mentioned. This was the *Ordinale*, or book containing the general rules relating to the *Ordo divini servitii*. It is the *Ordinarius* or *Breviarius* of many Continental churches. Its method was to go through the year and show what was to be done; what days were to take precedence of others; and how, under such circumstances, the details of the conflicting Services were to be dealt with. The basis of such a book would be either the well-known Sarum *Consuetudinarium*, called after St. Osmund, but really drawn up in the first quarter of the thirteenth century, the Lincoln *Consuetudinarium* belonging to the middle of the same century, or other such book. By the end of the fifteenth century Clement Maydeston's *Directorium Sacerdotum*, or Priests' Guide, had superseded all such books, and came itself to be called the Sarum *Ordinale*, until, about 1508, the shorter Ordinal, under the name of *Pica Sarum*, "the rules called the Pie," having been cut up and re-distributed according to the seasons, came to be incorporated in the text of all the editions of the Sarum Breviary.

H. B.

CAMBRIDGE,
March 17, 1881.

Mr Micklethwaite has kindly pointed out to me the following passage from the Cistercian *Consuetudines* (Guignard, *Documents inédits*, Dijon, 1878, p. 174), cap. LXXII, "Nullus ingrediatur coquinam excepto cantore et scriptoribus ad planandam tabulam, ad liquefaciendum incaustum, ad exsiccandum pergamenum...." That is, the kitchen fire might be used for melting the wax on the tablets, so that a fresh list of names could be written (see above, p. 8), for liquefying frozen ink, and for drying the vellum skins ready for writing on.

SOME PUBLICATIONS OF

The Cambridge University Press.

The Engraved Gems of Classical Times, with a Catalogue of the Gems in the Fitzwilliam Museum, by J. HENRY MIDDLETON, M.A., Slade Professor of Fine Art, and Director of the Fitzwilliam Museum, Cambridge. Royal 8vo. Buckram, 12s. 6d.

The Lewis Collection of Gems and Rings in the possession of Corpus Christi College, Cambridge, with an Introductory Essay on Ancient Gems by J. HENRY MIDDLETON, M.A. Royal 8vo. Buckram, 6s.

The Types of Greek Coins. By PERCY GARDNER, Litt.D., F.S.A. With 16 Autotype plates, containing photographs of Coins of all parts of the Greek World. Impl. 4to. Cloth extra, £1. 11s. 6d.; Roxburgh (Morocco back), £2. 2s.

Essays on the Art of Pheidias. By C. WALDSTEIN, Litt. D., Reader in Classical Archæology in the University of Cambridge. Royal 8vo. 16 Plates. Buckram, 30s.

A Catalogue of Ancient Marbles in Great Britain, by Prof. ADOLF MICHAELIS. Translated by C. A. M. FENNELL, Litt. D. Royal 8vo. Roxburgh (Morocco back), £2. 2s.

The Literary Remains of Albrecht Dürer, by W. M. CONWAY. With Transcripts from the British Museum MSS., and Notes by LINA ECKENSTEIN. Royal 8vo. Buckram, 21s. (*The Edition is limited to 500 copies.*)

The Woodcutters of the Netherlands during the last quarter of the Fifteenth Century. In 3 parts. I. History of the Woodcutters. II. Catalogue of their Woodcuts. III. List of Books containing Woodcuts. By W. M. CONWAY. Demy 8vo. 10s. 6d.

London: C. J. CLAY AND SONS,
CAMBRIDGE UNIVERSITY PRESS WAREHOUSE,
AVE MARIA LANE.

www.ingramcontent.com/pod-product-compliance
Lightning Source LLC
Chambersburg PA
CBHW031329230426
43670CB00006B/287